HEALTH PSYCHOLOGY RESEARCH FOCUS

EATING DISORDERS: CAUSES, DIAGNOSIS AND TREATMENTS

HEALTH PSYCHOLOGY RESEARCH FOCUS

Additional books in this series can be found on Nova's website under the Series tab.

Additional E-books in this series can be found on Nova's website under the E-books tab.

HEALTH PSYCHOLOGY RESEARCH FOCUS

EATING DISORDERS: CAUSES, DIAGNOSIS AND TREATMENTS

COLLEEN M. SHAPIRO
EDITOR

Nova Science Publishers, Inc.
New York

Library of Congress Cataloging-in-Publication Data

Eating disorders : causes, diagnosis and treatments / editors, Collen M. Shapiro.
p. cm.
Includes index.
ISBN 978-1-61209-746-6 (hardcover)
1. Eating disorders--Diagnosis. 2. Eating disorders--Treatment. I. Shapiro, Collen M.
RC552.E18E2827 2011
616.85'26--dc23

2011024896

Published by Nova Science Publishers, Inc. † New York

CONTENTS

Preface		**vii**
Chapter 1	Eating Disorders: Causes, Diagnosis and Treatments *Christine Courbasson, Leah Shapira, and Melissa Di Fonzo*	**1**
Chapter 2	Multimodal Perceptual and Emotional Integration in Eating Disorders *Anna M. Lomanowska and Matthieu J. Guitton*	**39**
Chapter 3	Eating Disorders and Menstrual Dysfunction – Implications On Bone Mineral Density *William W. K. To and Margaret W. N. Wong*	**61**
Chapter 4	Eating Disorders in Individuals with Developmental Disabilities *Efrosini Kalyva*	**83**
Chapter 5	Psychological Well-Being and Health Behaviors in College Females with Eating Disorders: Comparisons with A Non-Eating Disorder Cohort *Diane E. Mack, Philip M. Wilson, Benjamin D. Sylvester and Jenna D. Gilchrist*	**105**
Chapter 6	Multiple Family Group Therapy for Young Adolescents with Anorexia Nervosa: A Descriptive Study *Catherine Doyen, Solange Cook-Darzens and Marie-Christine Mouren*	**127**

Chapter 7 Risk Factors of Eating Disorders in Females **141**
Tamara Yousef Mousa

Chapter 8 Dissociation and the Escape from Awareness of Appearance Threats **155**
Matthew Fuller-Tyszkiewicz and Alexander J. Mussap

Chapter 9 Commentary: Motivation for Exercise in Eating Disorders: New Insight Gives Relevance for the Diagnostic Criteria **167**
S. Bratland-Sanda

Index **177**

PREFACE

This new book presents current research in the study of the causes, diagnosis and treatment of eating disorders. Topics discussed in this compilation include varied eating disorders and their diagnostic criteria; the multimodal perceptual and emotional integration in eating disorders; eating disorders and menstrual dysfunction; health behaviors in college females with eating disorders and in individuals with developmental disabilities; risk factors for women with eating disorders and excessive exercise associated with eating disorders.

Chapter 1 - Eating disorders are multidimensional illnesses characterized by clinical disturbances in eating behaviours and attitudes that pose very serious physiological and psychological health consequences. These consequences, including medical and psychiatric comorbidities, are associated with serious psychosocial sequelae and an economic burden on health care (Striegel-Moore, Leslie, Petrill, Garvin, and Rosenheck, 2000). This review delineates the different types of eating disorders and their according diagnostic criteria. The prevalence, epidemiology, prognosis, and etiology of the illness are explored, and the various empirically-supported treatment options that are available are enumerated.

Chapter 2 - Eating disorders are often characterized by multimodal perceptual and emotional alterations, including distorted perceptions and recurring negative emotional states. Perceptual distortions observed in eating disorder sufferers are not limited to the gustatory modality, but also affect other sensory modalities. For instance, sufferers may experience alterations both in taste and body shape perception. The results of recent clinical and animal studies indicate that perceptual processes interact with altered emotional states, and that the integration of these modalities plays a critical role in the ontogeny and maintenance of eating disorders. The aim of this chapter is to examine current perspectives on the involvement of multimodal perceptual and emotional integration in these disorders and to highlight elements for future research and for innovative treatments. First, clinical observations of perceptual distortions and their interaction with emotional states of eating disorder sufferers will be considered. Second, the fundamental mechanisms of integration between taste perception and emotional states will be examined from the perspective of recent studies in animal models. Finally, new therapeutic avenues that take advantage of a multimodal approach will be explored, with special emphasis on the use of virtual environments as therapeutic tools. In conclusion, understanding the interactions between multimodal perceptual and emotional processes may offer important avenues for future research into the ontogeny of eating disorders and the development of innovative treatments.

Chapter 3 - Eating disorders have been associated with a high incidence of menstrual dysfunction in the form of oligomenorrhea and amenorrhea, particularly in adolescent populations. Such abnormal menstrual patterns, in turn, bear direct implications on bone health. In the treatment of these women, although bone mass accrual usually improves with weight gain and menstrual recovery, residual deficits may persist. Women with a history of early onset eating disorders are more likely to suffer from osteoporosis / osteopenia in later life even years after recovery, and those with persistent eating disorders are likely to have continued low body weight and decreased bone density. In the female athlete triad, where menstrual dysfunction and eating disorders are essential components, bone health concerns are also important considerations in the management. The best treatment options remains controversial. At present, there is no good evidence in the literature to guide medical interventions for the treatment and prevention of osteoporosis and osteopenia in these women suffering from eating disorders.

Chapter 4- Eating disorders refer to abnormal eating habits that may involve excessive or insufficient food intake and affect not only the physical but also the emotional and psychological health of the individual. It is estimated that 5-10% of the adolescent population worldwide exhibit eating disorders, such as anorexia nervosa, bulimia nervosa, and binge-eating disorder, while the mortality rate is alarming. However, limited studies have explored the eating disorders of individuals with developmental disabilities. Therefore, this chapter starts with some general information about the prevalence, nature, and the outcomes of eating disorders. The remaining of the chapter deals with eating problems in individuals with developmental disabilities, such as autism spectrum disorders, intellectual disabilities, attention deficit/hyperactivity disorder, Prader-Willi syndrome and other disabilities. At the end of the chapter some prominent treatment programs for these populations are reviewed and critically evaluated.

Chapter 5 – Background: The peak onset of eating disorders (ED) arises predominantly between 15 to 21 years old (American Psychiatric Association, 2010). Given the alarming rates of mortality and functional impairment associated with ED (Berkman et al., 2006), it is not surprising that health professionals are targeting university/college students as an important cohort for addressing health issues stemming from ED (American College Health Association, 2000). Objectives: The purpose of this investigation was to examine differences across indices of psychological health, weight loss strategies, and health promoting behaviors between college females self-reporting a diagnosis of anorexia nervosa (AN) or bulimia (BN) with an age-matched comparison cohort not reporting a diagnosis of an ED. Methods: Data were derived from the 2000 – 2004 survey period from the American College Health Association–National College Health Assessment (ACHA-NCHA). Female undergraduate students who self-reported a diagnosis of AN (n = 880) or BN (n = 1410) were compared with those not reporting a diagnosis of AN/BN (n = 56965). Participants completed a self-report instrument on a single occasion. Results: Analyses of the data demonstrated lower perceived health, more frequent negative thoughts, and greater frequency of health promoting behaviors for individuals diagnosed with AN/BN when compared to those not reporting a diagnosis ($p < .005$). Specifically, individuals with AN or BN reported lower perceptions of overall (Cohen d's = 0.07 - 0.16) and psychological health (γ's ranged from 0.05 – 0.09) and greater use of weight loss strategies (phi's = 0.07 to 35.67) than individuals not reporting AN/BN. Finally, individuals living with AN/BN reported engaging in more frequent health promoting behaviors (d's = 0.33 – 0.40) than individuals in the comparison group. Conclusion: In summary, college females with AN/BN reported greater psychological health concerns and use of potentially harmful weight loss strategies. Greater reported use of health promoting behaviors reported by those with AN/BN is encouraging. As colleges and universities have been recognized as effective settings for health promotion interventions (Center for Disease Control and Prevention, 1997) because of their ability to reach a large proportion of young adults, consideration of psychological health and health promoting behaviors is essential for all members of the college community.

Chapter 6 – Objective: Multiple Family Group Therapy (MFGT) was recently developed for eating disordered patients and notably for adolescents with anorexia nervosa (AN). The aim of this study was to compare anorectic adolescents treated with MFGT with those treated without MFGT. Method: BMI z-scores were obtained for two groups of anorectic adolescents at discharge. Results: BMI z-scores showed greater improvement in the MFGT group than in the control group at 12 months. Conclusion: MFGT seems particularly useful for severe forms of AN or for fragile or dysfunctional families.

Chapter 7 - Eating disorders are described as a persistent disturbance in eating behavior intended to control body weight and accompanied by body image dissatisfaction. These disturbances impair both physical health and psychosocial functioning. Hence, the recognition of risk factors of eating disturbances and vulnerable groups is considered an effective intervention before developing eating disorders. This is important to prevent the health hazards related to eating disorders such as amenorrhea and osteopenia. The current paper, therefore, will discuss the predisposing factors of eating disorders in females including biological variables, particularly genetic predisposition, individual, familial and social variables, as well as westernization. Individual variables such as low self-esteem, pubertal timing in adolescent girls and negative body image, as well as parental pressures towards thinness and negative family relations have influenced eating disorders occurrence. Similarly, socio-cultural variables including socioeconomic status, exposure to thin media messages, and pressure from peers have increased the risk of exhibiting eating disorders.

Chapter 8 - Although extant literature demonstrates a link between dissociation and disordered eating symptomatology, the nature of this relationship remains unclear. One prominent explanation is based on an 'escape from awareness' model of dissociation, in which binge eating reflects a maladaptive cognitive response to the appearance-threatening aspects of certain foods. This is typically conceptualized as an initial hyper-vigilance aimed at detecting a potential appearance threat – for example, an item of high calorie food identified by an individual who is preoccupied with her/his weight, currently dieting, and hungry – followed by a rapid cognitive disengagement from awareness of the identified threat. In this chapter, we review evidence for this two stage model in individuals with elevated levels of disordered eating symptomatology. In addition, we report on our own findings that suggest that dissociation in the context of food and bingeing may be more closely related to the initial hyper-vigilance stage of threat processing. This chapter concludes with recommendations for future research into the role of threat processing in binge eating.

Chapter 9 - Exercise is defined as one of several possible weight compensatory behaviors in the DSM-IV criteria for bulimia nervosa. However, little knowledge exists about other reasons for exercise among patients with eating disorders. Aim: To review the literature about reasons for exercise among patients with eating disorders compared to non-clinical controls. Methods: Literature search in PubMed and ISI Web of Science was carried out. To be included the studies had to involve patients diagnosed with DSM-IV anorexia nervosa, bulimia nervosa or eating disorders not specified. Results: A total of six papers met the inclusion criteria. Of these, four had examined a wider range of motives for exercise than just weight and shape. One paper found weight and shape as a more important reason for exercise among patients than controls. Three papers found exercise for regulation of affects and mood as more important among the patients than the controls. Furthermore, one study found exercise for affect regulation, but not weight regulation, as a more important motive among the excessive exercising patients compared to the non-excessive exercisers. Conclusion: Exercise in eating disorders is not necessarily all about the body weight, especially not among patients with longstanding eating disorders. These findings suggest that the DMS-IV criteria should emphasize assessment of all types of exercise among the patients, regardless of the exercise motives.

In: Eating Disorders
Editor: C. M. Shapiro, pp. 1-38
ISBN 978-1-61209-746-6

Chapter 1

EATING DISORDERS: CAUSES, DIAGNOSIS AND TREATMENTS

***Christine Courbasson*[*1, 2], *Leah Shapira*[3], *and Melissa Di Fonzo*[2]**

INTRODUCTION

Eating disorders are multidimensional illnesses characterized by clinical disturbances in eating behaviours and attitudes that pose very serious physiological and psychological health consequences. These consequences, including medical and psychiatric comorbidities, are associated with serious psychosocial sequelae and an economic burden on health care (Striegel-Moore, Leslie, Petrill, Garvin, and Rosenheck, 2000). This review delineates the different types of eating disorders and their according diagnostic criteria. The prevalence, epidemiology, prognosis, and etiology of the illness are explored, and the various empirically-supported treatment options that are available are enumerated.

[*] Correspondence: Christine M. Courbasson, Ph.D., C. Psych. Head, Eating Disorders and Addiction Clinic, Center for Addiction and Mental Health, Assistant Professor, Department of Psychiatry, University of Toronto. 33 Russell Street. Toronto Ontario. M5S 2S1. Phone: 416-535-8501 ext. 6620. Fax: 416-595-6399. Email: christine_courbasson@camh.net

[1] Centre for Addiction and Mental Health

[2] University of Toronto

[3] York University

The Diagnostic and Statistical Manual of Mental Disorders, fourth edition (DSM-IV-TR) recognizes two types of eating disorders: Anorexia Nervosa (AN) and Bulimia Nervosa (BN) (APA, 2000). A separate category is devoted to Eating Disorders Not Otherwise Specified (ED-NOS) which includes disorders of eating that do not meet the criteria for any of the other eating disorders (APA, 2000). Binge Eating Disorder (BED) is a provisional diagnosis in the DSM-IV-TR and currently falls under the diagnosis of ED-NOS.

To meet diagnosis for any of the eating disorders, an individual must conform to the diagnostic criteria listed in the DSM-IV-TR (APA, 2000). The following describes the guidelines used to diagnose a patient with an eating disorder:

Diagnostic Criteria for each Eating Disorder (APA, 2000)

Anorexia Nervosa

A. Refusal to maintain body weight at or above a minimally normal weight for age and height (e.g., weight loss leading to maintenance of body weight less than 85% of that expected; or failure to make expected weight gain during a period of growth, leading to body weight less than 85% of that expected).
B. Intense fear of gaining weight or becoming fat, even though underweight.
C. Intense fear of gaining weight or becoming fat, even though underweight.
D. Disturbance in the way in which one's body weight or shape is experienced, undue influence of body weight or shape on self-evaluation, or denial of the seriousness of the current low body weight.
E. In post-menarchal females, amenorrhea, i.e., the absence of at least three consecutive menstrual cycles. (A woman is considered to have amenorrhea if her periods occur only following hormone administration (e.g., estrogen). Some have period after criteria, some don't – be consistent.

There are two subtypes of AN:

- *Restrictive Type:* During the current episode of AN, the person has not regularly engaged in binge-eating or purging behaviour (i.e., self-induced vomiting or the misuse of laxatives, diuretics, or enemas).
- *Binge-Eating/ Purging Type:* During the current episode of AN, the person has regularly engaged in binge-eating or purging behaviour (i.e., self-induced vomiting or the misuse of laxatives, diuretics, or enemas).

Bulimia Nervosa

A. Recurrent episodes of binge eating. An episode of binge eating is characterized by both of the following:
   i. Eating, in a discrete period of time (e.g., within any 2-hour period), an amount of food that is definitely larger than most people would eat during a similar period of time and under similar circumstances.
   ii. A sense of lack of control over eating during the episode (e.g., a feeling that one cannot stop or control what or how much one is eating.
B. Recurrent inappropriate compensatory behaviour in order to prevent weight gain, such as self-induced vomiting; misuse of laxatives, diuretics, enemas, or other medications; fasting; or excessive exercise.
C. The binge eating and inappropriate compensatory behaviours both occur, on average, at least twice a week for 3 months.
D. Self-evaluation is unduly influenced by body shape and weight.
E. The disturbance does not occur exclusively during episodes of AN.

There are also two subtypes of BN:

- *Purging Type:* the person regularly engages in self-induced vomiting or the misuse of laxatives, diuretics, or enemas.
- *Nonpurging Type:* the person uses other inappropriate compensatory behaviours, such as fasting or excessive exercise, but does not regularly engage in self-induced vomiting or the misuse of laxatives, diuretics, or enemas.

Eating Disorder Not Otherwise Specified

The Eating Disorder Not Otherwise Specified category is for disorders of eating that do not meet all the criteria for any specific Eating Disorder. Examples include:

A. For females, all of the criteria for AN (see re email regarding writing names in full) are met except that the individual has regular menses.
B. All of the criteria for AN are met except that, despite significant weight loss, the individual's current weight is in the normal range.
C. All of the criteria for BN are met except the binge eating and inappropriate compensatory mechanisms occur at a frequency of less than twice a week or for a duration of less than 3 months.
D. The regular use of inappropriate compensatory behaviour by an individual of normal body weight after eating small amounts of food (e.g., self-induced vomiting after the consumption of two cookies).
E. Repeatedly chewing and spitting out, but not swallowing, large amounts of food.
F. Binge-eating disorder: recurrent episodes of binge eating in the absence of the regular use of inappropriate compensatory behaviours characteristic of BN.

Binge Eating Disorder

A. Recurrent episodes of binge eating. An episode of binge eating is characterized by both of the following:
    i. Eating, in a discrete period of time (e.g., within any 2-hour period), an amount of food that is definitely larger than most people would eat in a similar period of time under similar circumstances
    ii. A sense of lack of control over eating during the episode (e.g., a feeling that one cannot stop eating or control what or how much one is eating).
B. The binge-eating episodes are associated with three (or more) of the following:
C. Eating much more rapidly than normal
D. Eating until feeling uncomfortably full
E. Eating large amounts of food when not feeling physically hungry
F. Eating alone because of being embarrassed by how much one is eating

G. Feeling disgusted with oneself, depressed, or very guilty after overeating
H. Marked distress regarding binge eating is present
I. The binge eating occurs, on average, at least two days a week for six months
J. The binge eating is not associated with the regular use of inappropriate compensatory behaviours (e.g purging, fasting, excessive exercise) and does not occur exclusively during the course of AN or BN.

EPIDEMIOLOGY AND PROGNOSIS

Anorexia Nervosa

The lifetime prevalence of AN is estimated to be 0.5% (Striegel-Moore and Franko, 2003). While there has been an increasing rate of males suffering from AN, it occurs much more commonly among women (with a male-to-female ratio ranging from approximately 1:10 to 1:15;Golden and Miller, 2010) and Caucasians (Striegel-Moore and Franko, 2003). Typically, the onset of AN occurs during mid-adolescence (Walsh et al., 2006) with a better prognosis for early onset cases (APA, 2000). Due to severe malnutrition and being underweight, frequent hospitalization is typical. The recovery rate is highly variable, typically fewer than half of individuals recover and one-fifth of individuals still remain chronically ill (Steinhausen, 2002). AN also has the highest mortality rate out of any of the other eating disorders, often either due to suicide or the physical effects associated with starvation (Walsh et al., 2006).

Bulimia Nervosa

While BN occurs much more commonly than AN with a lifetime prevalence between 1-3% (over double than that of AN; Gauvin, Steiger and Brodeur, 2009), its recovery rate is much higher. A 5-year follow-up study of individuals with BN, suggested that more than half recovered, with residual psychological symptoms gradually decreasing over time (Keski-Rahkonen, 2009). As with AN, the majority of BN sufferers are women (with the male-to-female ratio estimating between 1:15 to 1:20; Golden and Miller, 2010). Typically, the onset of BN occurs in individuals in late adolescence and early adulthood (Walsh et al., 2006), and often begins after periods of dieting or food restriction (in many cases after AN; Eddy et al., 2008).

Note that although the binge/purge type of AN may sound similar to BN, it is primarily different from BN as individuals with the binge/purge type of AN are amenorrehic and at a low body weight (Eddy et al., 2008)

Eating Disorder Not Otherwise Specified

Due to the rigidity of the diagnostic criteria for AN and BN, ED-NOS is the most commonly diagnosed eating disorder for those individuals who do not endorse the full symptom profile for AN or BN (Fairburn and Bohn, 2005). Often, just one criteria may be missing from a AN or BN diagnosis to warrant the label of ED-NOS, such as a patient who meets every criteria to be diagnosed with AN except for having a current weight that is more than 85% of the average body weight for their age and height (Anderson et al., 2001; APA, 2000). Unfortunately, very little empirical research has been conducted involving persons with ED-NOS despite the fact that many patients with ED-NOS , with time, end up meeting full diagnostic criteria for AN or BN (Fairburn et al., 1995). Furthermore, in the upcoming fifth version of the DSM, which is expected to be released in 2013, BED will become its own category of an eating disorder and AN and BN will become more inclusive (e.g. amenorrhea will no longer be a criteria necessary for AN diagnosis; APA 2000).

Binge Eating Disorder

Although Binge Eating Disorder is not a currently recognized as a stand alone eating disorder in the DSM-IV- TR, it is becoming increasingly acknowledged as a disorder itself as it is associated with a high prevalence rate (approximately 1% to 3% of the general population suffer from BED; Nolen-Hoeksema and Rector, 2008) and increased health care utilization (APA, 2000; Bruce and Agras, 1992; Striegel-Moore et al., 2005). BED resembles BN in a variety of ways, however, unlike with BN, individuals with BED do not regularly engage in purging, exercising, or fasting to compensate for binge eating; Nolen-Hoeksema and Rector, 2008). Individuals suffering from BED are often significantly overweight, although there are individuals diagnosed with BED who are not obese (Monteleone, 2006). Although women are 1.5 times more likely to be diagnosed with BED, the gender differences compared to AN and BN are less pronounced, with BED occurring at a later age (Mitchell, Deblin, de Zwaan, Crow and Peterson, 2008; Walsh et al., 2006).

ETIOLOGY

The etiology of eating disorders is multifactorial; a combination of over 30 biological, psychological, and sociocultural risk factors are posited to play a role in the development of the illness (Jacobi, Hayward, de Zwaan, Kraemer and Argas, 2004). It is worthy of note that being predisposed to risk factors does not necessarily mean an individual will develop an eating disorder definitively, but highlights the need to monitor and be aware of potential risk variables (Walsh et al., 2006). Some of the more commonly occurring biological, psychological, and sociocultural risk factors are highlighted below.

Biological Risk Factors

A genetic component contributing to an individual's risk of developing an eating disorder has been identified. Twin studies with large samples have shown the heritability of AN to be between 48% and 74%, and the genetic effect of BN to range from 59% to 83% (Nolen-Hoeksema and Rector, 2008). It has also been reported that individuals with an eating disorder often have family members who evidence greater psychopathology (Lilenfeld, Ringham, Kalarchian and Marcus, 2008).

The hypothalamus and its regulatory chemicals are posited to play a substantial role in controlling eating behaviour. Studies have shown that individuals with AN have a lower functioning hypothalamus and unregulated levels of serotonin and dopamine, chemical known to connect with the hypothalamus to regulate eating (Brambilla, Bellodi, Arancio, Ronchi, and Limonta, 2001). To date, it is inconclusive whether these brain-related findings are a cause or consequence of AN. In addition, patients with BN evidence low serotonin levels, a neurochemical state that has been postulated to cause the body to crave foods high in carbohydrates (and may explain why sufferers of BN often binge on these types of foods) (Wurtman, 1987; Nolen-Hoeksema and Rector, 2008). Thus, both genetic and neurochemical components can play a critical role in increasing an individual's risk for an eating disorder.

Psychological Risk Factors

Some of the most prominently reported psychological risk factors associated with the development of an eating disorder include body dissatisfaction, low self-esteem, perceived pressure to be thin, internalization of the thin-ideal, and using food to cope with negative emotions (Homan, 2010; Masheb and Grilo, 2006; Smith, 2010; Stice, 2010). In an experiment conducted by Abbate-Daga (2010) involving 586 outpatients with AN, BN-P, and ED-NOS, eating disorders were highly correlated with body dissatisfaction. Specifically, the patients with BN illustrated the most body dissatisfaction, followed respectively by ED-NOS, AN-BP, and AN-R. In another study comparing 197 adolescent primary care patients between the ages of between 14 and 19 with and without low self esteem, the patients with low self esteem were 4 times more likely to develop eating disorder symptomology (Courtney, 2008). Thus, individuals with low self-esteem and body dissatisfaction may be at an increased risk for developing an eating disorder.

Studies also suggest that individuals who have difficulty coping with negative emotions are more likely to develop an eating disorder. For example, Sim (2006) found that adolescent girls who experienced chronic aversive emotion and had difficulties labeling their emotions were more likely to illustrate disordered eating behaviours. In particular, there was a positive correlation between experiencing negative affect and disordered eating ($r = .35$); as negative affect increased, so did disordered eating. On the other hand, the correlation between constructive coping with negative affect and disordered eating was negative ($r = -.32$); as constructive coping increased, disordered eating decreased. This example highlights that difficulties controlling negative emotions can put an individual at risk for an eating disorder.

Moreover, certain personality factors may also predispose an individual to developing an eating disorder. For example, perfectionism (Gallucci, 2009) and a rigid, dichotomous thinking style are personality factors that often can carry over to the weight domain (e.g. wanting the perfect body and seeing being thin as good and being "fat" as bad) (Nolen-Hoeksema and Rector, 2008).

Individuals who diet, restrict their food intake (Stice, 2010), or have had early digestive problems, such as gastrointestinal problems and fussy eating, are also at an increased risk of later developing an eating disorder (Gendall, Joyce, Carter, McIntosh and Bulik, 2005; Marchi and Cohen, 1990). Lastly, although controversial, being a victim of sexual abuse is also a possible psychological risk factor (Jacobi et al., 2004).

Sociocultural Risk Factors

Exposure to the western ideal of thinness is a salient factor in the development of an eating disorder (Canals, 2009). As the ideal shape for women has been getting thinner, more women are becoming increasingly driven to meet the societal standards of beauty and thinness. According to the sociocultural model, individuals who internalize the thin ideal are at an increased risk for body dissatisfaction which may lead to negative affect and dieting behaviours, all of which increase the risk of developing an eating disorder (Canals, 2009). It was reported that exposure to images of ultra-thin models resulted in negative affect and body dissatisfaction in women (Nolen-Hoeksema and Rector, 2008). Stice and colleagues (2001) conducted an experiment which illustrated the effects of chronic exposure to thin-deal images in fashion magazines on adolescent girls. Following a 15-month subscription to a fashion magazine, girls who were already experiencing body dissatisfaction prior to the experiment and who also had little social support were affected the most by the extremely thin images in the magazines. In fact, they became even more dissatisfied with their bodies, dieted more, and showed bulimic symptomology.

Unfortunately, the adverse effects associated with being exposed to the thin ideal are not exclusive to individuals in North America. Highlighting the pernicious effects of Westernized media, a study done in Fiji showed that following the introduction of television, the prevalence of eating attitudes and behaviours among young adolescent girls dramatically increased (VanderWal, 2008). Studies involving the negative effects of the thin ideal also extend to immigrants to western culture. Immigrants who adapt their cultural identity and join western culture, and internalize its thin ideals are also at high risk for developing an eating disorder. For example, Abrams, Allen and Gray (1993) reported that African Americans who shunned their African identity and reported greater idealization of a westernized identity were more likely to endorse eating disorder behaviours and attitudes. Thus, regardless of an individual's place of origin or where an individual is situated in the world, exposure to the western ideal of thinness appears to be a significant factor in the development of an eating disorder.

Individuals who are involved in physically-focused activities that place extensive importance on thinness and/or weight, such as modeling, or body-focused sports like ballet, wrestling, gymnastics, and judo, are also at high risk for developing an eating disorder (Walsh et al., 2006; Nolen-Hoeksema and Rector, 2008). A study was conducted by Sundgot-Borgen (1994) to assess the prevalence of eating disorders amongst female athletes between the ages of 12 and 35, and found that the prominence of eating disorders amongst female athletes varied depending on the type of sports they participated in. For example, athletes involved in sports classified as "aesthetic" (e.g., gymnastics, figure skating) or "weight dependent" (e.g., judo, wrestling) were more likely to have AN or BN, while ball game sports, such as volleyball, were the least likely to show a link with eating disorders.

Parental attitudes about weight, shape, and food, are also known to influence the development of an eating disorder. Specifically, a maternal drive for thinness and body dissatisfaction and a paternal perfectionism have been shown to increase the likelihood of developing an eating disorder (Stice, 2010). Additionally, family dynamics characterized by over-controlling parents who do not allow the expression of emotion, also place individuals at risk (Nolen-Hoeksema and Rector, 2008). Thus, it is important to educate parents about potential risk factors in order in efforts to prevent potential eating disorders in their offspring.

Homosexual males are a specific sub-population at great risk for experiencing eating disorders. It has been theorized that just as heterosexual women want to attract men, so do homosexual males and therefore, they may become vulnerable to similar pressures and standards of beauty that women experience (Feldman and Meyer, 2007) Furthermore, women in their post-partum period are also at an increased risk for developing an eating disorder, or for eating disorder symptoms to get worse if present already (Astrachan-Fletcher, Veldhuis, Lively, Fowler and Marcks, 2008). This increase can be attributed to the weight changes associated with pregnancy (Stein and Fairburn, 1996) which can cause increased body dissatisfaction; this in turn predicts more eating problems (Gjerdingen et al., 2009).

EATING DISORDERS AND MEDICAL RISK

Malnutrition and critical changes in body weight are just two of the adverse health consequences associated with eating disorders. Many other physiological and organ systems are affected, including but not limited to, the endocrine, cardiovascular, skeletal, musculoskeletal, neurological, gastrointestinal, haematological, and fluid and electrolyte balance systems (Forman, 2010; Walsh et al., 2006). The following briefly outlines some of the medical comorbidities that can be associated with eating disorders, although it is important to note that having an eating disorder does not necessarily mean an individual will experience all of these potential medical complications.

In AN, the reproductive system can be significantly affected (Walsh et al., 2006). Secondary amenorrhea, defined as the absence or suppression of periods (menstruation) for at least 6 months in a woman who has previously menstruated (Welt, 2008), affects more than 90% of females with AN (Mehler, 2001). The consequences associated with this secondary amenorrhea can include infertility, osteoporosis, and the failure to undergo puberty if the amenorrhea presents early enough in life (Slupik, 1999). Furthermore, both sufferers of AN and BN can experience growth problems such as delayed puberty, growth retardation and short stature, especially in younger individuals who have not yet completed puberty (Swenne, 2005). It has been reported that if an eating disorder occurs before menarche, that is, if the individual develops the eating disorder prior to their first period, and also experience weight loss, the individual is at an increased risk for growth retardation and short stature (Swenne, 2005). A longitudinal study conducted by Swenne (2005) which investigated stunted growth in female children with eating disorders of premenarcheal onset, found that catch-up growth is possible if these individuals gain weight before the ability to grow is lost with age. Thus it is extremely important that these individuals revert back to healthy eating and gain weight (if they are underweight) immediately as the capacity for growth eventually declines.

Another condition linked to AN or BN is hypotension (low blood pressure when changing body position) (Walsh et al., 2006). Sufferers of BED on the other hand commonly develop hypertension, which can lead to abnormal thickening of the heart and kidney failure (Walsh et al., 2006; Domino and Kaplan, 2010). In addition, individuals who starve themselves, induce vomiting, or abuse laxatives, often develop hypoglycemia or low blood sugar, while binge-eating and over-eating can cause hyperglycemia or high blood sugar (Walsh et al., 2006).

Individuals with AN may develop anemia (Cleary, 2010), and its associated complications include a weakened immune system, shortness of breath, heart palpitations, and weakness and fatigue (Zeiger, 2007). Lastly, during the early stages of feeding severely malnourished patients with AN, a serious, common, and potentially life-threatening condition called refeeding syndrome may occur. This condition is characterized by significant fluid shifts and electrolyte disturbances, primarily driven by the change in insulin secretion as a result of the shift from protein metabolism to carbohydrate metabolism (Whitelaw, 2010). This can be avoided by increasing the nutritional support slowly and gradually (i.e. using liquid meal supplements), and closely monitoring electrolyte and organ status.

EATING DISORDERS AND PSYCHOLOGICAL COMORBIDITY

In addition to potentially deleterious physiological consequences, it is also common for individuals with eating disorders to present with numerous other concurrent psychological diagnoses such as depression, anxiety, and substance use disorders. Interestingly, many of these disorders deal with dysregulated affect (i.e. anxiety and depression) or, like eating disorders, can serve as a means to control negative affect (i.e. substance use) (Aldao, 2010; De Young, 2010; Wiser and Telch, 1999).

Braun, Sunday and Halmi (1994) reported that 51% of inpatients with eating disorders also suffered from concurrent depression, highlighting the commonality of comorbid mood and eating disorders. Do eating disorders cause depressive symptoms, or vice versa? A study longitudinal study conducted by Marmorstein (2008) investigating the relationship between eating disorders and depression in adolescence during two time intervals (from ages 11-14 and from 14-17), found that adolescent's eating disorder attitudes and behaviours predicted later depression symptomology, but not the reverse. On the contrary, Measelle, Stice and Hogansen (2003) found that over the course of four years, depression symptomology predicted eating disorder pathology for adolescent girls. However, although not conclusive, recent findings suggest that depression usually predates the onset of an eating disorder (Sihvola et al., 2009). Thus, future research is needed to determine the causal relationship between depression and eating disorders.

Anxiety disorders including obsessive compulsive disorder (OCD), social phobia, and generalized anxiety disorder (GAD), are also common amongst individuals suffering from eating disorders. Godart et al. (2003) reported that 71% of individuals with eating disorders also have endorsed at least one anxiety disorder, and that co-morbid anxiety disorders precede the onset of an eating disorder (75% in AN and 88% in BN). Specifically looking at OCD, research suggests that up to 40% of patients with AN and BN also meet diagnosis for OCD. Additionally, 13% to 42% of patients with primarily diagnosed OCD also have eating disorders (Godart et al., 2003).

In a study conducted by Godart (2003) investigating anxiety disorders in 271 females with AN and BN, it was reported that social phobia occurred most often before the onset of both types of disorders (51.2% in AN-R, 60.9% in AN-BP, 67.7% in BN-P and 71.4% in BN-NP). On the other hand, GAD appeared more often in the same year or after the onset of an eating disorder in AN-R, AN-BN, and BN-P (91.6%, 75%, and 67.1% respectively). Thus, these examples highlight the importance of early detection and treatment of mental disorders, including social phobia or eating disorders, to aid in the prevention of a following mental disorder that may end up occurring concurrently with the illness.

Substance use disorders (SUD) also are highly prevalent amongst individuals with eating disorders. Research shows that the prevalence of drugs and alcohol abuse is about 50% in individuals with eating disorders, compared to approximately only 9% in healthy populations (Bulik et al., 2010). The lifetime prevalence of SUD in patients with eating disorders is up to 23% in AN, and 55% in BN, with alcohol and stimulants (including tobacco and illicit drugs) making up the majority of the substances being abused. Moreover, it appears that patients with BN-P and AN-BP are more likely to have SUD compared to patients with other eating disorder subtypes (Calero-Elvira et al., 2007). When compared to healthy individuals, patients with AN-R are even less likely to have a SUD. Studies also show that the use of tobacco is more prevalent in patients with eating disorders than individuals in the general population (George and Waller, 2005), with patients with BN and AN-BP having the highest risk of smoking compared to patients with other eating disorder subtypes (Krug et al., 2008). Furthermore, individuals suffering with both SUD and an eating disorder also show a higher mortality rate and poorer prognosis (Thompson-Brenner, Eddy, Franko, Dorer, Vashchenko and Herzog, 2008). Lastly, individuals who suffer from eating disorders and SUD's concurrently tend to go through periods of decreasing the behaviours associated with one illness while turning more towards the behaviours associated with the other disorder. For example, individuals with ED-SUD may start to reduce their eating disorder behaviours but then increase their substance use (and vice versa)

Body dysmorphic disorder (BDD), which is characterized by excessive preoccupation with a body part an individual believes to be defective, often occurs co-currently with eating disorders and shares some similar clinical features (Didie, Reinecke, and Phillips, 2010). These features include body image dissatisfaction, obsessive thinking, chronic low self-esteem, and impairment in interpersonal functioning. While the prevalence of eating disorders in individuals with BDD varies across studies, it appears to be elevated compared to rates in the general population and more commonly found in ED-NOS. For example, in a study involving 200 individuals with lifetime BDD who were not seeking or receiving treatment as part of the study, 33% reported having a lifetime eating disorder (9%, 6.5%, and 17.5% of the cases had AN, BN, and ED-NOS respectively; Didie, Reinecke, and Phillips, 2010), compared to the reported 5% of the general population who reported suffering from an eating disorder alone (Treasure, Claudino, and Zucker, 2010). Eating disorders and their associated destructive behaviours, such as binge-eating, purging, dieting, and over-exercising, are posited to function as a means to help individuals control or deal with unpleasant emotions (De Young, 2010).

Just as with eating disorders, many of the mental health issues described above are connected to emotion regulation issues (Aldao, 2010). That is, many of these illnesses transpire as a means to deal with and control negative affect and sensations. Substance use, for example, is often used a means to avoid or "escape" the experience of emotions. Hence, providing an integrated program that (1) addresses the maladaptive behaviours associated with the eating disorder and concurrent mental health problem(s) and (2) teaches individuals more productive ways to deal with their emotions, not only plays an essential role in the recovery process of both disorders but can be more cost effective compared to sequential treatment. It is not surprising that medical and psychiatric comorbidities of eating disorders, such as the abovementioned, contribute to an economic burden on health care. Striegel-Moore, Leslie, Petrill, Garvin, and Rosenheck (2000) found that the annual cost of inpatient and outpatient treatment for females with eating disorders in the United States was estimated to be $12 214. While this estimation was found to be an underrepresentation of the costs, it is still even greater than the cost of treating obsessive compulsive disorder and also schizophrenia, with the later only compared to AN (Simon, 2005).

Treatment Options Available for Eating Disorders

Treatment Facilities

A variety of treatments have been developed for eating disorders, with the appropriate intensity and form of treatment depending on the patient's degree of severity (APA, 2006; Tylka, 1999). Weight, rate of weight loss, medical stability, and willingness to change (APA, 2006) should be examined before establishing which mode of treatment to use.

Inpatient Hospitalization

The initial goal to treating patients with severe eating disorders is to stabilize them medically, and often times, when outpatient therapy is ineffective or when the individual experiences low motivation to recover, inpatient hospitalization is the first step in doing so (Forman, 2010; Ametller, 2005). Involuntary inpatient hospitalization and forced feeding is most commonly needed in the cases involving patients with AN (Russell, 2001), especially when the patient weighs less than 75% of their expected weight (for their height and age), or when the patient continues to lose weight during outpatient treatment (Forman, 2010). Experts recommend that weight restoration to at least 90 to 92 percent of the target goal weight is considered a critical factor in the recovery from an eating disorder (Forman, 2010). Other forms of treatment, including outpatient therapy or day treatment are typically more appropriate, especially for patients with BN, as weight restoration is usually not an issue (Walsh et al., 2006). In cases where patients need to be put on medication to control their purging, or where the patient suffers from other psychiatric illnesses such as depression, anxiety disorders, substance abuse, suicide, or active psychosis, hospitalization may be required (Fennig, 2010; Steiger 2010). Furthermore, it is worthy to note that the success rates with patients who are involuntarily admitted to hospital for treatment appear to be no different than patients who admit themselves voluntarily. Watson (2000), found that eating disorder patients who were involuntarily admitted to hospital did just as well in treatment as patients who voluntarily admitted themselves to treatment (Watson, 2000). Put another way, being forced into hospital treatment does not hinder the recovery process any less than when individuals enter treatment by choice.

Day Patient Hospitalization

Day programs can help to ease a patient's transition from inpatient hospitalization to outpatient care, allowing patients to go home in the evening, while still providing structured eating routines and supervised meals during the day (APA, 2006).

Additionally, while the primary focus of inpatient hospitalization is to attain medical stability of a patient, the primary focus of day treatment is not only to help the patient maintain his/her medical stability, but also to provide a much more intensive active treatment intervention using group therapy, individual therapy, and family therapy (Schnaffner, 2008). With approximately one third of BN and AN patients relapsing (Keel et al., 2005) and treatment retention being quite low for patients with eating disorders, especially AN (Halmi et al., 1995), it can be important to offer stepped care for ED. For example, after inpatient treatment, transitioning to a day treatment program may be help to maintain the gains made in inpatient treatment.

Outpatient Treatment

Outpatient treatment usually includes both group and individual therapy for those individuals who experience mild to moderate eating disorder behaviours and symptoms (The American Psychiatric Association Work Group on Eating Disorders, 2006).

This form of treatment not only helps patients to focus on individual issues, but also allows them to receive group support, assisting individuals to work on their interpersonal relationships and helping them to decrease feelings of loneliness and isolation that they may experience as a result of their eating disorder (Arnold, 2007).

Outpatient treatment has been reported to demonstrate similar effectiveness in inpatient treatment for BN (Zeeck, 2009) and AN (Gowers et al., 2007). However, when outpatient therapy is not enough and patients need additional support (i.e. if the patient continues to lose weight and/or becomes medically unstable), hospitalization is strongly recommended (Forman, 2010).

PSYCHOLOGICAL TREATMENTS

In the abovementioned treatment facilities, different therapeutic modalities have been utilized and empirically tested in the treatment of eating disorders. The following delineates some of the treatment options currently utilized in ED treatment. As each client presents with unique characteristics, to maximize gains, it is important to find a treatment(s) that "fits" to the client rather than working to fit a client into a certain treatment framework.

Cognitive Behaviour Therapy (CBT)

CBT has received empirical support in the treatment of BN and BED, with its efficacy to treat AN still remaining in question (Pike et al., 2010; Walsh et al., 2006). This psychological treatment, usually lasting 10-20 sessions, focuses primarily on treating both the thoughts and behavioural factors that maintain eating disorders. For individuals who suffer from BN, the cognitive component of therapy involves disputing illogical cognitions that accompany disordered eating, binge eating and purging, and developing positive attitudes around weight and shape (Nolen-Hoeksema and Rector, 2008). The behavioural component of treatment promotes healthy eating and helps to introduce forbidden foods that often trigger binge eating and purging (often resulting from dichotomous thinking such as feeling the need to binge if the attempt to avoid the forbidden food fails(Nolen-Hoeksema and Rector, 2008). Moreover, in AN, the behaviour component is typically used during the period of achieving medical stability, and in fact, helps patients to achieve it (Nolen-Hoeksema and Rector, 2008). This is often done by making rewards contingent on weight gain. For example, during hospitalization, privileges, including weekend-passes to go home or allowing the patients to choose their own meals and/or snacks, are rewarded to patients who cooperate with the program and meet the appropriate weight gain requirements. While studies show that behaviour therapy helps patients gain 15 percent of their ideal body weight, most patients relapse and return to their eating disorder behaviours quickly once therapy ends (Fairburn, 2005). Thus, it is beneficial to incorporate additional therapeutic options that help deal with cognitive issues associated with weight gain so that relapse and weight loss can be prevented.

CBT has also shown promise in the treatment for BED. In fact, studies show that CBT for BED is a more effective treatment option than using antidepressant medication or no treatment at all (Ruhl, 2005). The downfall to this treatment option, however, is that patients undergoing CBT often do not experience significant weight loss, even though CBT helps to reduce the binge-eating frequency (Munsch et al., 2007). Although other therapy options have been shown to reduce weight loss, such as behavioural weight loss (BWL), where weight loss is the primary goal of treatment, numerous studies have explicated that the weight reduction from these altnerate treatments is only short-term. Therefore, further emphasis should be placed on integrating effective weight management options into traditional CBT techniques in efforts to increase healthy lifestyle patterns and exercise.

Moreover, despite the fact that CBT is considered a superior form of treatment for BN compared to drug and other psychological therapies in reducing eating disorder behaviours as well as preventing relapse (Ruhl, 2005), only about 40-50% of individuals completely stop binge-purging behaviours following treatment (Fairburn et al., 1995). Thus, to address the individuals who do not recover from BN, other treatment options need to be explored, including the possibility of treatment integration in targeting resistant ED clients.

Interpersonal Psychotherapy (IPT)

IPT is another short-term therapy, typically ranging from 15-20 sessions (Klerman, Weissman, Rounsaville and Chevron, 1984). This therapeutic option is based on the notion that interpersonal factors affect and perpetuate eating disorder symptomatology (Klerman et al., 1984). The model primarily focuses on four interpersonal factors that influence the development of an eating disorder: grief, interpersonal disputes, interpersonal deficits, and role transitions (McIntosh, 2000). The goal of IPT is to help improve factors such as these, thus helping to decrease the problematic behaviours associated with eating disorders (McIntosh, 2000). With this said, it is unfortunate that there is little empirical research exploring the effectiveness of IPT for AN. Instead, research pays particularly more attention to the benefits of IPT for BN and BED. Findings support the use of IPT for the treatment of BN which appears to work quickly at eliminating eating disorder behaviours (Arcelus, 2009). In a pilot study conducted by Arcelus (2009), IPT significantly reduced binge eating and purging amongst BN patients within 8 sessions of treatment. However, IPT is not as fast in producing symptomatic improvements in BN patients when compared to CBT in the short term (Arcelus, 2009). Nonetheless, in the long term, there appears to be no significant differences of recovery rates in patients between the two treatments (Agras et al., 2000). Additionally, IPT has also been compared to CBT when it comes to treating BED; studies show that IPT is equally effective as CBT, even in the long term (Fairburn et al., 1997; Wilfley et al. 2002). Lastly, along with CBT, IPT, like most other psychotherapies, is more successful at reducing binge eating and purging behaviours than decreasing the weight of overweight individuals with BED (Nolen-Hoeksema and Rector, 2008).

Family Therapy

Family therapy is considered an effective treatment for treating patients with AN, especially when the patient is a child or an adolescent (Eisler, 2010). This therapeutic model holds that the patient with AN and his/her family are treated as a unit, without blaming anyone for causing the eating disorder (Rhodes, 2003). The Maudsley Approach is a commonly used form of family therapy for younger and adolescent patients as it involves having the parents of the patient with AN initially take the primary role in their child's nutritional recovery and weight restoration (Lock et al., 2001). This model holds that at first, parents must take full responsibility over meal planning and the supervision of meals. However, as recovery progresses, patients are slowly provided with more control over their eating. Finally, once weight is completely restored, issues involving adolescent identity and parental relationships are examined.

Unfortunately, there is limited extant research investigating the differences between the effectiveness of family therapy compared to other forms of treatments. Currently, family therapy is not the therapy of choice for treating individuals with BN or BED as evidence supporting the effectiveness of family therapy for BN is limited and there has been no family based treatments for BED developed to date. However, as an individual's eating disorder can affect the entire family (Newell, 2010), further investigation into efficacious family oriented treatments is necessary. For example, family members often develop anxiety due to growing concern for their suffering family member's health (Maier, 2009). This anxiety often leads family members to dedicate constant attention to the ill individual, affecting family dynamics. In addition, family members often grow distant from each other and live in fear of saying something 'wrong' to their ill family member, especially if the suffer denies his/her illness (Maier, 2009).

Psychodynamic Therapy

Psychodynamic therapy for individuals with eating disorders focuses on bringing the unconscious conflicts that underline the eating disorder behaviours to the surface, so that the patient can experience and understand them (Cleaves, 2008). While there is only a limited amount of research conducted involving psychodynamic treatments with eating disorders due to the difficulties associated with standardizing the approach for empirical study, there have been some studies that illustrate the effectiveness of this therapeutic approach (Cleaves, 2008). For example, a study done by Murphy and colleagues (2005) illustrated that a time limited psychodynamic approach that incorporates behavioural techniques helps to reduce eating disorder symptoms in patients with BED and BN. Additionally, in a study involving 37 adolescents individuals with AN, ego-oriented psychotherapy (a form of psychodynamic therapy) helped significantly to improve individual's mood, relationship with food, and eating-related family conflict (Cleaves, 2008). Finally, when compared to other therapeutic treatments for eating disorders such as CBT, psychodynamic therapy appears at most to be just as effective in reducing eating disorder symptoms (Cleaves, 2008).

Mindfulness-Based Therapies

Mindfulness refers to paying attention to a particular stimulus with a non-judgmental attitude that is usually taught by engaging in medication exercises (Kabat-Zinn, 1990). Mindfulness-based therapies encourage this perspective, with training aimed to help individuals make adaptive choices about responding to aversive experiences, all the while helping to reduce the intensity with which individuals react to certain emotions and thoughts (Lineham, 1993).

Mindfulness-based eating awareness training (MB-EAT) incorporates both mindfulness-based stress reduction (MBSRand MBCT with guided eating meditations into daily activities related to food cravings and eating, to help individuals cultivate mindful awareness of their destructive eating patterns, and then help them to remove negative reactivity (Kristeller, Baer, and Quillian-Wolever, 2006; Kristeller and Hallett, 1999). Kristeller and Hallet (1999) conducted an experiment to study the efficacy of a group-based MB-EAT on obese women suffering from BED over a 6 week period. Not only did these women experience a decrease in the severity and frequency of binge eating, but also evidenced reductions in depression and anxiety symptoms. Specifically, the frequency of the binge eating decreased from approximately slightly over 4 times a week to approximately less than 2 times a week. These results suggest that MB-EAT can be an effective treatment for BED.

Mindfulness-based cognitive therapy (MBCT), originally developed to prevent relapse from depression, has become an effective treatment for treating BED (Baer, Fischer, and Huss, 2005; Ma and Teasdale, 2004). MBCT encourages the non-judgmental acceptance of bodily sensations, cognitions, emotions, and perceptions (sights and sounds), as well as assisting individuals to acknowledge and let go of negative thoughts without treating them as an unchangeable reality (Baer, Fischer, and Huss, 2005). Additionally, Mindfulness-Action Based Cognitive Therapy (MACBT) has been found to treat individuals with concurrent BED and SUD (Courbasson, Nishikawa, and Shapira, in press). This method of treatment puts particular focus on emotional regulation, helping individuals to find alternative coping mechanisms for dealing with distressing emotions rather than turning to food or substances. Following a 16-week group of MABCT, individuals suffering from BED and comorbid SUD showed significant improvements in eating disorder attitudes, drug and alcohol severity, depression, the ability to resist negative emotions, and a reduction in objective binge-eating episodes and emotional eating.

Another psychological therapy that also incorporates elements of mindfulness training in the treatment of eating disorders is acceptance and commitment therapy (ACT) (Hayes, Strosahl, and Wilson, 1999). ACT, which helps tp promote the ability to make adaptive choices when experiencing strong emotions, has been demonstrated to be effective at treating eating pathology.

For example, Juarascio (2010) compared the effectiveness of standard CBT (i.e. Beck's cognitive therapy; CT) with ACT amongst 55 participants who illustrated eating disorder symptomology and found ACT to be the superior treatment for eating disorders. In fact, ACT produced a large decrease in eating pathology while CT only produced a modest decrement.

In addition to effectively treating individuals with BED, mindfulness-based therapies can also be used to treat AN (Kristeller, Baer, and Quillian-Wolever, 2006). The approach when treating AN is to present the individual with AN with related eating disorder thoughts such as "my stomach is gross" and then encourage the individual to not act in accordance to them. Unfortunately however, to date, little is known about the effectiveness of mindfulness-based therapies when treating BN (Kristeller, Baer, and Quillian-Wolever, 2006), highlighting the focus of future research.

PHARMACOLOGICAL TREATMENTS

When evaluating the different therapeutic options available for eating disorders, there are no pharmacological interventions that are cited as the "cure" for eating disorders, and many side effects are prominent. However, there are pharmacological treatments that, in tandem with psychological treatments, may help to treat eating disorders. The following discusses these treatments.

Anorexia Nervosa

There are no psychotropic medications that specifically benefit individuals with AN, yet some medications that serve to improve other comorbid disorders (such as depression and anxiety) may impact AN (Forman, 2010; Walsh et al., 2006). For example, the antidepressant Fluoxetine, a selective-serotonin reuptake inhibitor (SSRI), was not found to significantly affect time to relapse or weight maintenance above a BMI of 18.5 in a group of weight-restored individuals with AN who were concurrently receiving CBT, in comparison to placebo (Walsh et al., 2006). These results differ from a previous study where weight maintenance with Fluoxetine was observed (compared to placebo), possibly due to its small sample size and the fact that the placebo group did not receive CBT and had a high drop-out rate (Kaye et al., 2001). Though the American Psychiatric Association does not recommend the use of psychoactive drugs as a first line of treatment for AN, it suggests that they can be considered to treat potentially comorbid disorders such as obsessive compulsive behaviour (OCD) and depression (Forman, 2010).

Bulimia Nerovsa

In contrast to AN, pharmacological treatment of BN is recommended, despite being shown to be inferior to treatment with CBT (Walsh et al., 2010). The only drug approved by the US Food and Drug Administration for the treatment of BN is Fluoxetine (Forman, 2010). The recommended dose is 60mg/day, higher than that used to treat depression, because numerous studies have shown a significantly better response to fluoxetine at this dosage (Archives of General Psychiatry, 1992); Forman, 2010; Shapiro et al., 2007; Walsh et al., 2010; Williams, Goodie and Motsinger, 2008).

Binge Eating Disorder

SSRI's and appetite suppressants such as Sibutramine have been demonstrated to improve the symptoms of BED (Appolinario et al., 2003; Forman, 2010; Hudson et al., 1998); however there are drawbacks to these medications. For example, Fluoxetine was found to be ineffective when compared to placebo in a study conducted by Grilo et al. (2005), and thus, the NICE (National Institute for Clinical Excellence) guidelines (2004) stated that there is insufficient information to conclude that weight loss and binge eating are positively influenced by medication. Sibutraminne on the other hand, while found to reduce weight loss and binge-eating, is associated with many different side effects such as headache, insomnia, and dizziness (Wilfley et al., 2008).

EATING DISORDERS IN OLDER ADULTS

While eating disorders are more commonly found in adolescents and younger adults (Stein, 2009), their prevalence is not limited to this population. In fact, although controversial, eating disorders amongst the older adult population (defined as 50 years and older) have become increasing prevalent, again more commonly in females (Gadalla, 2008; Lapid, 2010). Lapid (2010) reported that 88% of eating disorder cases in an older adult population were female. In addition, it was also reported that older adults with eating disorders showed higher rates of late onset (69%) versus early onset (which continues from an earlier period or re-occurs in an older age). Furthermore, the majority of this population (81%) met every criteria of AN except amenorrhea, which needs to be considered in light of the fact that the average age for menopause is approximately 51 years old; Casper, 2009). Moreover, just as with young adults and adolescents, older adults also evidence concurrent psychiatric disorders alongside eating disorders, including anxiety disorders, SUD's (mostly alcohol dependence), and especially depression (Gadalla, 2008).

While the clinical features of eating disorders amongst older adults are similar to that of younger adults and adolescents, the mechanisms leading to the development of an eating disorder can differ. For example, Gupta (1995) found that the aging physical appearance associated in older adults is correlated with preoccupation with weight, dieting, and exercise, all of which are factors that can increase the likelihood of developing an eating disorder. In addition, aging may lead individuals to feel that they are devalued by society and have lost a sense of control; this may in turn trigger the development of an eating disorder in older adults because of the perceived gain in power that the disorder offers (Lapid, 2010). Furthermore, nutritional rehabilitation plays an essential role in reducing the symptoms associated with an eating disorder and helping the individual to gain weight (if needed) (Berry, 2000; Taylor, 2008). Finally, older adults often may experience a loss of appetite due to the side-effects of some medications as well as their loss of taste and smell due to their old age, thereby leading them to reduce their food intake (Morely, 2003; Ofo, 2006;Satoh-Kuriwada, 2009), which can result in significant weight loss that can perpetuate AN.

As with younger adults with eating disorders, older adults can benefit from the use of similar types of pharmacological and psychological treatments (Lapid, 2010). However, it is important to note that there are some issues associated with eating disorders in older adults that make this population's treatment unique. For example, while young adolescents can benefit from their parent's support and involvement in recovery, older adults are encouraged to have their spouses and children contributing to their care (Lapid, 2010). In addition, older adults may suffer from cognitive and hearing impairment due to old age, and thus may have a difficult time participating in psychological therapies. Thus, including a separate category of eating disorders in older adults in the DSM can be quite beneficial as this population shows unique psychological mechanisms leading to an eating disorder and unique treatment needs.

EATING DISORDERS AND ITS ASSOCIATED STIGMA

Although awareness of the causes and consequences of eating disorders is growing, the general public, and even some clinicians, still stigmatize eating disorders, which may hinder the extent to which individuals seek treatment or promote prevention endeavours. While empirical research has made it clear that biological factors (eg. genetic factors) play an important role in the development of an eating disorder, the general public tends to hold that the illness is caused exclusively through environmental factors. For example, in a poll study commissioned by the National Eating Disorder Association (NEDA), it was found that the vast majority of American adults blame dieting, media, and families as causal factors in eating disorders (O'Hara and Smith, 2007). Other researchers have found that not only does the general public fail to see the seriousness of this illness, but many of them think that the individuals suffering from an eating disorder are to blame for their own illness, and thus, should just 'get better.' In a poll study conducted by Crisp (2005) in the UK, 33% of subjects blamed the sufferer for their own eating disorder. Furthermore, in a study conducted by Murray, Touyz, and Beaumont (1990) which assessed the knowledge of eating disorders in adults up to age 30, it was found that only 3% of these subjects viewed eating disorders as having medical consequences. Additionally, it was reported that up to 50% of eating disorder cases go unrecognized amongst general clinicians (Becker, Grinspoon, Klibanski, and Herzog, 1999), and thus, are thus left untreated. Surprisingly, even when an eating disorder diagnosis is made, it has been reported that many doctors simply tell their patients to eat better, highlighting that the stigma associated with eating disorders are not limited to the general public (Wahl, 1995).

Moreover, due to the stigma associated with eating disorders, many suffers have reported to feel too ashamed and afraid to seek help, resulting in the avoidance of support and treatment of their illness in fear that their condition will be discovered (O'Hara and Smith, 2007). Thus, being exposed to family members, friends, or general clinicians who hold these stereotypical views on the illness may impede early diagnosis and subsequent treatment of eating disorders.

CONCLUSION

Eating disorders are serious psychological disorders with widespread negative health and psychosocial consequences. Therefore, destigmatization and appropriate treatment of the illness is vital to an individual's recovery. Biological, psychological, and social risk factors, both isolated and in combination, may contribute to the development of an eating disorder. While there is some substantial evidence supporting the effectiveness of psychological therapies for eating disorders (e.g. CBT for BN), there is still a great need for more controlled empirical studies to further delineate what type of treatment most benefits each type of eating disorder. It may be that treatments are more efficacious for certain individuals depending on the constellation of risk factors they present, highlighting an area for future research. Additionally, although more research is critical, pharmacological treatments show some efficacy treating the symptoms of BN. The adverse social, psychological and health consequences, along side rising prevalence rates, argues for the necessity of early recognition, detection, prevention, and subsequent treatment of eating disorders.

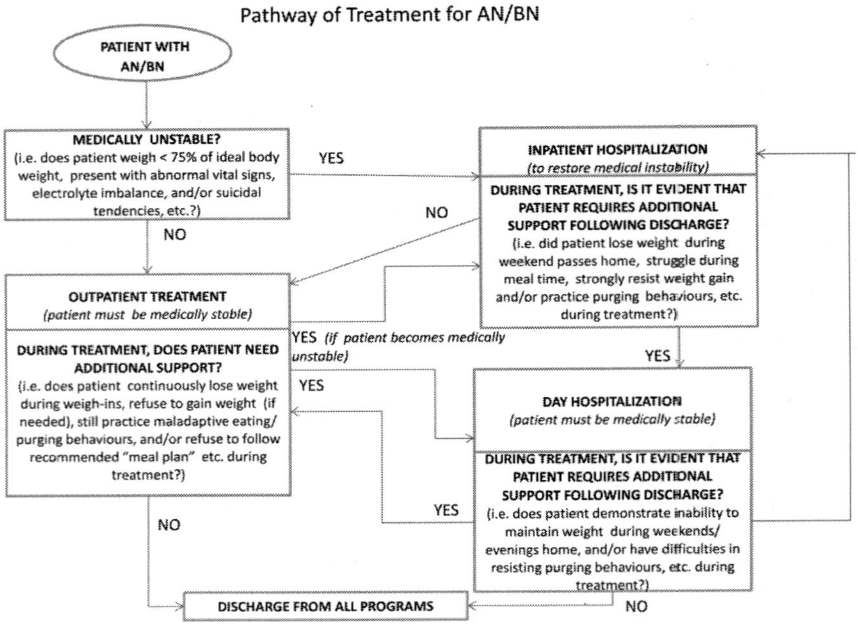

Figure 1. Fennig, 2010; Forman, 2010; Nolen-Hoeksema and Rector, 2008; Steiger 2010.

REFERENCES

Abrams, K., Allen, L., and Gray, J.J. (1993). Disordered eating attitudes and behaviours, psychological adjustment, and ethnic identity: A comparison of black and white female college students. *International Journal of Eating Disorder, 14,* 49-57.

Abbate-Daga, G. (2010). Attachment Insecurity, Personality, and Body Dissatisfaction in Eating Disorders. *Journal of nervous and mental disease, 198(7),* 520-524.

Adolescent Medicine Committee and Canadian Pediatric Society. (1998). Eating disorders in adolescence: principals of diagnosis and treatment. *Pediatrics and Child Health, 3(3),* 189-192.

Agras, W. S., Walsh, T., Fairburn, C., Wilson, T., and Kraemer, H.C. (2000). A multicenter comparison of cognitive–behavioral therapy and interpersonal psychotherapy for bulimia nervosa. *Archives of General Psychiatry, 57(5)*, 459-466.

Agras W. S. (1984). Eating disorders: management of obesity, bulimia, and anorexia nervosa. New York: Pergamon Press.

Aldao, A. (2010). Emotion-regulation strategies across psychopathology: A meta-analytic review. Clinical Psychology Review, 30(2), 217-237.

American Psychiatric Association. (2000). Diagnostic and statistical manual of mental *disorders*(4th ed., text revision). Washington, DC: APA.

Arnetller, L. (2005). Readiness to recover in adolescent anorexia nervosa: prediction of hospital admission. *Journal of child psychology and psychiatry, 46(4)*, 394-408.

Andersen, A.E., Bowers, W.A., and Watson, T. (2001). A slimming program for eating disorders not otherwise specified: Reconceptualizing a confusing, residual diagnostic category. *Psychiatric Clinics of North America, 24(2)*, 271-280.

Appolinario, J C, Bacaltchuk, J, Sichieri, R, et al. (2003). A randomized, double-blind, placebo-controlled study of sibutramine in the treatment of binge-eating disorder. Archives of general psychiatry, 60(11), 1109-1116.

Arcelus, Jon. (2009). A Case Series Evaluation of A Modified Version of Interpersonal Psychotherapy (IPT) For The Treatment of Bulimic Eating Disorders: A Pilot Study. *European eating disorders review, 17(4)*, 260.

Archives of General Psychiatry. (1992). Fluoxetine in the treatment of bulimia nervosa. A multicenter, placebo-controlled, double-blind trial. *Fluoxetine Bulimia Nervosa Collaborative Study Group, 49(2)*, 139-149.

Astrachan-Fletcher, E., Veldhuis, C., Lively, N., Fowler, C., and Marcks, B. (2008). The reciprocal effects of eating disorders and the postpartum period: A review of the literature and recommendations for clinical care. *Journal of Women's Health, 17(2)*, 227-239.

Baer, R. A., Fischer, S., and Huss, D. B. (2005). Mindfulness-based cognitive therapy applied to binge eating: A case study. *Cognitive and Behavioral Practice, 12*, 351–358.

Becker, A.E., Grinspoon, S.K., Klibanski, A., and Herzog, D.B. (1999). Eating disorders. *New England Journal of Medicine, 340(14)*, 1092–1098.

Berry, E M. (2000). Disorders of eating in the elderly. *Journal of adult development, 7(2)*, 87-99.

Bissada, H., Tasca, G.A., Barber, A.M., and Bradwejn, J. (2008) Olanzapine in the treatment of low body weight and obsessive thinking in women with anorexia nervosa: a randomized, double-blind, placebo-controlled trial. *American Journal of Psychiatry, 165 (10),* 1281-1265.

Brambilla, F, Bellodi, L, Arancio, C, Ronchi, P., and Limonta. (2001). Central dopaminergic function in anorexia and Bulimia nervosa: a psychoneuroendocrine approach. *Psychoneuroendocrinology, 26(4),* 393-409.

Braun, D. L., Sunday, S. R. and Halmi, K.A. (1994). Psychiatric comorbidity in patients with eating disorders. Psychological Medicine: *A Journal of Research in Psychiatry and the Allied Sciences, 24 (4),* 859-867.

Broft, A., Berner, L.A., and Walsh, T.B. (2010). Pharmacotherapy for bulimia nervosa. In *Grilo,* C.M. and Mitchell, J.E. (Eds). *The Treatment of Eating Disorders: A Clinical Handbook.* (pp. 338 401). New York: Guilford Press.

Bruce, B., and Agras, W.S. (1992). Binge-eating in females: a population-based investigation. *International Journal of Eating Disorders, 12*, 365-373.

Bulik, C.M., Thornton, L.M., Root, T.L., Pisetsky, E.M., Lichtenstein, P., and Pedersen, N.L. (2010). Understanding the relation between anorexia nervosa and bulimia nervosa in a Swedish national twin sample. *Biological Psychiatry*, *67*(1), 71-77.

Buresh, C.T. and Graber, M.A. (2006). Unusual Causes of Recurrent Abdominal Pain. *Emergency Medicine*, 38(5), 11-18.

Calero-Elvira, Krug, I., Davis, K., Lopez, C., Femandez-Aranda, F., and Treasure, J., (2007). Meta-analysis on drugs in people with eating disorders. *European Eating Disorders Review, 17(4),* 243-259.

Canals, J1. (2009). Influence of a parent's eating attitudes on eating disorders in school adolescents. *European Child and Adolescent Psychiatry, 18(6),* 353-359.

Casper, R. F. (2009). Clinical manifestations and diagnosis of menopause. In *UpToDate 18.2.*

Cleary, B S. (2010). Interpreting the complete blood count in anorexia nervosa. *Eating disorders, 18(2),* 132-139.

Cleaves, D H. (2008). Evidence-based therapies for children and adolescents with eating disorders. In *Handbook of evidence-based therapies for children and adolescents : bridging science and practice : Issues in clinical child psychology.* (pp. 335-353).

Cockfield, A., and Philpot U. (2009). Feeding size 0: the challenges of anorexia nervosa. Managing anorexia from a dietitian's perspective. *PubMed, 68(3),* 281-288.

Conrado, L. (2009). Body dysmorphic disorder in dermatology: diagnosis, epidemiology and clinical aspects. *Anais brasileiros de dermatología, 84(6)*, 569-579.

Courbasson, C., Nishikawa, Y., and Shapira, L.B. (in press). Mindfulness-action based cognitive behavioural therapy for concurrent binge eating disorder and substance use disorders.

Courtney, E A. (2008). Problematic eating behaviors in adolescents with low self-esteem and elevated depressive symptoms. *Eating behaviors, 9(4),* 408-414.

Crisp, A. (2005). Stigmatization of and discrimination against people with eating disorders including a report of two nationwide surveys. *European eating disorders review, 13(3),* 147-152.

De Young, K P. (2010). Prevalence and Correlates of Exercise Motivated by Negative Affect. *The international journal of eating disorders, 43(1),* 50-58.

Didie, E, Reinecke, M, and Phillips, K. (2010). Case Conceptualization and Treatment of Comorbid Body Dysmorphic Disorder and Bulimia Nervosa. *Cognitive and Behavioral Practice, 17(3),* 259-269.

Domino, F. J., and Kaplan, N. M. (2010). Overview of hypertension in adults. In *UpToDate* 18.2.

Dresser, L.P., Massey, E.W., Johnson, E.E., Bossen, E. (1992). Ipecac myopathy and cardiomyopathy. Journal of Neurology, Neurosurgery, and Psychiatry, 55, 560-562.

Eddy, K.T., Dorer, D.J., Franko, D.L., Tahilani, K.,Thomson-Brenner, H., and Herzog, D.B. (2008). Diagnostic crossover in anorexia nervosa and bulimia nervosa: Implications for DSM-V. *The American Journal of Psychiatry, 165(2),* 245-250.

Eisler, I. (2010). Family-based treatments for adolescents with anorexia nervosa: Single-family and multifamily approaches. In *Treatment of Eating Disorders: A Clinical Handbook,* 150-174.

Fairburn, C.G., and Bohn, K. (2005). Eating disorder NOS (EDNOS): An example of the troublesome "not otherwise specified" (NOS) category in DSM-IV. *Behaviour Research and Therapy, 43(6),* 691-701.

Fairburn, C.G., Cooper, Z., and Shafran, R. (2003). Cognitive behaviour therapy for eating disorders: A "transdiagnostic" theory and treatment. *Behaviour Research and Therapy*, *41*(5), 509-528.

Fairburn, C.G., Welch, S.L., Doll, H.A., Davies, B.A., and O'Connor, M.E. (1997). Risk factors for bulimia nervosa: A community-based case-control study. *Archives of General Psychiatry*, *54*(6), 509-517.

Fairburn, G., Norman, P.A., Welch, S.L., O'Connor, M.E., Doll, H.A., and Peveler, R.C. (1995). A Prospective study of outcome in bulimia nervosa and the long-term effects of three psychological treatments. *Archives of General Psychiatry, 52(4),* 304-312.

Feldman, M.B., and Meyer, I.H. (2007). Eating disorders in diverse lesbian, gay, and bisexual populations. *International Journal of Eating Disorders, 40(3),* 218-226.

Fennig, S. (2010). Suicidal behavior and depression in adolescents with eating disorders. *Nordic journal of psychiatry, 64(1),* 32-39.

Forman S. F. (2010). Eating disorders: Epidemiology, pathogenesis, and clinical features. In *UpToDate Online 18.2..*

Forman S. F. (2010). Eating disorders: Treatment and outcome. In *UpToDate Online 18.2.*

Frisch, M J. (2006). Residential treatment for eating disorders. *International Journal of Eating Disorders, 39(5),* 434.

Frisch, M.J., Herzog, D.B., and Franko, D.L. (2006). Residential treatment for eating disorders. *International Journal of Eating Disorders, 39(5),* 434-442.

Gadalla, T M. (2008). Eating disorders and associated psychiatric comorbidity in elderly Canadian women. *Archives of Women, 11(5-6),* 357-362.

Gauvin, L., Steiger, H., and Brodeur, J.M., (2009). Eating-disorder symptoms and syndromes in a sample of urban-dwelling Canadian women: Contributions toward a population health perspective. *International Journal of Eating Disorders, 42(2),* 158-165.

Gendall, K.A., Joyce, P.R., Carter, F.A., McIntosh, V.V., and Bulik, C.M. (2005). Childhood gastrointestinal complaints in women with bulimia nervosa. *International Journal of Eating Disorders, 37(3),* 256-260.

George, A., and Waller, G. (2005). Motivators for smoking in women with eating disorders. *European Eating Disorders Review, 13(6),* 417-423.

Gjerdingen, D., Fontaine, P., Crow, S., McGovern, P., Center, B., and Miner, M. (2009). Predictors of mothers' postpartum body dissatisfaction. *Women and Health, 49(6-7),* 491-504.

Godart, N T. (2003). Anxiety disorders in subjects seeking treatment for eating disorders: a DSM-IV controlled study. *Psychiatry Research, 117(3),* 245-258.

Godart, N. T., Flament, M. F., Curt, F., Perdereau, F., Lang, F., Venisse, J.L., Halfon, O., Loas, P.B.G., Corcos M., Jeammet P. and Fermanian, J. (2003). Anxiety disorders in subjects seeking treatment for Eating disorders: A DSM-IV controlled study. *Psychiatry Research, 117(3),* 245-258.

Golden, N.H., Jacobson, M.S., Schebendach, J., Solanto, M.H., Hertz, S.M., Shenker I.R. (1997) Resumption of menses in anorexia nervosa. *Archives of Pediatrics and Adolescent Medicine, 151(1),* 16-21.

Gowers, S.G., Clark, A., Roberts, C., Griffiths, A., Edwards, V., Bryan, C., Smethurst, N., Byford, S., and Barrett, B. (2007). Clinical effectiveness of treatment for anorexia nervosa in adolescents: Randomised control trial. *British Journal of Psychiatry, 191(4),* 427-435.

Grilo, C.M., and Masheb, R.M., and Wilson, G.T. (2005). Efficacy of Cognitive Behavioral Therapy and Fluoxetine for the Treatment of Binge Eating Disorder: A Randomized Double-Blind Placebo-Controlled Comparison. *Biological Psychiatry, 57(3),* 301-309.

Gupta, M A. (1995). Concerns about aging and a drive for thinness: A factor in the biopsychosocial model of eating disorders? *The international journal of eating disorders, 18(4),* 351-357.

Halmi, K.A., Agras, S.W., Crow, S., Mitchell, J.,Wilson, T.G., Bryson, S.W., and Kraemer H.C. (1995). Predictors of treatment acceptance and completion in anorexia nervosa: Implications for future study designs. *Archives of General Psychiatry, 62(7),* 776-781.

Harris, M, and Cumella, E. (2006). Eating disorders across the life span. *Journal of Psychosocial Nursing and Mental Health Services, 44(4),* 21-26.

Hayes, S. C., Strosahl, K. D., and Wilson, K. G. (1999). Acceptance and commitment therapy: An experiential approach to behavior change. New York: Guilford Press.

Homan, K. (2010). Athletic-ideal and thin-ideal internalization as prospective predictors of body dissatisfaction, dieting, and compulsive exercise. *Body Image, 7(3),* 240-245.

Hudson, J.I., McElroy, S.L., Raymond, N.C., Crow, S., Keck, P.E., et al. (1998). Fluvoxamine in the treatment of binge-eating disorder: A multicenter placebo-controlled, double-blind trial. *American Journal of Psychiatry (155),* 1756-1762.

Jacobi, C., Hayward, C., de Zwaan, M., Kraemer, H.C., and Agras, S.W. (2004). Coming to terms with risk factors for eating disorders: Application of risk terminology and suggestions for a general taxonomy. *Psychological Bulletin, 130(1),* 19-65.

Juarascio, A S. (2010). Acceptance and commitment therapy versus cognitive therapy for the treatment of comorbid eating pathology. *Behavior modification, 34(2),* 175-190.

Kabat-Zinn, J. (1990). Full Catastrophe Living. New York: Delacorte.

Kaye, W.H., Nagata, T., Weltzin, T.E., Hsu, G.L.K., Sokol, M.S., McConaha, C., Plotnicov, K.H., Weise, J., and Deep, D. (2001). Double-blind placebo-controlled administration of fluoxetine in restricting-and restricting-purging-type anorexia. *Biological Psychiatry*, *49*(7), 644-652.

Keel, P.K., Dorer, D.K., Franko, D.L., Jackson, S.C. and Herzog, D.B. (2005). Postremission predictors of relapse in women with eating disorders. *The American Journal of Psychiatry, 162(12),* 2263-2268.

Kelly, A.M., Wall, M., Eisenberg, M.E., Story, M., and Neumark-Sztainer, D. (2005). Adolescent girls with high body satisfaction: Who are they and what can they teach us? *Journal of Adolescent Health, 37(5),* 391-396.

Keski-Rahkonen, A1. (2009). Incidence and outcomes of bulimia nervosa: A nationwide population-based study. *Psychological Medicine, 39(5),* 823-831.

Kessler, R.C., Nelson, C.B., McGonagle, K.A., Edlund, M.J., Frank, R.G. and Leaf, P.J. (1996) The Epidemiology of Co-Occurring Addictive and Mental Disorders: Implications for Prevention and Service Utilization. *American Journal of Orthopsychiatry, 66(1)*, 17-31.

Klerman, G.L., Weissman, M.M., Rounsaville, B.J. and Chevron (1984). Interpersonal psychotherapy of depression. New York: Basic Books.

Kristeller, J. L., Baer, R. A., and Quillian-Wolever, R. (2006). Mindfulness-based Approaches to Eating Disorders. In *Baer, R. (Ed.) Mindfulness and acceptance-based interventions: Conceptualization, application, and empirical support*. San Diego, CA: Elsevier.

Kristeller, J. L. and Hallett, C. B. (1999). An exploratory study of a meditation-based intervention for binge eating disorder. *Journal of Health Psychology, 4(3),* 357- 363.

Krug, I., Treasure, J., Anderluh, M., Bellodi, L., Cellini, M.B. et al., (2008). Present and lifetime comorbidity of tobacco, alcohol and drug use in eating disorders: A European multicenter study. *Drug and Alcohol Dependence, 97(1-2),* 169-179.

Laine, L., Fauci, A.S., Braunwald, E., Kasper, D.L., Hauser, S.L., Longo, D.L., Jameson, J.L., and Loscalzo, J. (2006). Chapter 42: Gastrointestinal Bleeding. In *Harrison's Principles of Internal Medicine, 17.*

Lapid, M I. (2010). Eating disorders in the elderly. International *Psychogeriatrics, 22(4),* 523-536.

Lavender, A., Shubert, I., de Silva, and Treasure, J.. (2006). Obsessive-compulsive beliefs and magical ideation in eating disorders. *British Journal of Clinical Psychology, 45(3),* 331-342.

Lilenfeld, L.R.R., Ringham, R., Kalarchian, M.A., and Marcus, M.D. (2008). A Family history study of binge-eating disorder. *Comprehensive Psychiatry*, *49*(3), 247-254.

Lock, J., le Grange, D., Agras, S.W., and Dare, C. (2001). *Treatment manual for anorexia* nervosa: A family based approach. New York: Guilford Press.

Lucas, A.R., Melton, L.J., Crowson, C.S., O'Fallon, W.M. (1999). Long-term fracture risk among women with anorexia nervosa: a population-based cohort study. *Mayo Clinic Proceedings, 74(10),* 972-977.

Ma, S.H., and Teasdale, J.D. (2004). Mindfulness-based cognitive therapy for depression: Replication and exploration of differential relapse prevention effects. *Journal of Consulting and Clinical Psychology, 72,* 31-40.

Maier, A S. (2009). Family therapy with eating disorders: Creating an alliance for change. In *Effective Clinical Practice in the Treatment of Eating Disorders*. (pp. 95-109).

Malina, A., Gaskill, J., McConaha, G.K., Frank, M., Scholar, L., and Kaye, W.H. (2003). Olanzapine treatment of anorexia nervosa: A retrospective study. *International Journal of Eating Disorders, 33,* 234-237.

Marchi, M., and Cohen, P. (1990). Early childhood eating behaviors and adolescent eating disorders. *Journal of the American Academy of Child and Adolescent Psychiatry, 29(1),* 112-117.

Marmorstein, N R. (2008). Prospective associations between depressive symptoms and eating disorder symptoms among adolescent girls. *The international journal of eating disorders, 41(2),* 118-123.

Masheb, R. M. and Grilo, C. (2006) Emotional overeating and its sssociations with eating disorder psychopathology among overweight patients with binge eating disorder. *International Journal of Eating Discrders, 39(2),* 141-146.

McCabe, M P. (2010). Impact of a healthy body image program among adolescent boys on body image, negative affect, and body change strategies. *Body Image, 7(2),* 117-123.

McIntosh, V. (2000). Interpersonal psychotherapy for anorexia nervosa. *International Journal of Eating Disorders, 27(2),* 125.

Measelle J.R., Stice E., Hogansen J.M. (2006). Developmental trajectories of co-occurring depressive, eating, antisocial, and substance abuse problems in female adolescents. *Journal of Abnormal Psychology, 115(3),* 524–538.

Mehler, P.S. (2001). Diagnosis and care of patients with anorexia nervosa in primary care settings. *Annals of Internal Medicine, 134 (11),* 1048-1059.

Miller C.A. and Golden N. H. (2010). An Introduction to Eating Disorders: Clinical Presentation, Epidemiology, and Prognosis. *Nutrition in Clinical Practice.*

Mitchell, J.E., Devlin, M.J., de Zwann, M., Crow, S.J., and Peterson, C.B. (2008). A cognitive-behavioural treatment program for binge eating disorder. *Binge Eating disorder: Clinical Foundations and Treatment,* New York: Guilford Press.

Monteleone, P. (2006). Eating Disorders; A functional serotonin transporter gene polymorphism is associated with binge eating disorder. *Health and Medicine Week,* 627.

Munsch, S., Biedert, E., Meyer, A., Michael, T., Schlup, B., Turch, A., and Margraf, J. (2007). A randomized comparison of cognitive behavioral therapy and behavioral weight loss treatment for overweight individuals with binge eating disorder. *International Journal of Eating Disorders, 40(2),* 102-113.

Murphy, S., Russell, L., and Waller, G., (2005). Integrated psychodynamic therapy for bulimia nervosa and binge eating disorder: Theory, practice and preliminary findings. *European Eating Disorders Review, 13(6),* 383-391.

Murray, S., Touyz, S., and Beaumont, P. (1990). Knowledge about eating disorders in yhr community. *The international journal of eating disorders, 9(1),* 87-93

National Institute for Clinical Excellence. (2004*). Eating Disorders – Core interventions in the* treatment and management of anorexia nervosa, bulimia nervosa and related eating disorders (*Clinical Guideline No. 9).* London.

Newell, C. (2010). Early recognition of eating disorders: eating disorders can have a devastating effect on both individual and family. Although most treatment is on an outpatient basis, primary care can help with early recognition, referral and essential monitoring of the patient. Practice Nurse; *The Journal for Nurses in General Practice, 39(12),* 20-26.

Nolen-Hoeksema, S., and Rector, N. A. (2008). *Abnormal Psychology* (Canadian Edition). New York: McGraw-Hill.

Ofo, E. (2006). Olfactory Loss: 10-Minute Consultation. BMJ. *British medical journal (Compact ed.), 334(7590),* 423-423.

O'Hara, S.K., and Smith, C.S. (2007). Presentation of eating disorders in the news media: What are the implications for patient diagnosis and treatment? *Patient Education and Counseling, 68(1),* 43-51.

Pike, K.M., Carter, J.C., and Olmsted, M.P. (2010). Cognitive-behavioral therapy for anorexia nervosa. In C.M. Grilo and J.E. Mitchell (Ed.), *The Treatment of Eating Disorders: A Clinical Handbook* (pp. 83-107). New York, NY: Guilford Press.

Pokrajac-Bulian, A., Zivcic-Becirevic, I., Calugi, S., and Dalle Grave, R. (2006). School prevention program for eating disorders in Croatia: A controlled study with six months of follow-up. *Eating and Weight Disorders, 11(4),* 171-178.

Powers, P.S., Santana, C.A., and Bannon, Y.S. (2002). Olanzapine in the treatment of anorexia nervosa: An open label trial. *International Journal of Eating Disorders*, *32*(2), 146-154.

Quiroga, S. (2002). Comparative study on the therapeutic efficacy for eating disorders. Psicoterapia e Istituzioni: *Review of Psychoanalytical Methodological Research and Clinical Experiences, 9(1),* 37-62.

Rhodes, P. (2003). The Maudsley model of family therapy for children and adolescents with anorexia nervosa: theory, clinical practice, and empirical support. *Australian and New Zealand Journal of Family Therapy, 24(4),* 191-198.

Rosen, J. C., and Ramirez, E. (1998). A comparison of eating disorders and body dysmorphic disorder on body image and psychological adjustment. *Journal of Psychosomatic Research, 44,* 441–449.

Ruhl, U. (2005). Cognitive-behavioral psychotherapy for adolescents with eating disorders. *Praxis der Kinderpsychologie und Kinderpsychiatrie, 54(4),* 286-302.

Russell, G. (2001). Involuntary treatment in anorexia nervosa. *Psychiatric Clinics of North America, 24(2),* 337-349.

Sallet, P C. (2010). Eating Disorders in Patients with Obsessive-Compulsive Disorder: Prevalence and Clinical Correlates. *The international journal of eating disorders, 43(4),* 315-325.

Sassaroli, S. (2008). Perfectionism in depression, obsessive-compulsive disorder and eating disorders. *Behaviour Research and Therapy, 46(6),* 757.

Satoh-Kuriwada, S. (2009). Hyposalivation Strongly Influences Hypogeusia in the Elderly. *Journal of healthscience, 55(5),* 689-698.

Schaffner, A.D. (2008). Integrating evidence-based treatments with individual needs in an outpatient facility for eating disorders. *Eating Disorders, 16(5)*, 378-392.

Shapiro, J.R., Reba-Harrelson, L., Dymek-Valentine, M., Woolson, S.L., Hamer, R.M., and Bulik, C.M. (2007). Feasibility and acceptability of CD-ROM-based cognitive-behavioural treatment for binge-eating disorder. *European Eating Disorders Review, 15* 175-184.

Sim, L. (2006). The contribution of emotion regulation to body dissatisfaction and disordered eating in early adolescent girls. *Journal of Youth and Adolescence, 35(2),* 219-228.

Simon, J. (2005). The health service use and cost of eating disorders. *Psychological Medicine, 35(11),* 1543-1551.

Singer, G.G., Brenner, B.M., Fauci, A.S., Braunwald, E., Kasper, D.L., Hauser, S.L., Longo, D.L., Jameson, J.L., and Loscalzo, J. (2006). Chapter 46: Fluid and Electrolyte Disturbances. Chapter 76 in *Harrison's Principles of Internal Medicine, 17.*

Slupik, R. (1999). Managing adolescents with eating disorders. *International Journal of Fertility and Women, 44(3),* 125-130.

Smith, A J. (2010). Body image, eating disorders, and self-esteem problems during adolescence. In *Self-esteem Across the Lifespan.* (pp. 125-141).

Smolak, L. (1998). Lessons from lessons: An evaluation of an elementary school prevention program. In *The prevention of eating disorders.* (pp. 137-172).New York, NY, US: New York University Press.

Steiger, H. (2010). Treatment of psychiatric comorbidities. In *Treatment of Eating Disorders : A Clinical Handbook.* (pp. 447-457).

Stein, A., and Fairburn, C.G. (1996). Eating habits and attitudes in the postpartum period. *Psychosomatic Medicine, 58(4)*, 321-325.

Stein, D. (2009). Eating disorders: From Etiology to Treatment. *International journal of child and adolescent health, 2(2),* 139-151.

Steinhausen, H. (2002). The outcome of anorexia nervosa in the 20th century. *The American Journal of Psychiatry, 159(8),* 1284-1293.

Stice, E. (2010). Risk factors and prodromal eating pathology. *Journal of child psychology and psychiatry, 51(4),* 518-525.

Stice, E., and Shaw, H. (2004). Eating disorder prevention programs: A meta-analytic review. *Psychological Buletin, 130(2),* 206-227.

Stice, E., Spangler, D., and Agras, S.W. (2001). Exposure to media-portrayed thin-ideal images adversely affects vulnerable girls: A longitudinal experiment. *Journal of Social and Clinical Psychology, 20(3),* 270-288.

Striegal-Moore, R.H., Dohm, F.A., Kramer, H.C., Schreiber, G.B., Crawford, P.B., and Daniels, S.R. (2005). Health services use of women with a history of bulimia nervosa or binge eating disorder. *International Journal of Eating Disorders*, 37(1), 11-18.

Striegal-Moore, R.H, and Franko, D.L., (2003). Epidemiology of binge eating disorder. *International Journal of Eating Disorders, 34,* 19-29.

Striegel-Moore, R. H., Leslie, D., Petrill, S. A., Garvin, V. and Rosenheck, R. A. (2000). One-year use and cost of inpatient and outpatient services among female and male patients with an eating disorder : evidence from a national database of health insurance claims. *International Journal of Eating Disorders 27(4),* 381–389.

Sundgot-Borgen, J. (1994). Risk and trigger factors for the development of eating disorders in female elite athletes. *Medicine and science in sports and exercise, 26(4),* 414-419.

Swenne, I. (2005). Weight requirements for catch-up growth in girls with eating disorders and onset of weight loss before menarche. *The international journal of eating disorders, 38(4),* 340-345.

Taylor, F. (2008). Eating disorders are not just a problem for the young. *Working With Older People, 12(3),* 31.

Thompson-Brenner, H., Eddy, K.T, Franko, D.L, Dorer, D.E, Vashchenko, M., and Herzog, D.B. (2008). Personality pathology and substance abuse in eating disorders: a longitudinal study. *International Journal of Eating Disorders, 41(3),* 203-208.

Treasure, J., Claudino, A., and Zucker, N. (2010). Eating disorders. *The Lancet, 375 (9714),* 583-593.

Trost, A S. (2007). The Healthy Image Partnership (HIP) parents program: The role of parental involvement in eating disorder prevention. *Dissertation abstracts international, 68(6-A),* 2327-2327.

Tylka, T L. (1999). Exploring the construct validity of the eating disorder continuum. *Journal of counseling psychology, 46(2),* 268-276.

VanderWal, J.S. (2008). The sociocultural model of eating disorder development : Application to a Guatemalan sample. *Eating behaviors, 9(3),* 277-284.

Wahl, O. F. (1995). Media madness: public images of mental illness. New Bruns-wick, NJ: *Rutgers University Press;* 1995.

Walsh B.T., Fauci A.S., Braunwald E, Kasper D.L., Hauser S.L., Longo D.L., Jameson J.L., Loscalzo J. (2006). In *Harrison's Principles of Internal Medicine, 17e.*

Watson, T.L., Bowers, W.A., and Andersen, A.E. (2000). Involuntary treatment of eating disorders. *American Journal of Psychiatry, 157,* 1806-1810.

Welt, C. K. (2008). Patient information: Menstrual cycle disorders (absent and irregular periods). In *UpToDate Online 18.2.*

Wilfley, D.E., Crow, S.J., Hudson, J.I., Mitchell, J.E., Berkowitz, R.I. et al., (2008). Efficacy of subutramine for the treatment of binge eating disorder: A randomized multicenter placebo-controlled double-blind study. *The American Journal of Psychiatry, 165 (1),* 51-58.

Wilfley, D.E., Welch, R., Stein, R.I., Spurrell, E.B., Cohen, L.R., Saelens, B.E., Counchis, J.Z., Frank, M.A., Wiseman, C.V., and Matt, G.E. (2002). A randomized comparison of group cognitive- behavioral therapy and group interpersonal psychotherapy for the treatment of overweight individuals with binge-eating disorder. *Archives of General Psychiatry, 59,* 713-721.

Williams, P.M., Goodie, J., Motsinger, C.D. (2008). Treating eating disorders in primary care. *American Family Physician, 77(2),* 187-195.

Wilson, G. T. (1999). Cognitive behavior therapy for eating disorders : progress and problems. *Behaviour Research and Therapy, 37*, S79-S95.

Whitelaw, M. (2010). Does aggressive refeeding in hospitalized adolescents with anorexia nervosa result in increased hypophosphatemia? *Journal of adolescent health, 46(6),* 577-582.

Wilksch, S. M. (2009). Reduction of Shape and Weight Concern in Young Adolescents: A 30-Month Controlled Evaluation of a Media Literacy Program. *Journal of the American Academy of Child and Adolescent Psychiatry, 48(6),* 652.

Wurtman, J. (1897). Disorders of food-intake: excessive carbohydrate snacking intake among a class of obese people. *Annals of the New York Academy of Sciences, 499,* 197-202.

Zeeck, A. (2009). Inpatient versus Day Clinic Treatment for Bulimia Nervosa : A Randomized Trial. *Psychotherapy and Psychosomatics, 78(3),* 152-160.

Zeeck, A., Wietersheim, J., Armin, H., Einsele, S. and Heinz, W., et al. (2009). Inpatient or day clinic treatment? Results of a multi-site-study. *GMS Psycho-Social Medicine, 6,* 1-11.

Zeiger, R. F. (2007). Anorexia Nervosa in *McGraw-Hill's Diagnosaurus 2.0.*

In: Eating Disorders
Editor: C. M. Shapiro, pp. 39-61
ISBN 978-1-61209-746-6

Chapter 2

Multimodal Perceptual and Emotional Integration in Eating Disorders

***Anna M. Lomanowska*[1,2] *and Matthieu J. Guitton*[1,2*]**

Abstract

Eating disorders are often characterized by multimodal perceptual and emotional alterations, including distorted perceptions and recurring negative emotional states. Perceptual distortions observed in eating disorder sufferers are not limited to the gustatory modality, but also affect other sensory modalities. For instance, sufferers may experience alterations both in taste and body shape perception. The results of recent clinical and animal studies indicate that perceptual processes interact with altered emotional states, and that the integration of these modalities plays a critical role in the ontogeny and maintenance of eating disorders. The aim of this chapter is to examine current perspectives on the involvement of multimodal perceptual and emotional integration in these disorders and to highlight elements for future research and for innovative treatments. First, clinical observations of perceptual distortions and their interaction with emotional states of eating disorder sufferers will be considered.

* Address for correspondence: Dr Matthieu J. Guitton, Address:CRULRG, 2601 chemin de la Canardière F-6517, Québec, QC, G1J 2G3, Canada. Phone: 1 418 663 5747, Fax: 1 418 663 8756, Email: matthieu.guitton@pha.ulaval.ca

[1] Centre de Recherche Université Laval Robert Giffard,Quebec City, QC, Canada

[2] Faculty of Pharmacy, Laval University, Quebec City, QC, Canada

Second, the fundamental mechanisms of integration between taste perception and emotional states will be examined from the perspective of recent studies in animal models. Finally, new therapeutic avenues that take advantage of a multimodal approach will be explored, with special emphasis on the use of virtual environments as therapeutic tools. In conclusion, understanding the interactions between multimodal perceptual and emotional processes may offer important avenues for future research into the ontogeny of eating disorders and the development of innovative treatments.

Keywords: anorexia, bulimia, eating disorders, perception, social interactions, virtual reality.

INTRODUCTION

One of the most striking symptoms of eating disorders, including anorexia and bulimia nervosa, is the drastic disturbance of eating behavior resulting from pathological efforts of sufferers to control their body weight and shape. However, eating disorders are also characterized by other persistent symptoms, most notably multimodal perceptual and emotional alterations. These include significant distortions in the perception of taste, body shape, and food-related cues, as well as disturbances in emotional regulation and social interactions (Skrzypek et al, 2001; Klein and Walsh, 2004; Giel et al., 2010). The occurrence of these diverse symptoms reflects the complexity of the physiological, psychological, and social processes that contribute to eating disorders.

According to recent clinical and animal studies, perceptual distortions interact with altered emotional states, and the integration of these modalities plays a critical role in the ontogeny and maintenance of eating disorders (Klein and Walsh, 2004; Guitton et al., 2008). These are thought to be multifactorial processes, with considerable interactions between internal (biological or psychological) and external (social or environmental) risk factors (Klein and Walsh, 2004). It is important to consider the nature of these interacting processes in order to advance our understanding of the mechanisms underlying eating disorders and to develop effective treatments.

The aim of this chapter is to examine current perspectives on the involvement of multimodal perceptual and emotional integration in eating disorders and to highlight elements for future research and for innovative treatments. The first part will focus on the clinical observations of perceptual distortions and their interaction with emotional states of eating disorder sufferers. The second part will examine the fundamental mechanisms of integration between taste perception and emotional states from the perspective of studies performed in animal models. Finally, the third part will describe new therapeutic avenues that take advantage of a multimodal approach, particularly the use of virtual environments as therapeutic tools.

1. MULTIMODAL PERCEPTUAL DISTURBANCES IN EATING DISORDER SUFFERERS

Perceptual alterations associated with eating disorders encompass different modalities involved in the perception of body shape, taste, food-related cues, and interoceptive signals (Skrzypek et al, 2001; Klein and Walsh, 2004; Giel et al., 2010). These multimodal alterations are accompanied by emotional and social disturbances (Klein and Walsh, 2004). The clinical evidence reviewed below highlights the integrated relationship between perceptual and emotional alterations in eating disorders and its effects on behavioral functioning.

One of the core features of eating disorders – and one of the defining symptoms – is the disturbance of body image (Cash and Deagle, 1997; Skrzypek et al., 2001; Klein and Walsh, 2004). Body image is defined as the picture that individuals form in their minds of the size, shape, and form of their own body and specific body parts, as well as their attitude regarding these characteristics (Slade, 1988). Sufferers of anorexia or bulimia nervosa often consider themselves as too heavy, even if underweight (Skrzypek et al., 2001; Klein and Walsh, 2004). They may even exhibit an intense fear of gaining weight, and thus impose on themselves a very low weight threshold (Skrzypek et al., 2001; Klein and Walsh, 2004). Many sufferers exhibit perceptual body size distortions when presented with images of their own bodies (Probst et al., 1998; Cash and Deagle, 1997; Skrzypek et al., 2001). Specifically, they show erroneous self-evaluation of their body shape and size, which is especially pronounced for images of the whole body compared to individual body parts (Probst et al., 1998; Gardner and Bokenkamp, 1996; Cash and Deagle, 1997; Skrzypek et al., 2001). An important consideration is whether these body image disturbances are attributable to actual sensory deficits in body size estimation, or whether they are related to the cognitive and affective components of perception. Research findings favor the latter explanation, that distorted perception of body image is rooted in cognitive and affective processes (Gardner and Bokenkamp, 1996; Cash and Deagle, 1997; Skrzypek et al., 2001). Brain imaging studies of patients with eating disorders support this hypothesis: exposure to morphed images of their own bodies is associated with abnormal activation of two brain regions particularly involved in sensory and emotional integration and cognitive aspects of emotional processing, the amygdala and the prefrontal cortex, respectively (Miyake et al., 2010). Furthermore, in anorexic patients, exposure to real images of their own bodies is associated with a global reduction in brain activation, without the typical activation of the insula, one of the brain regions involved in the processing of self-referential information (Sachdev et al., 2008). Taken together, these differences in brain activation patterns indicate that the perceptual disturbances of body image observed in eating disorder sufferers likely reflect alterations in the way that sensory information is integrated with emotional, cognitive and self-referential processes.

In addition to body image distortions, eating disorder sufferers exhibit altered reactivity to food-related visual cues (Faunce, 2002; Klein and Walsh, 2004; Giel et al., 2010). Food cues appear to be highly salient for individuals with anorexia or bulimia nervosa, but reactions to these cues differ depending on the assessment method and the type of eating disorder (Giel et al., 2010). Specifically, patients with anorexia and bulimia nervosa report that they perceive images of food as unpleasant (Uher et al., 2004; Santel et al., 2006). Conversely, they also exhibit increased attentional bias towards both pictorial and linguistic food cues in comparison to neutral stimuli presented in a Stroop task (Faunce, 2002; Stormark and Torkildsen, 2004). This increase in selective attention towards food cues may reflect the allocation of cognitive resources in preparation for disengagement from eating-related behavior and avoidance of food (Giel et al., 2010). However, selective attention may be mediated by different processes in patients with different eating disorders. For instance, bulimia patients exhibit an increased appetitive response towards food cues (characterized by reduced startle reactivity), whereas anorexia patients fail to exhibit any activation of the appetitive motivation system (Friederich et al., 2006). Nevertheless, both groups report that food cues are anxiety provoking (Friederich et al., 2006). Indeed, bulimic patients may initially perceive food cues as appetitive, but the cues may also elicit a negative emotional state associated with the inability to inhibit binge eating behavior (Giel et al., 2010; Klein and Walsh, 2004). Once again, brain imaging supports this hypothesis: when compared to anorexic patients or control subjects, bulimic patients show decreased brain activation in response to food stimuli in the anterior and lateral prefrontal cortex, areas associated with inhibition of undesirable behavior

(Uher et al., 2004). Thus, the nature of neural processing of food cues may differ between anorexic and bulimic individuals.

The above findings demonstrate that visual food cues elicit different subjective and physiological responses in eating disorder sufferers compared to healthy controls. These responses appear to be rooted in altered cognitive and emotional functioning marked by greater allocation of attentional and affective resources to the processing of food-related stimuli.

Another perceptual process affected in eating disorder sufferers is taste perception (Drewnowski et al., 1987; Klein and Walsh, 2004). Rather than a global perceptual shift, anorexic and bulimic individuals show selective alterations related to different components of taste perception, including the intensity of taste, signaling of the caloric value of food, and hedonia. The ability to detect the intensity of sweet taste is generally intact in eating disorder sufferers (Drewnowski et al., 1987; Sunday and Halmi, 1990), but bulimics have some difficulties with perceiving the intensity of fat content (Sunday and Halmi, 1990). Both anorexics and bulimics show a substantial aversion to fat content in food (Drewnowski et al., 1987; Sunday and Halmi, 1990; Simon et al., 1993), which is thought to reflect a conditioned response to the perceived calories in fatty foods (Klein and Walsh, 2004). Conversely, both groups tend to report increased preference for sweet taste compared to controls, despite the fact that sweet taste can also be a signal for calories (Drewnowski et al., 1987; Sunday and Halmi, 1990; Franko et al, 1994). These findings indicate that information regarding the caloric value of food may not be the main factor in altered taste perception, and that changes in the hedonics of taste may also be involved. Taste hedonics refer to the relative a priori pleasantness of a given taste, often referred to as “liking” or palatability, and reflect an emotional component of taste perception (Kelley et al., 2002; Berridge, 2009). In fact, separate neural pathways appear to be involved in mediating the sensory and hedonic components of taste (Sewards, 2004). Currently, there is limited information regarding the neural processing of taste signals by eating disorder patients. An electrophysiological study of anorexic patients provides evidence that altered taste perception is related to differences in neural activation to both sweet and bitter taste stimuli (Toth et al., 2004). Furthermore, a neuroimaging study shows that in response to a sweet taste, anorexic patients exhibit altered activation of insular-striatal circuits, areas which may be involved in integrating self-referential information with the incentive and/or hedonic properties of taste (Wagner et al., 2008). Overall, the disturbances in taste perception observed in eating disorder sufferers appear to be critically influenced by emotional processes related to taste hedonics.

The hedonics of taste can be modulated by interoceptive signals related to hunger and satiety (Yeomans et al., 2004). For instance, feeding to satiety on a specific type of food (sensory-specific satiety) can reduce the subsequent hedonic value of that food (Sorensen et al., 2003). The processes involved in the signaling of hunger and satiety also appears to be affected in individuals with eating disorders (Klein and Walsh, 2004). Anorexic individuals generally report lower ratings of hunger and higher ratings of satiety during test meals (Halmi and Suday, 1991; Hetherington and Rolls, 1991) and show lower correlations between measures of gastric contents and hunger (Robinson, 1989). On the other hand, bulimic individuals show the opposite pattern of increased hunger ratings and decreased satiety ratings during a meal (Klein and Walsh, 2004), and fail to show sensory-specific satiety (Hetherington and Rolls, 1989). Bulimic individuals also exhibit greater gastric capacity, impairments in gastric emptying, and reduced gastric relaxation, which may interfere with signaling satiety (Klein and Walsh, 2004). Thus, disruptions in the way that internal signals are perceived by eating disorder sufferers may play a role in altered hedonic evaluation of food. Additionally, interoceptive signals may also independently contribute to the symptoms of eating disorders, such as the tendency to purge in bulimics. Because the relationship between hedonics and satiety does not appear to be direct (Yeomans et al., 2004), further study of the interaction of these emotional and perceptual factors in eating disorders is necessary.

The evidence presented above demonstrates the extent of the multimodal perceptual alterations observed in eating disorder sufferers and how they may interact with emotional processes to produce pathological eating behavior. An important consideration in understanding the contribution of these processes to eating disorders is their role in the ontogeny of the disorders and maintenance of the symptoms (Klein and Walsh, 2004). This issue is difficult to disentangle because most studies of emotional and perceptual disturbances in sufferers are retrospective. Certain perceptual alterations, such as enhanced preference for sweet taste, may persist after treatment (Drewnowski et al., 1987; Sunday and Halmi, 1990). This may be indicative of an underlying trait in individuals susceptible to eating disorders (Klein and Walsh, 2004). Furthermore, emotional disturbances may be an underlying factor in the onset of eating disorders. In particular, symptoms of anxiety often precede the onset of both anorexia and bulimia nervosa (Deep et al., 1995; Bulik et al., 1997; Godart et al., 2000). At the same time, the maintenance of eating disorder symptoms is associated with the presence of anxiety and other mood alterations, and with general difficulty in regulating emotional states (Godart et al., 2000; Klein and

Walsh, 2004; McElroy et al., 2005; Whiteside et al., 2007). For instance, in the case of bulimia nervosa, negative emotions (e.g., feelings of anxiety, rejection, frustration, or low mood) often precede binges. Some have proposed that binge episodes may become learned responses to negative emotional states in an associative context (Abraham and Beumont, 1982; Heatherton and Baumeister, 1991; Klein and Walsh, 2004). Thus, negative emotional states likely play a role in the onset of eating disorders, but they may also be critically involved in the reinforcement of pathological eating behavior and persistence of symptoms.

It is also important to consider the relationship of interacting perceptual and emotional disturbances with other, seemingly unrelated, symptoms of eating disorders, such as overactivity and social withdrawal. Overactivity is commonly observed in individuals suffering from anorexia (Klein and Walsh, 2004; Arun, 2008). Interestingly, in the activity-induced animal model of anorexia, when animal are given the choice between restricted access to food or access to a running wheel, which allows them to increase their physical activity, they will progressively choose activity over feeding, leading to substantial weight loss (Smith, 1989). This points to the existence of a conserved biological mechanism related to the reinforcing effects of physical activity in times of limited nutritional resources (Arun, 2008). While emotional and perceptual disturbances and overactivity may reflect independent components of the disorder, it is possible that they may interact at the level of reward functioning. Overactivity in anorexia is thought to reflect a pathological outcome resulting from starvation-induced sensitization of the reward system, involving both the opioid and the dopamine systems (Carr and Papadouka, 1994; Carr 1996; 2002). Similarly, the hedonic aspects of food intake are also dependent on reward-related mechanisms involving the opioid system (Kelley, 2002; Berridge, 2009). Therefore, potential interactions between emotional processes and overactivity may be mediated at the level of the neural reward system.

The disturbance of social behavior is another prevalent symptom of eating disorders (Kaye et al., 2004; Klein and Walsh, 2004; Guitton, in press). Alterations of social behavior can take on various forms. For instance, evidence from clinical studies indicates that both anorexia and bulimia nervosa have significant comorbidity with social phobia (Kaye et al., 2004). Social avoidance following progressive weight loss has also been frequently described, particularly in relation to irritability experienced during an underweight state (Kaye, 1997). Finally, anorexia can also be characterized by social withdrawal triggered by food consumption, or by the fact (averred or inferred) that others know that food was ingested (Kaye et al., 2004; Guitton, in press). Interestingly, alterations of perception not related to food intake and body weight regulation can also trigger substantial modifications of social behavior, for instance, in the case of abnormal auditory perception (Guitton, 2009). This similarity suggests a link between perceptual processes and social behavior, which may also be relevant to eating disorders. Negative emotional states, such as anxiety, are also associated with social withdrawal (File and Seth, 2003; Neal and Edelmann, 2003). These parallels suggest that the potential relationship between interacting perceptual and emotional processes and disruptions in social behavior in sufferers of eating disorders are important to consider.

2. Basic Mechanisms of Multimodal Integration between Emotion and Taste Perception

In order to understand the biological mechanisms underlying human disorders, and thus aid in the development of effective therapies, appropriate animal models are required. One of the challenges in studying the behavioral and neurobiological processes underlying the ontogeny of psychological disorders in humans is the difficulty in eliciting symptoms of these disorders in model organisms (Guitton and Dudai, 2004; Puel and Guitton, 2007). This is particularly true for human eating disorders such as anorexia. Indeed, not only is it nearly impossible to induce a general avoidance of food in animals; but also, the involvement of perceptual and emotional processes in eating disorders makes them difficult to study. This section will outline some of the basic processes involved in the interaction between emotional states, taste perception, and food intake, and highlight novel approaches to studying these processes using animal models.

The relationship between taste perception and emotional states in mammals involves a unique associative process. Perceiving a taste is the actualization, at the cognitive level, of the detection of molecules, which serve as cues of the chemical nature of the ingested food. This represents an early stage of food identification, which can be used to predict the physiological effects that ingestion of a particular food will have. Thus, taste perception is intimately linked with subsequent positive or negative physiological states, which also elicit respective emotional states (comfort and pleasure vs. sickness and anxiety). This link is facilitated by a specific learning mechanism. In typical associative learning situations involving conditioned stimuli that activate other sensory modalities, such as sight or hearing, the delay between the cue (conditioned stimulus, CS) and the outcome (unconditioned stimulus, US) has to be as short as possible, usually counted in seconds. In contrast, taste-dependent learning involves a unique feature: the delay between the CS and US can be extremely long – up to several hours (Garcia et al., 1966; Berman and Dudai, 2001; Dudai, 2002). This long delay is likely related to the fact that ingestion-induced malaise usually requires several hours to develop. Furthermore, tolerating such a long delay in mammalian taste-dependant learning allows taste to associate not only with unconditioned physiological states, but also with emotional states (Guitton and Dudai, 2004), and even social responses (Guitton et al., 2008).

Food exposure can have various effects on social behavior in mammals (for review see Guitton, in press). Specifically, food exposure can increase the frequency of social interactions related to the exchange of taste-related information on the nature of "safe" foods (Guitton et al., 2008; Guitton, in press). Conversely, food exposure can also trigger immediate or delayed social withdrawal, linked to the on-line (real) or off-line (perceived or remembered) toxicity. Food-related social withdrawal may be the result of an evolved strategy to avoid predators while vulnerable (by avoiding being at the same place as other conspecifics that may also be targets of the predator) or to avoid fights with conspecifics that may lead to the loss of social status within the group social hierarchy. It may also be part of an evolutionary protective mechanism, which prevents the transmission of false information regarding the relative safety of a newly ingested food to other conspecifics (Guitton, in press). Interestingly, alteration of social behavior is also a feature of the pathology observed in patients suffering from eating disorders (Kaye et al., 2004; Klein and Walsh, 2004). This suggests that mechanisms mediating the social effects of food exposure may also be involved in food-related pathologies.

Social withdrawal in mammals is typically associated with the negative emotional state of anxiety (File and Seth, 2003). Anxiety is also co-morbid with the onset and maintenance of the symptoms of eating disorders in humans (Godart et al., 2000). Furthermore, one of the main neurotransmitter systems implicated in anxiety, the serotonergic system, plays a major role in eating disorders (Kaye, 2008). In animals, anxiety is also related to decreased food intake (Donohoe, 1984; Dulawa and Hen, 2005) and this effect is known to involve the serotonergic system (Compan et al., 2004; Bechtholt et al., 2007). Recent studies have identified some of the critical brain regions and serotonin receptors involved in decreased food intake (hypophagia) in rodents. These include the hypothalamus, a key brain region involved in the neuroendocrine regulation of food intake (Dietrich and Horvat, 2009), and the nucleus accumbens, a region considered to be critical in the translation of perceptual and emotional signals into motivated action (Cardinal et al., 2002). Specifically, pharmacological activation of the serotonin receptors 5-HT_{1B} and 5HT_{2C} in the hypothalamus was shown to induce hypophagia (Heisler et al., 2002; 2006). A similar effect was observed following activation of 5-HT_4 receptors in the nucleus accumbens (Jean et al., 2007). Further understanding of the involvement of the serotonergic system in the relationship between emotional processes and food intake is required to shed more light on the role of these brain regions in disordered eating.

Animal models of eating disorders have to take into account the multimodal integration of the perceptual, emotional, and behavioural processes described above. In the case of anorexia, some early models focus primarily on the physical symptoms of the disorder, including physical overactivity or food restriction-induced weight loss (Smith, 1989; Siegfried, 2003). A more recent model focuses on the interaction between perceptual and emotional processes related to the psychological components of anorexia. In this model rats display food avoidance and alterations in social behaviour induced by pairing a particular food with an anxiety-like state (Guitton and Dudai, 2004; Guitton et al., 2008). Conditioning of general food avoidance in rats is nearly impossible, but producing avoidance of specific food is relatively easy (Garcia et al., 1966; Berman and Dudai, 2001; Guitton and Dudai, 2004). This phenomenon, named conditioned taste aversion (CTA), involves pairing a taste with delayed visceral pain and malaise. Subsequent exposure to this taste triggers substantial aversion to the related food (Garcia et al., 1966; Berman and Dudai, 2001). However, in this situation, the exposure to the conditioned taste does not trigger any changes in the social behavior of rats (Guitton et al., 2008). In contrast, social withdrawal can be triggered, in addition to food avoidance, when a taste is paired with a diffuse emotional state, such as anxiety (Guitton and Dudai 2004; Guiton et al., 2008). Specifically, a serotoninergic agent, 5HT_{2C} receptor agonist meta-chlorophenylpiperazine (mCPP), can be used to induce an anxiety-like state in rats following exposure to a new taste. Subsequent exposure to this taste produces food avoidance and social withdrawal specifically linked to the time period following taste exposure (Guitton et al., 2008). This model provides a novel approach to studying the mechanisms involved in the interaction between perceptual and emotional processes in relation to some of the symptoms of eating disorders.

An important consideration in any animal model of eating disorders is individual variability in behavior. In humans, although many individuals engage in dieting and food-restricting behavior, only a small proportion develop eating disorders such as anorexia or bulimia nervosa. Of interest to studying the mechanisms of eating disorders are the factors underlying susceptibility to developing pathological outcomes.

Genetic differences are a likely contributor to individual differences in susceptibility (Bulik et al., 2007; Monteleone and Maj, 2008), but differences in life experience may also account for a substantial portion of individual variability (Klump et al., 2002). In the context of perceptual and emotional integration in eating disorders, the influence of prior experience on emotional regulation is important to consider. Indeed, in both humans and animals, adverse early life social experience is known to have long-term consequences on behavioral and physiological manifestations of stress and anxiety (Sanchez et al., 2001; Lomanowska et al., 2006).

Similar effects are observed following psychosocial stress in later life (Buwalda et al., 2005; Razzoli et al., 2009), although different neurobiological processes may be affected depending on the animal's age (Andersen, 2003; Lomanowska et al., 2010).

In humans, there is evidence that anxiety often precedes the onset of eating disorders (Godart et al., 2000). Therefore, further study of the relationship between social factors and anxiety, as well as the influence of this relationship on the multimodal integration of perceptual and emotional signals related to food intake, may provide an important step in the progress towards understanding the etiology of eating disorders.

3. The Use of Virtual Reality Technologies in the Context of Eating Disorders

Virtual environments are inherently multimodal settings that allow for the integrated three-dimensional (3D) computerized representations of multiple sensory and/or cognitive dimensions of real-life experience (Riva, 1997; Botella et al., 1998; Gaggioli et al., 2003). Besides the obvious recreational uses, virtual reality also has clinical applications. In particular, virtual settings provide a means to expose patients to ecologically valid settings and circumstances in a safe and convenient environment, such as a clinic, without substantially limiting interactivity and flexibility (Botella et al., 1998; Gregg and Tarrier, 2007). However, in contrast to real life settings, virtual environments can be constantly controlled and adapted to the therapeutic needs of individual patients. Thus, virtual reality represents an intriguing option as a therapeutic tool for the treatment of human psychopathology, and has been successfully used in the treatment of several disorders (Rose et al., 2005; Freeman 2008), including phobias (Vincelli et al., 2002; Bouchard et al., 2006), and addiction (Girard et al., 2009). Considering the perceptual disturbances associated with eating disorders, such as distortion of body image and reactivity to visual and gustatory food cues, treatment approaches involving virtual reality technologies may offer a valuable alternative to other conventional therapies (Gaggioli et al., 2003). Indeed, virtual instead of real stimuli have been used in several studies to assess and treat eating behaviors in eating disorder patients (Riva, 1997; Alcaniz et al., 2000; Lozano et al., 2002). The effectiveness of these virtual stimuli relies on the quality and realism of the virtual interface (Gaggioli et al., 2003). Importantly, the virtual approach should be considered as a putative treatment of eating disorders only if exposure to real and virtual settings elicits a comparable subset of behavioral, perceptual, and emotional responses in the subjects. Several studies have investigated this issue.

For individuals suffering from eating disorders, including anorexia and bulimia nervosa, food is clearly a stimulus that can elicit emotional responses (Carter et al., 2002; Legenbauer et al., 2004; Friederich et al., 2006). Several studies have focused on the capacity of food-related stimuli presented in virtual environments to trigger emotional responses in eating disorder sufferers (Gutierrez-Maldonado et al., 2006; Ferrer-Garcia et al., 2009; Gorini et al., 2010). The results demonstrated that 3D virtual representations of food were as effective as real food, and more effective than 2D photographs, in triggering emotional responses, as assessed by psychological and physiological measures (Gutierrez-Maldonado et al., 2006; Ferrer-Garcia et al., 2009; Gorini et al., 2010). Furthermore, exposure to food-related stimuli in virtual environments allowed for the expression of behaviors that were more complex than simple emotional responses, such as actions related to purchasing food in a virtual supermarket (Nederkoorn et al. 2009).

Virtual technologies also allow for the multimodal representation of the self and other individuals in a virtual setting (Gaggioli et al., 2003; Guitton, 2010). When considering computerized human representations, realism and beauty represent two important factors that enhance the virtual experience (Giard and Guitton, 2010). These two factors also form the basis of virtual representations of the body developed for psychophysiological rehabilitation of eating disorders sufferers (Riva, 1997; Alcaniz et al., 2000). Body image distortion is one of the symptoms of eating disorders for which virtual reality represents a powerful assessment and therapeutic tool (Gaggioli et al., 2003). Assessment of body image distortion can be performed by presenting patients with detailed 3D virtual body models that vary from underweight to overweight, but are fundamentally based on the patients' real body structure. In this context, patients may choose which body shape they perceive as the closest to their current body shape (Riva, 1997). The 3D representations significantly improve the capacity to evaluate human shapes, specifically for body parts most affected by body image distortion in eating disorders patients, including the breasts, stomach, hips, and thighs (Riva, 1997). In contrast to 2D static tools, such as photographs, advanced virtual settings can use 3D morphing techniques to achieve real time deformation of body models that correspond to individual patients (Alcaniz et al., 2000).

With respect to treatment strategies, the virtual representations allow patients to witness changes in their body shape in a safe and controlled setting. This may be used in exposure and desensitization exercises to aid in changing patients' attitudes and behaviors related to body image (Myers et al., 2004).

The virtual experience can be further enhanced by incorporating more complex components of the environment, such as rooms in which patients can choose to eat and drink virtual food or monitor caloric intake and changes in weight while under the guidance of a therapist (Myers et al., 2004). Initial clinical results using such approaches are promising (Alcaniz et al., 2000; Riva et al., 1999; 2000; 2002).

Representations of other individuals in the virtual environment may also be used in therapeutic exercises (Gaggioli et al., 2003).

As discussed, the disturbance of social behavior is a prevalent symptom of eating disorders (Kaye et al., 2004; Klein and Walsh, 2004). Virtual reality enables patients to confront distressing social situations and manage their emotional and behavioral responses under the guidance of a therapist (Vincelli et al., 2002). Further development of the physical, behavioral, and interactive characteristics of virtual human representations holds promise for a more realistic recreation of social experiences in the virtual setting (Gaggioli et al., 2003).

Overall, the appeal of virtual reality-based therapies is that they can simultaneously stimulate multiple perceptual and emotional systems in a controlled manner. This multimodal approach may be particularly beneficial for the assessment and treatment of eating disorders sufferers.

CONCLUSION

Based on the analysis of clinical and animal studies, it is clear that in order to enhance our understanding of eating disorders, it is necessary to consider the influence of multimodal sensory and emotional integration. Further investigation of the contribution of this process to the ontogeny and maintenance of eating disorders is required not only to gain greater insight into the mechanisms underlying eating disorders, but also to provide new avenues for the advancement of treatment strategies.

Modeling the cognitive and emotional aspects of eating disorders in animals clearly represents a challenge. However, as exemplified by the animal model of taste-dependent social avoidance, this research approach is valuable in studying the fundamental associative processes involved in the integration of external stimuli related to taste perception with internal physiological and emotional states, and their subsequent influence on complex behavior, such a social interactions.

Understanding of the neurobiological basis of these mechanisms is particularly important for the development of pharmacologically based therapeutics that address the perceptual, emotional, and socio-behavioral aspects of eating disorders.

The use of virtual reality also offers the possibility to integrate different sensory and emotional elements in the treatment of disordered eating. Indeed, this approach has already shown promise in cognitive-behavioral treatment paradigms. Along with the development of potential pharmacological treatments based on results from animal models, the use of virtual reality provides an attractive avenue for the future of eating disorder therapy. Overall, novel therapeutic strategies in this area should emphasize a multimodal approach that reflects the integrated nature of the perceptual, emotional, and behavioral processes involved in eating disorders.

ACKNOWLEDGMENTS

The present work was supported by the Natural Sciences and Engineering Research Council of Canada (NSERC – grant number 371644) and a Strategic Development Grant from the "Fonds de la Recherche en Santé du Québec" (FRSQ). MJG holds a Career Grant from the "Fonds de la Recherche en Santé du Québec" (FRSQ).

REFERENCES

Abraham, S. F., and Beumont, P. J. V. (1982). How patients describe bulimia or binge eating. *Psychological Medicine*, 12(3), 625-635.

Alcaniz, M., Botella, C., Perpina, C., Banos, R., Lozano, J. A., Montesa, J., et al. (2000). A new realistic 3D body representation in virtual environments for the treatment of disturbed body image in eating disorders. *Cyberpsychology and Behavior*, 3(3), 433-439.

Andersen, S. L. (2003). Trajectories of brain development: point of vulnerability or window of opportunity? *Neuroscience and Biobehavioral Reviews*, 27(1-2), 3-18.

Arun, C. P. (2008). Drive for leanness, anorexia nervosa, and overactivity: The missing link. Stress, Neurotransmitters, and Hormones: *Neuroendocrine and Genetic Mechanisms*, 1148, 526-529.

Bechtholt, A. J., Hill, T. E., and Lucki, I. (2007). Anxiolytic effect of serotonin depletion in the novelty-induced hypophagia test. *Psychopharmacology*, 190(4), 531-540.

Berman, D. E., and Dudai, Y. (2001). Memory extinction, learning anew, and learning the new: Dissociations in the molecular machinery of learning in cortex. *Science*, 291(5512), 2417-2419.

Berridge, K. C. (2009). 'Liking' and 'wanting' food rewards: Brain substrates and roles in eating disorders. *Physiology and Behavior*, 97(5), 537-550.

Botella, C., Perpina, C., Banos, R. M., and Garcia-Palacios, A. (1998). Virtual reality: a new clinical setting lab. *Stud Health Technol Inform*, 58, 73-81.

Bouchard, S., Cote, S., St-Jacques, J., Robillard, G., and Renaud, P. (2006). Effectiveness of virtual reality exposure in the treatment of arachnophobia using 3D games. *Technol Health Care*, 14(1), 19-27.

Bulik, C. M., Landt, M., van Furth, E. F., and Sullivan, P. F. (2007). The genetics of anorexia nervosa. *Annual Review of Nutrition*, 27, 263-275.

Bulik, C. M., Sullivan, P. F., Fear, J. L., and Joyce, P. R. (1997). Eating disorders and antecedent anxiety disorders: A controlled study. *Acta Psychiatrica Scandinavica*, 96(2), 101-107.

Buwalda, B., Kole, M. H. P., Veenema, A. H., Huininga, M., de Boer, S. F., Korte, S. M., et al. (2005). Long-term effects of social stress on brain and behavior: a focus on hippocampal functioning. *Neuroscience and Biobehavioral Reviews*, 29(1), 83-97.

Cardinal, R. N., Parkinson, J. A., Hall, J., and Everitt, B. J. (2002). Emotion and motivation: the role of the amygdala, ventral striatum, and prefrontal cortex. *Neuroscience and Biobehavioral Reviews*, 26(3), 321-352.

Carr, K. D. (1996). Feeding, drug abuse, and the sensitization of reward by metabolic need. *Neurochemical Research*, 21(11), 1455-1467.

Carr, K. D. (2002). Augmentation of drug reward by chronic food restriction: Behavioral evidence and underlying mechanisms. *Physiology and Behavior*, 76(3), 353-364.

Carr, K. D., and Papadouka, V. (1994). The role of multiple opioid receptors in the potentiation of reward by food restriction. *Brain Research*, 639(2), 253-260.

Carter, F. A., Bulik, C. M., McIntosh, V. V., and Joyce, P. R. (2002). Cue reactivity as a predictor of outcome with bulimia nervosa. *International Journal of Eating Disorders*, 31(3), 240-250.

Cash, T. F., and Deagle, E. A. (1997). The nature and extent of body-image disturbances in anorexia nervosa and bulimia nervosa: A meta-analysis. *International Journal of Eating Disorders*, 22(2), 107-125.

Compan, V., Zhou, M. M., Grailhe, R., Gazzara, R. A., Martin, R., Gingrich, J., et al. (2004). Attenuated response to stress and novelty and hypersensitivity to seizures in 5-HT4 receptor knock-out mice. *Journal of Neuroscience*, 24(2), 412-419.

Deep, A. L., Nagy, L. M., Weltzin, T. E., Rao, R., and Kaye, W. H. (1995). Premorbid onset of psychopathology in long-term recovered anorexia-nervosa. *International Journal of Eating Disorders*, 17(3), 291-297.

Dietrich, M. O., and Horvath, T. L. (2009). Feeding signals and brain circuitry. *European Journal of Neuroscience*, 30(9), 1688-1696.

Donohoe, T. P. (1984). Stress-induced anorexia - implications for anorexia-nervosa. *Life Sciences*, 34(3), 203-218.

Drewnowski, A., Halmi, K. A., Pierce, B., Gibbs, J., and Smith, G. P. (1987). Taste and eating disorders. *American Journal of Clinical Nutrition*, 46(3), 442-450.

Dudai, Y. (2002). Molecular bases of long-term memories: a question of persistence. *Current Opinion in Neurobiology*, 12(2), 211-216.

Dulawa, S. C., and Hen, R. (2005). Recent advances in animal models of chronic antidepressant effects: The novelty-induced hypophagia test. *Neuroscience and Biobehavioral Reviews*, 29(4-5), 771-783.

Faunce, G. J. (2002). Eating disorders and attentional bias: a review. *Eat Disord*, 10(2), 125-139.

Ferrer-Garcia, M., Gutierrez-Maldonado, J., Caqueo-Urizar, A., and Moreno, E. (2009). The validity of virtual environments for eliciting emotional responses in patients with eating disorders and in controls. *Behavior Modification*, 33(6), 830-854.

File, S. E., and Seth, P. (2003). A review of 25 years of the social interaction test. *European Journal of Pharmacology*, 463(1-3), 35-53.

Franko, D. L., Wolfe, B. E., and Jimerson, D. C. (1994). Elevated sweet taste pleasantness ratings in bulimia-nervosa. *Physiology and Behavior*, 56(5), 969-973.

Freeman, D. (2008). Studying and treating schizophrenia using virtual reality: A new paradigm. *Schizophrenia Bulletin*, 34(4), 605-610.

Friederich, H. C., Kumari, V., Uher, R., Riga, M., Schmidt, U., Campbell, I. C., et al. (2006). Differential motivational responses to food and pleasurable cues in anorexia and bulimia nervosa: a startle reflex paradigm. *Psychological Medicine*, 36(9), 1327-1335.

Gaggioli, A., Mantovani, F., Castelnuovo, G., Wiederhold, B., and Riva, G. (2003). Avatars in clinical psychology: A framework for the clinical use of virtual humans. *Cyberpsychology and Behavior*, 6(2), 117-125.

Garcia, J., Ervin, F. R., and Koelling, R. A. (1966). Learning with prolonged delay of reinforcement. *Psychonomic Science*, 5(3), 121-122.

Gardner, R. M., and Bokenkamp, E. D. (1996). The role of sensory and nonsensory factors in body size estimations of eating disorder subjects. *Journal of Clinical Psychology*, 52(1), 3-15.

Giard, F., and Guitton, M. J. (2010). Beauty or realism: The dimensions of skin from cognitive sciences to computer graphics. *Computers in Human Behavior*, 26(6), 1748-1752.

Giel, K. E., Teufel, M., Friederich, H. C., Hautzinger, M., Enck, P., and Zipfel, S. (2010). Processing of pictorial food stimuli in patients with eating disorders-A systematic review. *Int J Eat Disord.*

Girard, B., Turcotte, V., and Bouchard, S. (2009). Crushing virtual cigarettes reduces tobacco addiction and treatment discontinuation. *Cyberpsychology and Behavior*, 12(5), 477-483.

Godart, N. T., Flament, M. F., Lecrubier, Y., and Jeammet, P. (2000). Anxiety disorders in anorexia nervosa and bulimia nervosa: co-morbidity and chronology of appearance. *European Psychiatry*, 15(1), 38-45.

Gorini, A., Griez, E., Petrova, A., and Riva, G. (2010). Assessment of the emotional responses produced by exposure to real food, virtual food and photographs of food in patients affected by eating disorders. *Ann Gen Psychiatry*, 9, 30.

Gregg, L., and Tarrier, N. (2007). Virtual reality in mental health - A review of the literature. *Social Psychiatry and Psychiatric Epidemiology*, 42(5), 343-354.

Guitton, M. J. (2009). Tinnitus-provoking salicylate treatment triggers social impairments in mice. *Journal of Psychosomatic Research*, 67(3), 273-276.

Guitton, M. J. (2010). Cross-modal compensation between name and visual aspect in Socially active avatars. *Computers in Human Behavior*, 26(6), 1772-1776.

Guitton, M. J., and Dudai, Y. (2004). Anxiety-like state associates with taste to produce conditioned taste aversion. *Biological Psychiatry*, 56(11), 901-904.

Guitton, M. J., Klin, Y., and Dudai, Y. (2008). Taste-dependent sociophobia: When food and company do not mix. *Behavioural Brain Research*, 191(2), 148-152.

Guitton, M. J. (In Press). When taste triggers sociophobia. In: VR Preedy, RR Watson, CR Martin (Eds). International Handbook of Behavior, Diet, and Nutrition. New York : Springer.

Gutierrez-Maldonado, J., Ferrer-Garcia, M., Caqueo-Urizar, A., and Letosa-Porta, A. (2006). Assessment of emotional reactivity produced by exposure to virtual environments in patients with eating disorders. *Cyberpsychology and Behavior*, 9(5), 507-513.

Halmi, K. A., and Sunday, S. R. (1991). Temporal patterns of hunger and fullness ratings and related cognitions in anorexia and bulimia. *Appetite*, 16(3), 219-237.

Heatherton, T. F., and Baumeister, R. F. (1991). Binge eating as escape from self-awareness. *Psychological Bulletin*, 110(1), 86-108.

Heisler, L. K., Cowley, M. A., Tecott, L. H., Fan, W., Low, M. J., Smart, J. L., et al. (2002). Activation of central melanocortin pathways by fenfluramine. *Science*, 297(5581), 609-611.

Heisler, L. K., Jobst, E. E., Sutton, G. M., Zhou, L. G., Borck, E., Thornton-Jones, Z., et al. (2006). Serotonin reciprocally regulates melanocortin neurons to modulate food intake. *Neuron*, 51(2), 239-249.

Hetherington M., and Rolls, B. J. (1989). Sensory-specific satiety in anorexia and bulimia nervosa. *Annals of the New York Academy of Sciences*, 575, 387-398.

Hetherington, M. M., and Rolls, B. J. (1991). Eating behavior in eating disorders - response to preloads. *Physiology and Behavior*, 50(1), 101-108.

Jean, A., Conductier, G., Manrique, C., Bouras, C., Berta, P., Hen, R., et al. (2007). Anorexia induced by activation of serotonin 5-HT4 receptors is mediated by increases in CART in the nucleus accumbens. *Proceedings of the National Academy of Sciences of the United States of America*, 104, 16335-16340.

Kaye, W. (2008). Neurobiology of anorexia and bulimia nervosa. *Physiology and Behavior*, 94(1), 121-135.

Kaye, W. H. (1997). Anorexia nervosa, obsessional behavior, and serotonin. *Psychopharmacology Bulletin*, 33(3), 335-344.

Kaye, W. H., Bulik, C. M., Thornton, L., Barbarich, N., Masters, K., and Price Fdn Collaborative, G. (2004). Comorbidity of anxiety disorders with anorexia and bulimia nervosa. *American Journal of Psychiatry*, 161(12), 2215-2221.

Kelley, A. E., Bakshi, V. P., Haber, S. N., Steininger, T. L., Will, M. J., and Zhang, M. (2002). Opioid modulation of taste hedonics within the ventral striatum. *Physiology and Behavior*, 76(3), 365-377.

Klein, D. A., and Walsh, B. T. (2004). Eating disorders: clinical features and pathophysiology. *Physiology and Behavior*, 81(2), 359-374.

Klump, K. L., Wonderlich, S., Lehoux, P., Lilenfeld, L. R. R., and Bulik, C. M. (2002). Does environment matter? A review of nonshared environment and eating disorders. *International Journal of Eating Disorders*, 31(2), 118-135.

Legenbauer, T., Vogele, C., and Ruddel, H. (2004). Anticipatory effects of food exposure in women diagnosed with bulimia nervosa. *Appetite*, 42(1), 33-40.

Lomanowska, A. M., Ammari, N., and Kraemer, G. W. (2010). Interactions between the effects of early isolation rearing and complex housing on adult locomotor activity and sensitivity to amphetamine in rats involve noradrenergic neurotransmission. *Pharmacology Biochemistry and Behavior*, 95(1), 100-105.

Lomanowska, A. M., Rana, S. A., McCutcheon, D., Parker, L. A., and Wainwright, P. E. (2006). Artificial rearing alters the response of rats to natural and drug-mediated rewards. *Developmental Psychobiology*, 48(4), 301-314.

Lozano, J. A., Alcaniz, M., Gil, J. A., Moserrat, C., Juan, M. C., Grau, V., et al. (2002). Virtual food in virtual environments for the treatment of eating disorders. *Medicine Meets Virtual Reality*, 02/10, 85, 268-273.

McElroy, S.L., Kotwal, R., Keck, P.E., Jr., and Akiskal, H.S. (2005). Comorbidity of bipolar and eating disorders: distinct or related disorders with shared dysregulations? *Journal of Affective Disorders*, 86, 107-127.

Miyake, Y., Okamoto, Y., Onoda, K., Kurosaki, M., Shirao, N., and Yamawaki, S. (2010). Brain activation during the perception of distorted body images in eating disorders. *Psychiatry Research-Neuroimaging*, 181(3), 183-192.

Monteleone, P., and Maj, M. (2008). Genetic susceptibility to eating disorders: associated polymorphisms and pharmacogenetic suggestions. *Pharmacogenomics*, 9(10), 1487-1520.

Myers, T. C., Swan-Kremeier, L., Wonderlich, S., Lancaster, K., and Mitchell, J. E. (2004). The use of alternative delivery systems and new technologies in the treatment of patients with eating disorders. *Int J Eat Disord*, 36(2), 123-143.

Neal, J. A., and Edelmann, R. J. (2003). The etiology of social phobia: Toward a developmental profile. *Clinical Psychology Review*, 23(6), 761-786.

Nederkoorn, C., Guerrieri, R., Havermans, R. C., Roefs, A., and Jansen, A. (2009). The interactive effect of hunger and impulsivity on food intake and purchase in a virtual supermarket. *International Journal of Obesity*, 33(8), 905-912.

Probst, M., Vandereycken, W., Vanderlinden, J., and Van Coppenolle, H. (1998). The significance of body size estimation in eating disorders: Its relationship with clinical and psychological variables. *International Journal of Eating Disorders*, 24(2), 167-174.

Puel, J. L., and Guitton, M. J. (2007). Salicylate-induced tinnitus: molecular mechanisms and modulation by anxiety. Tinnitus: *Pathophysiology and Treatment*, 166, 141-146.

Razzoli, M., Carboni, L., and Arban, R. (2009). Alterations of behavioral and endocrinological reactivity induced by 3 brief social defeats in rats: Relevance to human psychopathology. *Psychoneuroendocrinology*, 34(9), 1405-1416.

Riva, G. (1997). Virtual reality as assessment tool in psychology. *Stud Health Technol Inform*, 44, 71-79.

Riva, G., Bacchetta, M., Baruffi, M., Cirillo, G., and Molinari, E. (2000). Virtual reality environment for body image modification: A multidimensional therapy for the treatment of body image in obesity and related pathologies. *Cyberpsychology and Behavior*, 3(3), 421-431.

Riva, G., Bacchetta, M., Baruffi, M., and Molinari, E. (2002). Virtual-reality-based multidimensional therapy for the treatment of body image disturbances in binge eating disorders: A preliminary controlled study. Ieee *Transactions on Information Technology in Biomedicine*, 6(3), 224-234.

Riva, G., Bacchetta, M., Baruffi, M., Rinaldi, S., and Molinari, E. (1999). Virtual reality based experiential cognitive treatment of anorexia nervosa. *J Behav Ther Exp Psychiatry*, 30(3), 221-230.

Robinson, P. H. (1989). Perceptivity and paraceptivity during measurement of gastric-emptying in anorexia and bulimia nervosa *British Journal of Psychiatry*, 154, 400-405.

Rose, F. D., Brooks, B. M., and Rizzo, A. A. (2005). Virtual reality in brain damage rehabilitation: Review. *Cyberpsychology and Behavior*, 8(3), 241-262.

Sachdev, P., Mondraty, N., Wen, W., and Gulliford, K. (2008). Brains of anorexia nervosa patients process self-images differently from non-self-images: An fMRI study. *Neuropsychologia*, 46(8), 2161-2168.

Sanchez, M. M., Ladd, C. O., and Plotsky, P. M. (2001). Early adverse experience as a developmental risk factor for later psychopathology: Evidence from rodent and primate models. *Development and Psychopathology*, 13(3), 419-449.

Santel, S., Baving, L., Krauel, K., Munte, T. F., and Rotte, M. (2006). Hunger and satiety in anorexia nervosa: fMRI during cognitive processing of food pictures. *Brain Research*, 1114, 138-148.

Sewards, T. V. (2004). Dual separate pathways for sensory and hedonic aspects of taste. *Brain Research Bulletin*, 62(4), 271-283.

Siegfried, Z., Berry, E. M., Hao, S. Z., and Avraham, Y. (2003). Animal models in the investigation of anorexia. *Physiology and Behavior*, 79(1), 39-45.

Simon, Y., Bellisle, F., Monneuse, M. O., Samuellajeunesse, B., and Drewnowski, A. (1993). Taste responsiveness in anorexia-nervosa. *British Journal of Psychiatry*, 162, 244-246.

Skrzypek, S., Wehmeier, P. M., and Remschmidt, H. (2001). Body image assessment using body size estimation in recent studies on anorexia nervosa. A brief review. *European Child and Adolescent Psychiatry*, 10(4), 215-221.

Slade, P. D. (1988). Body-image in anorexia-nervosa. *British Journal of Psychiatry*, 153, 20-22.

Smith, G. P. (1989). Animal-models of human eating disorders. *Annals of the New York Academy of Sciences*, 575, 63-74.

Sorensen, L. B., Moller, P., Flint, A., Martens, M., and Raben, A. (2003). Effect of sensory perception of foods on appetite and food intake: a review of studies on humans. *International Journal of Obesity*, 27(10), 1152-1166.

Stormark, K. M., and Torkildsen, o. (2004). Selective processing of linguistic and pictorial food stimuli in females with anorexia and bulimia nervosa. *Eat Behav*, 5(1), 27-33.

Sunday, S. R., and Halmi, K. A. (1990). Taste perceptions and hedonics in eating disorders. *Physiology and Behavior*, 48(5), 587-594.

Toth, E., Tury, F., Gati, A., Weisz, J., Kondakor, I., and Molnar, M. (2004). Effects of sweet and bitter gustatory stimuli in anorexia nervosa on EEG frequency spectra. *International Journal of Psychophysiology*, 52(3), 285-290.

Uher, R., Murphy, T., Brammer, M. J., Dalgleish, T., Phillips, M. L., Ng, V. W., et al. (2004). Medial prefrontal cortex activity associated with symptom provocation in eating disorders. *American Journal of Psychiatry*, 161(7), 1238-1246.

Vincelli, F., Choi, H., Molinari, E., Wiederhold, B. K., Bouchard, S., and Riva, G. (2002). Virtual reality assisted cognitive behavioral therapy for the treatment of panic disorders with agoraphobia. *Medicine Meets Virtual Reality*, 02/10, 85, 552-559.

Wagner, A., Aizenstein, H., Mazurkewicz, L., Fudge, J., Frank, G. K., Putnam, K., et al. (2008). Altered insula response to taste stimuli in individuals recovered from restricting-type anorexia nervosa. *Neuropsychopharmacology*, 33(3), 513-523.

Whiteside, U., Chen, E., Neighbors, C., Hunter, D., Lo, T., and Larimer, M. (2007). Difficulties regulating emotions: Do binge eaters have fewer strategies to modulate and tolerate negative affect? *Eating Behaviors*, 8, 162-169.

Yeomans, M. R., Blundell, J. E., and Leshem, M. (2004). Palatability: response to nutritional need or need-free stimulation of appetite? *British Journal of Nutrition*, 92, S3-S14.

In: Eating Disorders
Editor: C. M. Shapiro, pp. 61-82
ISBN 978-1-61209-746-6

Chapter 3

EATING DISORDERS AND MENSTRUAL DYSFUNCTION – IMPLICATIONS ON BONE MINERAL DENSITY

William W. K. To[1] and Margaret W. N. Wong[2]

ABSTRACT

Eating disorders have been associated with a high incidence of menstrual dysfunction in the form of oligomenorrhea and amenorrhea, particularly in adolescent populations. Such abnormal menstrual patterns, in turn, bear direct implications on bone health. In the treatment of these women, although bone mass accrual usually improves with weight gain and menstrual recovery, residual [1]deficits may persist. Women with a history of early onset eating disorders are more likely to suffer from osteoporosis / osteopenia in later life even years after recovery, and those with persistent eating disorders are likely to have continued low body weight and decreased bone density. In the female athlete triad, where menstrual dysfunction and eating disorders are essential components, bone health concerns are also important considerations in the management. The best treatment options remains controversial. At present, there is no good evidence in the literature to guide medical

[1] Department of Obstetrics and Gynaecology, United Christian Hospital, Hong Kong
[2] Department of Orthopaedics and TraumatologyPrince of Wales Hospital, The Chinese University of Hong Kong, Hong Kong

interventions for the treatment and prevention of osteoporosis and osteopenia in these women suffering from eating disorders.

INTRODUCTION

Menstrual dysfunction is a common feature of all eating disorders in females. The majority of cases of eating disorders occur in younger women before their third decade, when women are still in their reproductive age, and thus menstrual dysfunction becomes a prominent feature in the symptoms of their eating disorder. The etiology of menstrual dysfunction usually consists of multiple factors, and the degree of weight loss, exercises and psychological stress are all part of the scenario. The eating disorder by itself may be directly or indirectly be associated with various medical conditions. However, the additional occurrence of menstrual dysfunction in these women may add to the metabolic and endocrine abnormalities. Thus, the direct impact of abnormal nutrient intake, particularly of calcium, the metabolic complications resulting from this low caloric intake, and the endocrine effects of menstrual dysfunction will all add together to bring an impact on the bone health and bone mineral density (BMD) of these individuals. Data are emerging to show the long term impact of the effects of eating disorders on the bone health of these individuals in later life, particularly when they reach menopausal age groups. Various studies have attempted to evaluate whether eating disorders in younger age would imply a higher incidence of menopausal osteoporosis, or more importantly, a higher fracture risk in menopause. However, the clinical management of these adolescents and young women with eating disorders seemed to be elusive at the moment, and the efficacy of current management protocols on BMD changes remains dubious. This chapter will discuss the intricate relationship between eating disorders and menstrual dysfunction, and how the interaction of these two factors would influence BMD in these women. Current management modalities of these young women will be described and the limitations of such treatment on effectively preventing the negative impact of eating disorders on BMD will be presented.

THE DIAGNOSTIC CRITERIA FOR EATING DISORDERS – A GYNECOLOGICAL PERSPECTIVE

According to the Diagnostic and Statistical Manual of Mental Disorders 4th edition text revision)(DSM-IV-TR)[1], eating disorders fall into one of the following three categories: anorexia nervosa, bulimia nervosa and eating disorders not otherwise specified. Anorexia nervosa is associated with low body weight and affects up to 1% of young women, while bulimia nervosa can be found in women of any body weight and affects 2-5% of young women. Eating disorders not otherwise specified are a conglomeration of subtypes of eating disorders that are not necessarily less serious than the other two diagnoses and may affect up to 15% of young women [2], of which binge eating with obesity is the most common type. Apparently, all eating disorders arose from the same underlying pathological belief of slimness or shape change, with a dominant and morbid fear of becoming obese, a relentless drive for thinness, and a distortion of body image [3]. Young women may be triggered into active eating disorders at times of profound body changes, and puberty and pregnancy are common settings for adolescents and young women.

While strict criteria for these disorders are available, the application of these criteria remains problematic, and in a gynecological setting where women present for primary medical care with menstrual dysfunction, the current criteria of anorexia nervosa for 3 months of amenorrhea or a bodyweight below 85% of healthy women for age and height might not have been met. In particular, a weight loss criterion would assume the individual have a normal weight range to start off with, which is often not the case in practice. On the other hand, the DSM IV –TR criteria of a BMI below 17 also appears to be very strict, and unless the eating disorder is well established and chronic, many such women might not fit into the diagnostic criteria.

In young women or adolescents around the age of menarche, the application of the diagnostic criteria could be even more controversial, when body mass criteria are variable, cognitive and verbal appraisal are not well developed, and particularly if they are pre-menarchal or have delayed menarche. In a cohort of British children with eating disorders, it was found that the Great Ormond Street criteria, which was designed and developed for children's age range, was much more applicable and reliable compared to the DSM, as the DSM would classify over 50% of the cases as eating disorders not otherwise specified or could not be classified at all [4]. A list of possible changes to the classification strategies for these children and adolescents around menarche has recently been proposed [5].

Should Amenorrhea Be a Diagnostic Criterion for Anorexia Nervosa?

The inclusion of amenorrhea as a criterion for diagnosing anorexia nervosa has long been the subject for debate, and the removal of this criterion has been considered for the fifth edition of the DSM (DSM-V). From a gynecological perspective, this criterion is useful as it is objective and clear-cut, and is an important indicator of physical health status, often prompting the patient to seek medical consultation. It is also useful to help to avoid possible misdiagnosis of anorexia nervosa by providing a marker of abnormal physiology to distinguish constitutionally thin women who are underweight but still menstruating [6]. However, it can also be seen that many women with genuine anorexia will fail to meet this criterion, and will thus be classified as eating disorders otherwise not specified.

A large survey of the menstrual history of 1705 women presenting with eating disorders showed that menstrual dysfunction occurred across all eating disorder subtypes. The menstrual dysfunction came as a spectrum and individuals with normal menstrual history reported the highest lifetime body mass index (BMI), while those with amenorrhea the lowest. Normal menstruation and oligomenorrhea groups reported greater binge eating, vomiting and appetite suppressant use. Amenorrhea was associated with lower caloric intake and higher exercise levels. The authors concluded that menstrual dysfunction was not limited to anorexia nervosa only, and that menstrual status was strongly associated with BMI, caloric intake and exercise levels [7].

While a clear association between reduced body weight and amenorrhea exists, the concept of a critical percentage of body fat for normal menses has not been supported by evidence, and significant differences in the percentage of body fat can be seen amongst those that are amenorrheic and those that continue to menstruate [8]. In a retrospective review of 230 women with full syndrome of anorexia nervosa and 28 who were menstruating but weighed less than 85% of ideal body weight, the menstruating group had lower expected body weight, shorter hospitalization, lower scores in the Eating Attitudes test-26 and the Eating Disorder Inventory drive for thinness subscale than the amenorrheic controls. However, the two groups did not differ significantly on most clinical measures [9]. Similarly, another retrospective study of 240 consecutively admitted women with anorexia nervosa showed 140 of them were amenorrheic and only 47 were continuing to menstruate [10]. The two groups, however, differed only on the lowest lifetime and admission BMI, while other psychiatric inventory measures showed no differences at all, indicating that menstrual status carried no direct impact on their clinical course or outcome.

A study that examined 242 women with eating and "exercise' disorders (defined as excessive exercising due to mood disorder or for energy utilization) showed that those with oligomenorrhea or normal menses were more likely to have an exercise disorder compared to those that were amenorrheic. In addition, older age, higher BMI, were associated with a lower likelihood of amenorrhea, while higher weight loss and more exercises were associated with amenorrhea. Current BMI, weight loss age, and exercise for mood or energy utilization predicted 81% of amenorrhea cases and 82% of non-amenorrhea cases. The findings suggested that nutritional status is the best predictors of amenorrhea [11]. Again, in a large cohort of women including all types of eating disorders, Poyastro [7] compared menstrual status across the different diagnostic categories and found that menstruating participants had significantly higher values for highest and lowest lifetime BMI, greater binge and vomiting frequency, and more appetite suppressant use. On the other hand, amenorrheic women had the greatest caloric restriction, and the highest frequency of exercising and laxative abuse. The normal menstruating group scored significantly lower on personal standards, harm avoidance, but higher on novelty seeking, while other comorbid psychopathology scores did not differ.

From these studies, it can be seen that most of the observed differences between individuals with eating disorders who are amenorrheic or who continue to menstruate appear to reflect their nutritional status rather than psychopathological state.

Amenorrhea develops generally secondary to weight loss, malnutrition and exercise behavior rather than to a primary or predisposing psychopathology. In fact, some of the data points to higher scores indicating greater illness severity in the menstruating group, but this paradoxical finding may be explained by the fact that certain eating disorders such as binge eating may be associated with better nutritional states than those with anorexia nervosa [6].

How Does Anorexia Nervosa and Menstrual Dysfunction Affect BMD and Bone Health?

A variety of physiological mechanisms have been found to be conducive to low bone mass in young females with anorexia nervosa. The concept that there would be a critical level of stored energy or fat mass required for the initiation and maintenance of regular menstrual function was advocated more than 4 decades ago. With the discovery of leptin in the nineties, it has emerged as the important hormonal mediator between stored energy balance and hypothalamic- pituitary-ovarian axis function [12]. Anorexic women with low body fat characteristically had low leptin levels, and available data has suggested there was a leptin threshold level that permits menstruation. Other peripheral metabolic mediators such as ghrelin, insulin and cortisol, as well as central mediators such as corticotrophin-releasing hormone communicate with gonadotrophin-releasing hormone (GnRH)-producing neurons in the hypothalamus [3]. The result would be a loss of pulsatile GnRH secretion that interfered with normal ovarian follicular cycle development, ending in chronic anovulation and amenorrhea.

Insufficient caloric intake could directly be conducive to poor nutritional status and catabolic metabolism. Insufficient calcium intake could lead to insufficient biochemical stimuli for osteogenic activity [13], which can result from a simultaneous increase in bone resorption as well as decrease in bone formation in these women. In particular, levels of anabolic hormones such as insulin-like growth factors (IGF-1) are low, and a close correlation between IGF-1 levels and biochemical bone formation markers have been found [14]. The abnormal bone formation could be explained in part by abnormal osteoblast function found in these women with anorexia nervosa. In addition, the related menstrual dysfunction manifested as amenorrhea and oligomenorrhea could be a manifestation of hypothalamic-pituitary axis suppression and chronic anovulation, which would in turn lead to a hypo-osteogenic state similar to postmenopausal bone loss. Psychological stress and depression could also result in immobility and lack of adequate physical exercises to stimulate proper osteogenic activity. The low metabolic rate and catabolic metabolism might also retard proper age- appropriate bone accrual. Classical studies have shown that serum levels of dehydro-epiandrosterone was subnormal in patients with anorexia nervosa [15], and could correlate inversely with urinary levels of N-telopeptides, a bone resorption marker, indicating that the hormone may modulate the increased bone resorption in these women. Contrarily, serum levels of interleukin-6, tumour necrosis factor-alpha and other pro-resorptive cytokines, markers shown to contribute to increased bone resorption in postmenopausal women, were at very low or undetectable levels in adolescents with anorexia nervosa [13]. Thus, the mechanisms that are at work to produce bone loss in these young women could be somewhat different from the older postmenopausal woman. Further, when the BMD and biochemical profile of 113 anorexic patients were compared to 21 age matched controls, it was found that those with osteoporosis were significantly older, had longer disease and amenorrhea durations, lower weight and BMI, higher bone specific osteocalcin, and lower serum carboxyl-terminal telo-peptide collagen, IGF-1 and IGF- binding protein 3. The authors concluded that the aetiology of bone loss in anorexia nervosa was multifactorial. Hypo-oestrogenism alone could not account for the BMD loss or the biochemical changes, and nutritional factors, IGF-1 concentrations in particular, seemed to play an important role [16] [Table 1].

Table 1. Eating Disorders and relationship to BMD changes.

Cause	Clinical manifestation	Associated pathophysiology
Insufficient caloric intake	Low BMI	Poor nutritional status Catabolic metabolism
	Low body fat composition	Body fat mass below critical value Serum leptin levels below critical value
	Amenorrhea Chronic anovulation Hypo-estrogenism	Hypothalamic pituitary axis suppression Loss of pulsatile GnRH secretion Menopausal type bone loss
	Energy drain	Peripheral metabolic mediators below critical level – ghrelin,insulin, cortisol
Insufficient calcium intake	Decreased bone formation markers	Insufficient biochemical stimuli for osteogenic activity; decreased osteoblastic function Retardation of proper age-appropriate bone accrual
	Low metabolic rate	Low IGF-1 and other bone anabolic hormones
Psychological stress	Abnormal self image Depression Addictions	Immobility Lack of adequate physical exercises to stimulate proper osteogenic activity; Smoking and alcohol exert further negative impact on bone mass

AGE OF ONSET OF EATING DISORDER AND IMPACT ON BMD

Data have shown that adolescents who develop anorexia nervosa prior to menarche had lower BMD than those who develop the disorder later in adolescence. In a cross-sectional sample of adolescent girls with anorexia nervosa with a mean age of 14.7 years, low total body BMD was found in 23.7% of them and low spinal BMD was found in 36.6%. The age of menarche has been found to be the most important factor predicting BMD in these young anorexic women [17]. Similarly, in a detailed study of a cohort of adolescents with anorexia nervosa, when these girls are classified according to their stage of illness, it was found that osteopenia was more prevalent when patients presented at younger ages and when the duration of amenorrhea was longer [18]. Amenorrhea for 20 months was identified as a threshold above which the most severe osteopenia was seen. A further study that examined predictors of low bone density in young women with anorexia nervosa found a direct correlation between BMD and serum estradiol, weight, BMI and lean body mass [19]. As the duration of amenorrhea and dieting were associated with a low BMD, it was concluded that essentially it was the timing of onset of dieting that is most relevant to bone density. In addition, adolescents who both reported dieting at degrees not qualified to be anorexia nervosa and who also had amenorrhea were at similar risks for low bone density as those with true anorexia nervosa as judged by the standard diagnostic criteria. This implies that adolescents with eating disorders that do not qualify as anorexia nervosa still run similar risks of low bone density once they exhibit menstrual dysfunction.

It was estimated that 50% of adolescents with the diagnosis of anorexia nervosa have low BMD, though the terms of osteoporosis or osteopenia could not be applied to these young women as the definitions were for menopausal women. Thus, Z-scores should be used to compare with age-matched cohorts rather than T-scores. In addition, serial measurements would be particularly useful and more precise for this age-group as compared to cross-sectional measurements, as bone volume would be increasing with growth in adolescents up to 10-15% per year [20]. It was also estimated that bone growth would be impaired within the first year of diagnosis of anorexia nervosa, and those with over 6 years of amenorrhea would have a sevenfold increased risk of fractures compared to patients without anorexia. Those with primary amenorrhea had higher fracture risks than those with secondary amenorrhea, and permanent bone damage seemed to be likely [21]. Similarly, in a Danish nationwide register study, the incidence rate ratio of fractures after the diagnosis of anorexia nervosa was 1.98, and the increased risk persisted more than 10 years after the diagnosis. The risk ratio for bulimia nervosa was 1.31 and 1.44 before and after the diagnosis was made, and that for eating disorders not otherwise specified was 1.39 and 1.77 before and after the diagnosis [22]. Thus, all categories of eating disorders would bear a negative impact on bone health in these young women, albeit to different degrees.

Hormonal Treatment for Menstrual Dysfunction in Eating Disorders – Does it Improve Bone Mass?

While hypo-oestrogenism and disordered eating with poor nutrition are all associated with increased risks of bone loss in young women with anorexia nervosa, the appropriate management for preventing the development of osteoporosis is still controversial. In a randomized control trial, when postmenopausal doses of oestrogen replacement together with progestogens (Premarin 0.625 mg, days 1-25, Provera 5 mg days 16-25) were administered to a study group of 19 women and placebo was given to 25 controls, it was found that the oestrogen replacement was unable to prevent progressive osteopenia in these young women. Bone mass was found to increase only in a small subgroup of young women with the lowest initial body weight. However, recovery from anorexia nervosa was associated with significantly improved BMD in all subjects [23]. Moreover, in an open study that utilized contraceptive doses of ethinyl estradiol (50 ug) that are substantially more potent than postmenopausal hormonal replacement regimes, no demonstrable increase in BMD was observed after 12 months of treatment and partial weight recovery [24]. In a prospective observational study that compared a lower dosage of 20-35 ug ethinyl estradiol oral contraceptives with no hormones, it was again found that despite weight gain in both groups, there was no BMD increase seen in either group. Bone density was nevertheless maintained over the 2 year treatment period at both the spine and hip regions in those taking oral contraceptives [25]. When a 20 ug ethinyl estradiol oral contraceptive was compared with 50 mg of oral micronized dehydroepiandrosterone in a double-blinded randomized control trial, the investigators again found no significant increase in BMD over a period of 1 year, though maintenance of hip and spinal BMD was seen in both groups [26]. When the anabolic effects of IGF-1 combined with oestrogen and progestin was examined as an anti-resorptive agent and compared with standard oestrogen/progestin HRT, a significant increase in spinal BMD was seen after 9 months of combined therapy, but no significant changes in BMD was seen in the group on oestrogen/progestin HRT alone [14]. In an interesting longitudinal follow up of anorexic women, it was found that rapid BMD loss at a rate of around 2.5% occurred in women with active anorexia. While resumption of menstrual function was important for spine BMD recovery and weight gain was important for hip BMD recovery, the authors did not observe an increase in BMD with weight gain in women taking oral contraceptives. It was concluded that improvements in reproduction function and weight were more important for skeletal recovery for women with anorexia nervosa than hormonal therapy [27]. It appears that hormonal treatment alone would be ineffective.

NON-HORMONAL MANAGEMENT OF BONE HEALTH IN EATING DISORDERS

Weight restoration with resumption of menses is considered to be the key for long-term recovery of bone mass in anorexic women [28]. BMD may only partially improve with weight recovery if there is no resumption of regular ovulation. Over 85% of women would have spontaneous return to menses within 6 months of achieving a weight 90% of their ideal body weight [8]. Persistent amenorrhea might then reflect that these women merely have weight in normatives ranges, but were not truly weight restored. Once weight is normalized, follicular stimulating hormone, luteinizing hormone and progesterone levels would also normalize, but those with continued amenorrhea would have persistently lower estradiol and leptin levels than those who have resumed menstruation. It has also been described that the ultrasound morphology of the ovaries would be a useful adjuvant tool in discerning the appropriate final weight in women with persistent amenorrhea, as the ovaries would evolve from being small and amorphous in those who were underweight and hypo-estrogenic, to contain small follicles in those with some weight gain, to finally return to normal morphology with a dominant follicle in those who have restored premorbid weight [29].

Dietary supplementation of calcium and vitamin D has also been suggested as necessary components of therapy. The Society for Adolescent

Medicine in the United States supports the recommendation of a daily allowance of 1300-1500 mg/ calcium and 400 international units of vitamin D in anorexia nervosa [30]. It must be noted, however, that high rates of calcium and vitamin D deficiency have been found in adolescents without any eating disorders, and thus such supplements probably apply to all adolescents with such deficiencies.

While it is generally recognized that weight-bearing exercises should be recommended for osteoporosis to increase BMD, there is no consensus on the appropriate regimes that could be safely and effectively recommended in anorexia nervosa. Nevertheless, moderate weight-bearing exercises could be introduced if bone loss has not been severe, and when excessive exercise was not a cause of the menstrual dysfunction [3].

Biphosponates, such as risedronate [31] and alendronate [32] have been tested and the results encouragingly showed significant increases in BMD in the lumbar spine or hips respectively. However, while biphosphonates have been used in children with resorptive bone conditions, it is not approved yet for use in pre-menopausal women. The theoretical risks of using biphosponates in women of child-bearing age have been related to the fact that the drugs would be retained in the skeleton for long durations and might potentially affect fetal development. Moreover, the available data of biphosponates on young women were based on small studies with limited numbers that have no correlation to clinical fracture risks. Thus, the use of biphosphonates in this young age group should probably be confined to clinical trials.

Other treatment options to improve BMD that have been studied include dehydroepiandrosterone, testosterone, recombinant IGF-1 and recombinant leptin. Oral dehydroepiandrosterone 50 mg/day had been shown to maintain spine and hip BMD in anorexic women without any androgenic side effects up to 1 year of treatment, but there was no significant increase in BMD after accounting for the weight gain [26]. Short term, low dose transdermal testosterone has also been tested, but its efficacy ha yet to be confirmed. In addition, recombinant IGF-1 at doses of 100 ug/kg subcutaneously twice daily increased bone formation and resorption markers. Compared to oral contraceptive pills, IGF-1 30 ug/kg twice daily for 9 months was more effective in treating osteopenia in anorexic women with significant increases in BMD. Oral contraceptives alone were ineffective, but could enhance the effects of IGF-1 when administered together [14]. However, IGF-I is not widely available, the costs are prohibitive commercially, and the actual magnitude of BMD gain appeared small compared to other treatment measures, so that IGF-1 should remain within research protocols at present. Similarly, while recombinant leptin (r-metHuLeptin) could theoretically restore ovulation with normalization of the thyroid and gonadotrophin axis, further clinical studies would be needed to establish its clinical usage [28]. Thus, proper nutrition with supplements, restoration of weight, careful introduction of exercises, are probably more essential to increase BMD in these women.

THE FEMALE ATHLETIC TRIAD AND RELATIONSHIP TO BMD

The well known female athlete triad is a syndrome consisting of disordered eating, amenorrhea and osteoporosis, which in turn is well known for its association with osteoporosis [33] and an increased risk of stress fractures. Athletes with voluntary dieting and restricted calorie intake mimic the picture of young women with anorexia nervosa. In addition, they have high energy expenditures as a result of their physical exercises and thus can develop an imbalance of energy intake and output to result in "energy drain". Menstrual dysfunction in the form of amenorrhea or oligomenorrhea results as hypothalamic-pituitary-ovarian axis dysfunction occurs similar to patients with anorexia nervosa, and hypo-oestrogenism ensues with increased bone resorption and reductions on peak bone mass as in those with anorexia nervosa. Comparing exercising and sedentary women with anorexia nervosa, it has been shown that exercisers had a greater degree of menstrual dysfunction and took longer to resume menses following weight gain [34], showing that the effects of an eating disorder and intense exercises would probably be synergistic to produce amenorrhea.

On the other hand, positive effects of mechanical loading via exercise on bone mineral density (BMD) have been well documented in humans. Weight bearing exercise is known to be an important contributor to the establishment of peak bone mass and to maintenance of bone mass after this peak is attained [35]. It is commonly accepted that weight-bearing exercises provide an osteogenic stimulus to bones. The osteogenic stimulation of such activities could be seen in a variety of sports, such as athletics, weight lifting, high impact sports such as basketball or volley ball, and medium impact sports such as soccer or track. This effect was not observed in sports activities that involved extensive energy expenditure and muscle strength but no true weight bearing, such as in swimming [36]. Studies have also shown that the benefits of exercises in promoting bone accrual and a higher peak bone mass are greatest before the completion of puberty. Participation in exercises and training before the onset of menses appears to increase BMD significantly more than when started after initiation of menses. A study of Canadian children showed that physically active girls had a 17 % higher total body BMD as compared to sedentary peers [37]. However, when hypo-oestrogenism occurs together with menstrual dysfunction resulting from excessive exercises, the benefits of the physical activity may be lost and the net effects of these opposing forces may be difficult to predict.

Healthy athletes have been shown to have better than average BMD, but amenorrheic athletes have been shown to have vertebral BMD some 9-31% lower than eumenorrheic ones. Stress fractures were significantly associated with a long duration of amenorrhea in athletes [38]. In dancers, delayed menarche and prolonged amenorrhea was shown to be associated not only with increased risks of fractures, but also of scoliosis in these young women [39]. While it is still controversial whether eating disorders, low body weight, and low bone mineral density associated with prolonged hypo-estrogenic states are accountable for the increased incidence of scoliosis, the role of exercise in such amenorrheic states and the resulting impact on bone mineral density appears complex. Similar to athletes, dancers also fit into the high risk category for the development of the athlete triad, with a relatively high incidence of eating disorders due to the need for aesthetic body shapes, regular physical training that by its nature involves intensive weight bearing exercises and the resulting high rates of menstrual dysfunction [40]. A comparative study between young Chinese dancers and age matched non-athletic women that did not take into account eating disorders or menstrual status showed no difference in bone mineral density. The authors concluded that the dancers were significantly thinner than the controls and the negative effect of a lower bodyweight may neutralize the positive effects of the physical training, particularly in the femoral neck [41]. In contrast, a study on ballet dancers [33] demonstrated significantly lower areal bone mass in young ballet dancers with exercise-associated amenorrhea and delayed menarche despite their intensive exercises, pointing to the importance of normal hormonal function on bone mineral density in these young individuals, and the inability for exercises to compensate for the detrimental effects of menstrual dysfunction on bone mineral density. On the other hand, when comparing bone mineral density in ballet dancers with aged-matched amenorrheic young women with anorexia nervosa, it has been found that weight-bearing exercise might off-set the effects of hypogonadism at predominantly cortical weight-bearing sites. However, both non-weight bearing sites and weight bearing sites containing substantial amounts of trabecular bone, such as the lumbar spine, would still be adversely affected by the hypo-oestrogenism [42]. In all of these quoted studies, the female athlete triad with its essential component of eating disorders was implied as the basic pathophysiological mechanism. It appears therefore, that while exercise might have been able to offset some of the negative effects of hypoestrogen-ism on BMD, such protective effects could be incomplete [Figure 1].

TREATMENT MODALITIES FOR FEMALE ATHLETE TRIAD

In terms of therapy, weight gain and gradual resumption of menses with associated rises in endogenous oestrogen production are apparently still the best approaches to increasing bone density in these underweight exercising females. As in the case of hormonal treatment for anorexia nervosa induced menstrual dysfunction, the effect of oestrogen replacement in exercise-induced hypothalamic amenorrhea still remains controversial. In a controlled trial of ballet dancers with eating disorders and exercise induced menstrual dysfunction, an increase in lumbar spine BMD of 5.6% was seen after two years of Premarin/ Provera treatment, which did not differ significantly from the 4.5% increase in the placebo group. The authors concluded a lack of any beneficial effects after the prolonged hormonal treatment [43]. When oral contraceptives were given to a group of physically active women aged between 18-31 years, bone loss was still observed at the spine and hip [44]. To explain the lack of effect of hormonal replacement, it was speculated that endogenous gonadal oestrogen secretion was suppressed by oral contraceptive, but the replacement dose administered was inadequate for achievement of peak bone mass [45]. In a prospective series, BMD increased by 2.33% over 1 year in healthy young women with a 35 ug ethinyl estradiol norethindrone pill compared to a non-significant +0.33% increase in those on a 30 ug ethinyl estradiol desogestrol pill, while the untreated group had a -0.37% BMD loss. Apparently, the differences in BMD changes were small amongst the different groups [46]. Another randomized trial administered Trisequens plus calcium carbonate compared to calcium alone or placebo to oligo/amenorrheic elite runners for 9 months, and again failed to observe any significant BMD changes among women treated with estrogen at the hip or lumbar spine [47].

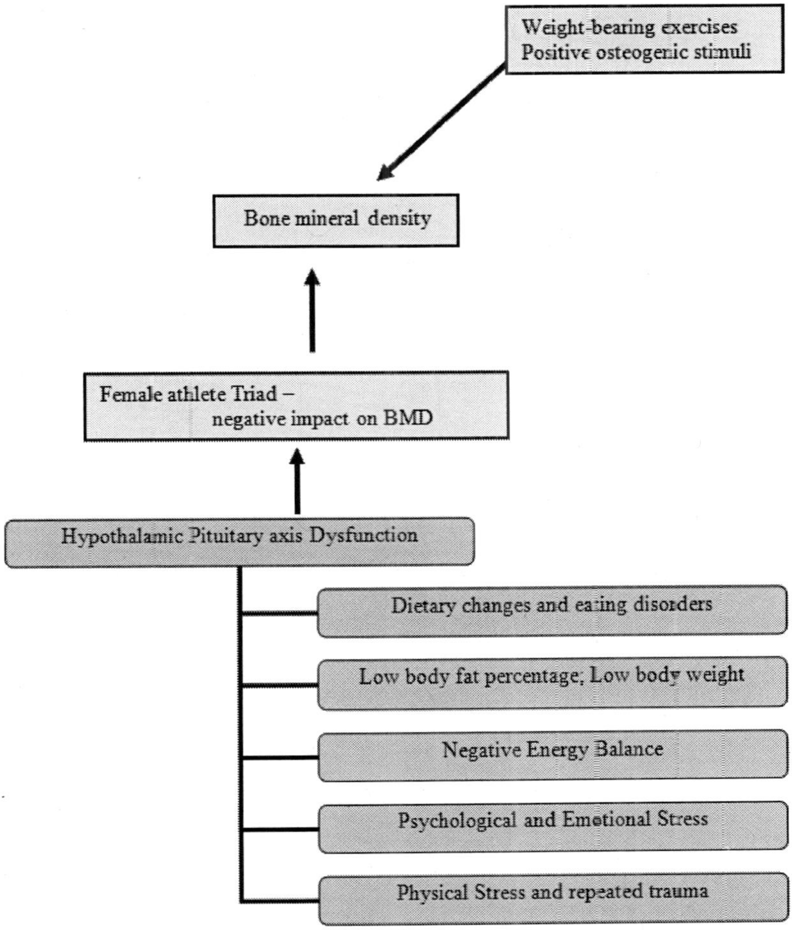

Figure 1. Female athlete triad and relationship to BMD.

Thus, it could be concluded that hormonal replacement therapy does not facilitate increase in BMD in exercising women with anorexia nervosa. The treatment would induce monthly menstrual bleeding, which may be incorrectly interpreted as an indication of adequate weight restoration. Such exogenous hormone-induced withdrawal would obscure resumption of spontaneous menses, an objective indicator often adopted by the medical team as well as the woman as a measure of restoration to biological health. Hormone induced withdrawal bleedings should particularly be avoided if the woman would use restoration of menses as a guide to her exercise and training levels, such as in the case of elite athletes or dancers.

Long Term Bone Health with Eating Disorders

As mentioned above, the adolescent years are critical for bone mass accrual, and anorexia and amenorrhea beginning at this time might be associated with greater bone mass deficits as compared to anorexia beginning at a later stage. In a 2-year follow-up of women with a 1-17 years of history of amenorrhea, the mean BMD at the end of the study did not differ between those who did or did not attain greater than 80% ideal weight, nor did it differ in those with or without resumption of menses [48], showing that weight restoration and correction of amenorrhea might not directly imply BMD improvements. Moreover, there was a 7.1 fold greater risk of non-spine fractures in those with anorexia during follow-up compared to controls. In another small cohort with teenage onset anorexia, after full recovery from the condition for 14-23 years, BMD at the femur, but not the spine, was still significantly lower than in controls [49].

More reassuringly, a recent longitudinal study measuring volumetric BMD have been able to demonstrate normalization of bone mass in the lumbar spine in a cohort of adolescents 2.7 years after their recovery from anorexia nervosa [50]. Similarly, another cohort showed no differences in BMD at various sites in teenage-onset anorexics compared to controls 11 years after the onset of anorexia, with only 2 out of the 36 in the cohort still not recovered from the condition (51). However, a much higher proportion of those with anorexia had osteopenia at follow-up compared to non-anorexic controls (45% Vs 25%) and there was an inverse relationship between spine BMD and the duration of anorexia, as well as a positive association with the lowest BMI. Nevertheless, the fracture risk between those with anorexia and controls did not differ. The authors suggested that there would be a higher risk of osteopenia in women with subchronic and chronic anorexia nervosa.

In a 1 to 4 year follow-up of a cohort between 15- 34 years old, it was found that those who had recovered from anorexia demonstrated a 0.5 -7.5% increase in BMD per year, while in the remaining with persistent disease, further decrease in BMD were observed, particularly in those who continued to lose weight [52]. Similarly, it was reported that 12 years after the diagnosis of anorexia nervosa, women who had recovery and good outcome had Z-scores of -0.26 and -0.68 at the spine and radius, while women with persistent disorder had Z –scores that were much lower at -1.7 and -2.2 respectively [53].

Thus, the data is consistent that eating disorders can frequently lead to long term detrimental effects on bone mass. It is apparent that those with shorter duration of anorexia and amenorrhea appear to have better outcome in bone health, as compared to those with chronic anorexia.

Conclusion

In summary, the diagnosis of an eating disorder should be considered when an adolescent female engages in potentially unhealthy weight-control practices, demonstrates obsessive thinking about food, weight, shape or exercise, or fails to attain or maintain a healthy weight, height, body composition or stage of sexual maturation for age. In particular, an eating disorder can still be present in the absence of established diagnostic criteria [30], and menstrual dysfunction in the form of amenorrhea or oligomenorrhea might or might not be present. Mental health intervention should be an integral part of the assessment, and a multidisciplinary approach consisting of medical, nursing, nutritional and mental health support is essential. Bone health and risks of osteoporosis should be an important part of the assessment and treatment. Gynecological hormonal treatment is not effective in maintaining BMD or restoring bone health. Depending on the age of onset and the duration of symptoms, eating disorders impose a genuine risk on bone health, but those with chronic anorexia nervosa probably run the highest risk of osteopenia, osteoporosis and fractures.

References

[1] American Paediatric Association 2000. Diagnostic and statistical manual of mental disorders, 4th Ed. Text revision (DSM-IV TR). American Psychiatric association, Washington DC.

[2] Pritts SD, Susman J. Diagnosis of eating disorders in primary care. *Am Fam. Physician* 2003; 67: 297-304.

[3] Andersen AE, Ryan GL. Eating disorders in the obstetric and gynecologic patient population. *Obstet. Gynecol.* 2009; 1353- 67.

[4] Nicholls D, Chater R, Lask B. Children into DSM don't go: a comparison of classification systems for eating disorders in childhood and early adolescence. *Int. J. Eat Disord* 2000; 28: 317- 24.

[5] Workgroup for classification of eating disorders in children and adolescents. Classification of child and adolescent eating disturbances. *Int. J. Eat Disord.* 2007; 40: S117-S122.

[6] Attia E, Roberto CA. Should amenorrhea be a diagnostic criterion for anorexia nervosa? *Int J Eat Disord* 2009; 42: 581- 9.

[7] Poyastro PA, Thornton LM, Plotonicov KH, Tozzi F, Klump KL, Berrettini WH et al. Patterns of menstrual disturbance in eating disorders. *Int J Eat Disord* 2007; 40: 424- 34.

[8] Golden N, Carlson J. The pathophysiology of amenorrhea in the adolescent. *Ann N Y Acad Sci* 2008; 1135: 163-78.

[9] Watson T, Andersen A. A critical examination of the amenorrhea and weight criteria for diagnosing anorexia nervosa. *Acta Psychiatr Scand* 2003; 108: 175 – 82.

[10] Roberto CA, Steinglass J, Nayer LE, Attia E, Walsh BT. The clinical significance of amenorrhea as a diagnostic criterion for anorexia nervosa. *Int. J. Eat. Disord.* 2008; 41: 559-63.

[11] Abraham S, Pettigrew B, Boyd C, Russell J. Predictors of functional and exercise amenorrhea among eating and exercise disordered patients. *Hum. Reprod.* 2006; 21: 257-61.

[12] Pineli G, Tagliabue A. Nutrition and fertility. *Minerva Gastroenterol Dietol* 2007; 53: 375- 82.

[13] Gordon CM, Goodman E, Emans SJ, Grace E, Becker KA, Rosen CJ, Gundberg CM, LeBoff MS. Physiologic regulators of bone turnover in young women with anorexia nervosa. *J. Pediatr.* 2002; 141: 64-70.

[14] Grinspoon SK, Thomas L, Miller K, Herzog D, Klibanski A. Effects of recombinant human IGF-I and oral contraceptive administration on bone density in anorexia nervosa. *J. Clin. Endocrinol. Metab.* 2002; 87: 2883-91.

[15] Zumoff B, Walsh BT, Katz JL, Levin J, Rosenfeld RS, Kream J, Weiner H. Subnormal plasma dehydroepiandrosterone to cortisol ratio in anorexia nervosa: a second hormonal parameter of ontogenic regression. *J. Clin. Endocrinol. Metab.* 1983; 56: 668-71.

[16] Legroux-Gerot I, Vignau J, D'Herbomez M, Collier F, Marchandise X, Duquesnoy B, Cortet B. Evaluation of bone loss and its mechanisms in anorexia nervosa. *Calcif Tissue Int* 2007; 81: 174- 82.

[17] Jagielska G, Wolanczyk T, Komender J, Tomaszewicz-Libudzic C, Przedlacki J, Ostrowski K. Bone mineral density in adolescent girls with anorexia nervosa: a cross sectional study. *Eur. Child Adolesc. Psychiatry* 2002; 11: 57-62.

[18] Audi L, Vargas DM, Gussinye M, Yesye D, Marti G, Carrascosa A. Clinical and biochemical determinants of bone metabolism and bone mass in adolescent female patients with anorexia nervosa. *Pediatr. Res.* 2002; 51: 497-504.

[19] Turner JM, Bulsara MK, McDermott BM, Byrne GC, Prince RL, Forbes DA. Predictors of low bone density in young adolescent females with anorexia nervosa and other dieting disorders. *Int. J. Eat Disord* 2001; 30: 245-51.

[20] Stevens SL. Assessment and management of bone health in adolescents with anorexia nervosa. Part II: bone health in adolescents with anorexia nervosa. *J. Pediatr Adolesc Gynecol* 2008; 21: 221- 4.

[21] Bruni V, Filicetti MF, Pontello V. Open issues in anorexia nervosa prevention and therapy of bone loss. *Ann NY Acad Sci* 2006; 1092: 91-102.

[22] Vestergaard P, Emborg C, Stoving RK, Hagen C, Mosekilde L, Brixen K. Fractures in patients with anorexia nervosa, bulimia nervosa, and other eating disorders – a nationwide register study. *Int. J. Eat Disord.* 2002; 32: 301 - 8.

[23] Klibanski A, Biller BM, Schoenfield DA, Herzog DB, Saxe VC. The effects of oestrogen administration on trabecular bone loss in young women with anorexia nervosa. *J. Clin. Endocrinol. Metab* 1995; 80: 898-904.

[24] Munoz MT, Morande G, Garcia-Centenera JA, Hervas F, Pozo J, Argente J. The effects of estrogen administration on bone mineral density in adolescents with anorexia nervosa. *Eur J. Endocrinol.* 2002; 146: 45-50.

[25] Golden NH, Lanzkowsky L, Schebendach J, Palestro CJ, Jacobson MS, Shenker IR. The effect of estrogen-progestin treatment on bone mineral density in anorexia nervosa. *J. Adolesc. Gynecol.* 2002; 15: 135-43.

[26] Gordon CM, Grace E, Emans SJ, Feldman HA, Goodman E, Becker KA, Rosen CJ, Gundberg CM, LeBoff MS. Effects of oral dehydroepiandro-sterone on bone density in young women with anorexia nervosa: a randomized trial. *J. Clin. Endocrinol. Metab.* 2002A; 87: 4935- 41.

[27] Miller KK, Lee EE, Lawson EA, Misra M, Minhan J, Grinspoon SK, Gleysteen S, Mickley D, Herzog D, Kibanski A. Determinants of sleletal loss and recovery in anorexia nervosa. *J. Clin. Endocrinol. Metab* 2006; 91: 2931-7.

[28] Jayasinghe Y, Grover SR, Zacharin M. Current concepts in bone and reproductive health in adolescents with anorexia nervosa. *Br. J. Obstet Gynaecol* 2008; 115: 304- 15.

[29] Mitan LAP. Menstrual dysfunction in anorexia nervosa. *J. Pediatr. Adolesc. Gynecol.* 2004; 17: 81- 5.

[30] Golden NH, Katzman DK, Kreipe RE, Stevens SL, Sawyer SM, Rees J, Nicholls D, Rome ES. Society for Adolescent Medicine. Eating disorders in adolescents -position statement of the Society for adolescent medicine. *J. Adolesc. Health.* 2003; 33: 496-503.

[31] Miller KK, Grieco KA, Mulder J, Grinspoon S, Mickley D, Yehezkel R, Herzog DB, Klibanski A. . Effects of risedronate on bone mineral density in anorexia nervosa. *J. Clin. Endocrinol. Metab.* 2004; 89: 3903-6.

[32] Golden NH, Iglesias EA, Jacobson MS, Carey D, Meyer W, Schebendach J, hertz S, Shenker IR. Alendronate for the treatment of osteopenia in anorexia nervosa – a randomized, double blinded placebo-controlled trial. *J. Clin. Endocrinol. Metab.* 2005; 90: 3179- 85.

[33] Warren MP, Brooks-Gunn J, Fox RP, Holderness CC, Hyle EP, Hamilton WG. Osteopenia in exercise-associated amenorrhea using ballet dancers as a model: a longitudinal study. *J. Clin. Endocrin. Metab.* 2002: 3162-8.

[34] Litt IF, Glader L. Anorexia nervosa, athletics and amenorrhea. *J. Pediatr.* 1986; 109: 150- 3.

[35] Borer KT. Physical activity in the prevention an amelioration of osteoporosis I women: interaction of mechanical, hormonal and dietary factors. *Sports Med* 2005; 35: 779-830.

[36] Emslander HC, Sinaki M, Muhs JM, Chao EY, Wahner HW, Bryant SC, Riggs BL, Eastell R. Bone mass and muscle strength in female college athletes (runners and swimmers). *Mayo Clin. Proc.* 1998; 73: 1151-60.

[37] Bailey DA, McKay HA, Mirwald RL, Crocker PR, Faulkner RA. A six-year longitudinal study of the relationship of physical activity to bone mineral accrual in growing children: the University of Saskatchewan Bone Mineral Accrual study. *J. Bone Miner Res.* 1999; 14: 1672-9.

[38] Myburgh KH, Hutchins J, Fataar AB, Hough SF, Noakes TD. Low bone density is an etiologic factor for stress fractures in athletes. *Ann Intern Med* 1990; 113: 754-9.

[39] Warren MP, Brooks-Gunn J, Hamilton LH, Warren LF, Hamilton WG. Scoliosis and fractures in young ballet dancers; relation to delayed menarche and secondary amenorrhea. *New Engl. J. Med.* 1986; 314: 1348-50.

[40] To WWK, Wong MWN, Lam IYL. Bone mineral density differences between adolescent dancers and non-exercising adolescent females. *J. Pediatr Adolesc. Gynecol.* 2005; 18: 337- 42.

[41] Tsai SC, Hsu HC, Fong YC, Chiu CC, Kao A, Lee CC. Bone mineral density in young female Chinese dancers. *International Ortho* 2001; 25: 283 - 5.

[42] Young N, Formica C, Szmukler G, Seeman E. Bone density at weight-bearing and non-weight-bearing sites in ballet dancers: the effect of exercise, hypogonadism and body weight. *J. Clin. Endocrinol. Metab* 1994; 78: 449-454.

[43] Warren MP, Brooks-Gunn J, Fox RP, Holderness CC, Hyle EP, Hamilton WG, Hamilton L. Persistent osteopenia in ballet dancers with amenorrhea and delayed menarche despite hormone therapy: a longitudinal study. *Fertil Steril* 2003; 80: 398-404.

[44] Burr DB, Yoshikawa T, Teegarden D, Lyle R, McCabe G, Weaver CM. Exercise and oral contraceptive use suppress the normal age-related increase in bone mass and strength of the femoral neck in women 18-31 years of age. *Bone* 2000; 20: 855-63.

[45] Polatti F, Perotti F, Filippa N, Gallina D, Nappi RE. Bone mass and long-term monophasic oral contraceptive treatment in young women. *Contraception* 1995; 51: 221-4.

[46] Berenson AB, Radecki CM, Grady JJ, Rickert VI, Thomas A. A prospective controlled study of the effects of hormonal contraception on bone mineral density. *Obstet Gynecol.* 2001; 98: 576-82.

[47] Gibson JH, Mitchelle A, Reeve J, Harries MG. Treatment of reduced bone mineral density in athletic amenorrheic amenorrhea: a pilot study. *Osteoporos Int* 1999; 10: 284 - 9.

[48] Rigotti N, Neer R, Skates S, Herzog DB, Nussbaum SR. The clinical course of osteoporosis in anorexia nervosa: a longitudinal study of cortical bone mass. *JAMA* 1991; 265: 1133- 8.

[49] Hartman D, Crisp A, Rooney B, Rackow C, Atkinson R, Patel S. Bone density of women who have recovered from anorexia nervosa. *Int. J. Eat Disord.* 2000; 28: 107-12.

[50] Bass SL, Saxon L, Corral AM, Rodda CP, Strauss BJ, Reidpath D, Clarke C. Near normalization of lumbar spine bone density in young women with osteopenia recovered from anorexia nervosa: a longitudinal study. *J. Pediatr. Endocrinol. Metab.* 2005; 18: 897-907.

[51] Wentz E, Mellstrom D, Gillberg C, Sundh V, Gillberg IC, Rastam M. Bone density 11 years after anorexia nervosa onset in a controlled study of 39 cases. *Int. J. Eat Disord.* 2003; 34: 314 – 8.

[52] Hotta M, Shibasaki T, Sato K, Demura H. The importance of body weight history in the occurrence and recovery of osteoporosis in patients with anorexia nervosa: evaluation by dual X-ray absorptiometry and bone metabolic markers. *Eur. J. Endocrinol.* 1998; 139: 276- 83.

[53] Herzog W, Minne H, Deter C, Leidig G, Schellberg D, Wuster C, Gronwald R, Sarembe E, Kroger F, Bergmann G. Outcome of bone mineral density in anorexia nervosa patients 11.7 years after first admission. *J. Bone Miner Res.* 1993; 8: 597-605.

In: Eating Disorders
Editor: C. M. Shapiro, pp. 83-103
ISBN 978-1-61209-746-6

Chapter 4

EATING DISORDERS IN INDIVIDUALS WITH DEVELOPMENTAL DISABILITIES

Efrosini Kalyva
City College, Thesaloniki, Greece

ABSTRACT

Eating disorders refer to abnormal eating habits that may involve excessive or insufficient food intake and affect not only the physical but also the emotional and psychological health of the individual. It is estimated that 5-10% of the adolescent population worldwide exhibit eating disorders, such as anorexia nervosa, bulimia nervosa, and binge-eating disorder, while the mortality rate is alarming. However, limited studies have explored the eating disorders of individuals with developmental disabilities. Therefore, this chapter starts with some general information about the prevalence, nature, and the outcomes of eating disorders.

The remaining of the chapter deals with eating problems in individuals with developmental disabilities, such as autism spectrum disorders, intellectual disabilities, attention deficit/hyperactivity disorder, Prader-Willi syndrome and other disabilities. At the end of the chapter some prominent treatment programs for these populations are reviewed and critically evaluated.

DEFINITIONS OF EATING AND FEEDING DISORDERS

When lay people hear the term eating disorders, they typically think of anorexia nervosa, bulimia nervosa and binge eating disorders. Anorexia nervosa is characterized by the individual's inability to maintain a normal healthy body weight. Bulimia nervosa is marked by recurrent episodes of binge eating that are accompanied by some form of undesirable compensatory behavior (e.g., excessive exercising or vomiting). Individuals with binge eating disorder exhibit the same behaviors as those who suffer from bulimia without the accompanying compensatory behaviors (Berkman, Lohr, and Bulik, 2007). Evidence suggests that individuals at higher risk for developing eating disorders are females, children with eating and gastrointestinal problems, individuals who are very concerned with their shape and weight, individuals with low self-esteem and negative self-image, victims of sexual abuse, as well as individuals with general psychiatric comorbidity (Jacobi, Hayward, de Zwaan, Kraemer, and Agras, 2004). Anorexia and bulimia nervosa are not caused merely by problematic relations to food, the process of eating or body image. Before the manifestation of eating disorders some concerns and problems usually appear in connection with emotional reactions to situations, identity development and self-image (Buhl, 2002).

Eating and feeding problems are evident in 25–45% of typically developing children throughout their development (Cashdan, 1998), but they usually disappear without any adverse health effects and without professional guidance and treatment. The most severe feeding problem is food refusal, with the child refusing to accept certain foods and/or selecting specific foods that are restricted in terms of range and quantity (Luiselli, 1994). Chronic and severe food refusal can lead to malnutrition, growth retardation, dehydration and vulnerability to infectious diseases (de Moor, Didden, and Korzilius, 2007).

Despite the fact that the prevalence rates of eating and feeding problems in children with developmental disabilities range from 20% to 80% (Martins, Young, and Robson, 2008), there has been limited research on the topic. The eating and feeding problems that have been documented with a variety of children with developmental disabilities often go unnoticed, but they might become increasingly challenging and difficult as children grow older, stronger, and more independent (Ho, Eaves, and Peacoby, 1997). In case that these problems are not addressed adequately, these children can be at high risk for nutritionally related medical problems (Clark, Rhodes, and Turner, 1993). It is indicative that children with a feeding disorder in early childhood are likely to exhibit eating disorders, such as anorexia or bulimia nervosa in adolescence (Jacobi, Agras, Bryson, and Hamer, 2003; Rastam, 1992). The next section of the chapter is dedicated to the documentation of feeding and eating problems in individuals with developmental disabilities according to published studies. There will be reference to the following groups of disabilities: attention-deficit/hyperactivity disorder; cerebral palsy; Williams syndrome; Prader-Willi syndrome; autism spectrum disorders; and intellectual disabilities.

EATING DISORDERS AND ATTENTION-DEFICIT/HYPERACTIVITY DISORDER (ADHD)

A population that has been studied in relation to eating discrders was that of individuals with ADHD and there is evidence suggesting that there are some underlying common clinical features (Biederman, Ball, Monuteaux, Surman, Jahnoson, and Zeitlin, 2007; Cortese, Dalla Bernardina, and Mouren, 2007; Spencer, Biederman, and Mick, 2007; Surman, Randell, and Biederman, 2006). For example, lack of impulse control and low self-esteem are common characteristics of bulimia nervosa and ADHD (Dukarm, 2005). Biederman et al. (2006) found in their study, which had some important methodological limitations, that girls with ADHD had displayed marginally more eating disorders than their typically developing peers. Two relevant cross-sectional studies that have been conducted showed that there is high prevalence of bulimia amongst females with ADHD (Mattos, Saboya, Ayrao, Segrenreich, Duchesne, and Coutinho, 2004; Surman, et al., 2006). In fact, Wentz, Lacey, Waller, Rastam, Turk, and Gillberg (2005) conducted a pilot study with female patients with eating disorders and found that almost 1/5 manifested symptoms of ADHD. Moreover, Yates, Lunde, Johnson, Mitchell, and McKee (2009) attempted to determine the prevalence of childhood symptom-onset of ADHD in a group of women that were receiving clinical treatment for eating disorders. They found that these women presented more inattentive symptoms, while the reported current subjective symptoms of motor restlessness and fidgetiness could not be attributed to childhood-onset ADHD.

However, other studies reported contradictory findings, with only 3% of ADHD symptoms in inpatients with anorexia nervosa and 9% in those with bulimia nervosa (Blinder, Cumella, and Sanathara, 2006), or 5.4% and 3.4% for adolescent or young women respectively in the general population (Fayyad et al., 2007). Hudson et al. (2003) claimed that if there were overlapping clinical characteristics between bulimia nervosa and ADHD, they would both respond to the same medical treatment, but this was not the case.

There are two factors that might account for the lack of extensive research on the relationship between ADHD and eating pathology: a) there are many more males than females with ADHD (Hinshaw and Blachman, 2005), and b) most studies are conducted with children with ADHD rather than adolescents. However, most eating disorders affect females (Sweeting and West, 2002) during the postpubertal adolescence period (Stice, Presnell, and Bearman, 2001).

It is worth exploring why ADHD could be linked to the appearance of eating disorders. Girls with ADHD may be at risk for bulimia nervosa because they tend to express their distress through eating and internalizing disorders (Pajer, 1998). Moreover, impulsivity that is characteristic of ADHD can predict also bulimia (Fahy and Eisler, 1993; Wonderlich, Connolly, and Stice, 2004) among adolescent girls. The negative relationship between children with ADHD and their parents or peers that has been documented in relevant studies (Johnston and Mash, 2001; Peris and Hinshaw, 2003) has been associated also with the development of bulimia nervosa (Johnson, Cohen, Kasen, and Brook, 2002; Marchi and Cohen, 1990; Mikami, Hinshaw, Patterson, and Lee, 2008), although more research on the topic is still needed (Jacobi et al., 2004). Finally, the internalizing and disruptive behavioral problems exhibited by children with ADHD (Hinshaw, Owens, Sami, and Fargeon, 2006; Mannuzza and Klein, 2000) have been implicated in the appearance of bulimia nervosa symptoms and dissatisfaction with body image (Bearman, Presnell, Martinez, and Stice, 2006).

Eating Disorders and Cerebral Palsy (CP)

Children with cerebral palsy may exhibit feeding problems early in life due to the problems that they face in movement control (Spalding and McKeever, 1998; Motion, Northstone, Emond, Stucke, and Golding, 2002) that could lead even to undernourishment (Sleigh, 2005). These movement control problems are likely to impede also other self-help skills and speech development, which in turn deteriorate the existing feeding problems. Since most children with cerebral palsy live at home (Townsley and Robinson, 2000), their mothers are usually responsible for their feeding without necessarily receiving the appropriate support (Sullivan, Lambert, Rose, Ford-Adams, Johnson, and Griffiths, 2000). One resource that many parents choose to use in order to feed their children is a gastronomy feeding tube (G-tube) that has been found to be quite effective (Sleigh and Brocklehurst, 2004), although there are some studies providing contradictory evidence about its popularity among parents (Spalding et al., 1998). The majority of studies on feeding problems associated with cerebral palsy have focused primarily on neurological processes, such as sucking, swallowing and dribbling (Motion et al., 2002).

Webb, Morgan, and Lacey (2009) studied a woman with cerebral palsy who claimed that her anorexia nervosa resulted from the social handicap generated by cerebral palsy. An example that she provided was the lack of social support with people asking her to get out of the way instead of helping her. This behavior made her believe that if she could become very small and thin, then she would become less obtrusive and more accepted. Another factor that contributed further to her anorexia was the fact that her difficulties with swallowing and eating coordination made her feel embarrassed, because she was making a mess of herself and she felt disgusted with her own image. Therefore, she tried to avoid eating in public in order to lessen the dysphoria that she experienced. Webb and colleagues (2009) reported that the most important finding of their study was the realization that professionals need to identify and acknowledge the needs of every individual when designing the appropriate intervention.

Lalkhem's (2002) descriptive study attempted to explore how self-esteem and self-concept develop in adolescents with cerebral palsy. He stressed the importance of body image in shaping self-concept and self-esteem, given that adolescents with cerebral palsy often have to deal with the fact they may not be able to control their movement and their body. Therefore, low self-esteem coupled with negative body image can lead to anorexia nervosa or other eating disorders in adolescents with cerebral palsy.

Eating Disorders and Williams Syndrome (WS)

Williams syndrome is an autosomal dominant congenital disorder that has very distinct physical, neurodevelopmental and behavioral patterns (Howlin, Davies, and Udwin, 1998). Individuals with Williams syndrome have mental retardation, are short and have certain facial features that tend to be described as 'elfin'. They are outgoing and extremely friendly, while they may become very anxious and hyperactive (Einfeld, Tonge, and Florio, 1997). There are also many medical conditions associated with this syndrome, which lead to feeding problems (Gosch and Pankau, 1997) – with up to 60% of individuals with Williams syndrome classified as having feeding problems in an Irish sample (Lally, 1999). The feeding problems can be categorized either as behavioral (e.g., tantrums during mealtimes) or as both behavioral and medical (e.g., delay in feeding themselves, rumination and consumption of small amounts of food). The first category seems to be the most important, since almost half the children with Williams syndrome who are classified as having feeding problems are characterized primarily by behavioral mismanagement at mealtime that is caused by negative reinforcement contingencies (Cooper et al., 1995) and not by organic problems (Lally, 1999).

Eating Disorders and Prader-Willi Syndrome (PWS)

Prader-Willi syndrome is another neurodevelopmental disorder that is linked to missing material from the paternal chromosome 15 (Nicholls, Knoll, Butler, Karam, and Calande, 1989) and is considered to be the most common genetic cause of life-threatening obesity (Young et al., 2006). Eating disorders, such as food preoccupations and hyperphagia are basic symptoms of Prader-Willi syndrome and can be detected from the second year of life (Dimitropoulos, Feurer, Butler, and Thompson, 2001), although poor suck reflex leads to gavage feeding long before the onset of eating disorders (Dimitropoulos et al., 2000). Individuals with Prader-Willi syndrome are often obese, due to their persistent hunger, their lack of satiation, their never ending food seeking, and the accompanying hypotonia (Holland, Whittington, and Hinton, 2003). A lot of studies (e.g., Hilton et al., 2006; Shapira, Lessig, He, James, Driscoll, and Liu, 2005) have explored the biological basis of hyperphagia in Prader-Willi syndrome, but it is still unclear to which extent the preference of individuals with Prader-Willi syndrome for high calorie foods contributes to the anomalies in their hunger system (Dimitropoulos and Schultz, 2008).

Despite the evidence of preliminary studies that individuals with Prader-Willi syndrome eat without making any discrimination (Pipes and Holm, 1973), later research revealed that when quantity is controlled for, they prefer to consume foods high in fat or carbohydrate instead of healthy options (Glover, Maltzman, and Williams, 1996; Joseph, Koppekin, and Thompson, 2002). Parents often report that their children with Prader-Willi syndrome engage in atypical eating behaviors, such as sneaking and gorging food or eating food that has gone bad or is not to be consumed by humans (Holm and Pipes, 1976; Sarimski, 1996). Dykens (2000) actually found that individuals with Prader-Willi syndrome are more likely to want to eat food that is contaminated or highly unusual food combinations in comparison to peers matched for IQ or typically developing peers, despite the fact that they acknowledged that these foods should not be consumed. However, when provided with the opportunity, their cognition did not match their behavior and they chose to eat inedible food.

In a comprehensive review of relevant studies Dimitropoulos and her colleagues (2000) concluded that

> "It has become increasingly clear that the behavioral phenotype of Prader–Willi Syndrome includes compulsive symptoms similar to obsessive compulsive disorder, which in all probability interact with the incessant hunger and lack of satiation to engender the intense preoccupation and food seeking characteristic of Prader-Willi syndrome." (p. 129).

EATING DISORDERS AND AUTISM SPECTRUM DISORDERS (ASD)

Autism spectrum disorders constitute a pervasive developmental disorder that is characterized primarily by impairments in communication, social interaction, and the range of interests and activities (American Psychiatric Association, 2000). Although aberrant eating habits are not incorporated in the contemporary early diagnostic criteria, they were reported even by Hans Asperger himself (1944), who noted that two of his three original patients were underweight. These eating problems have been documented over time by many studies and with a range of children with autism spectrum disorders (e.g., Ahearn, Castine, Nault, and Green, 2001; Schreck, Wiliams, and Smith, 2004).

There is plenty of evidence that many children with autism spectrum disorders are picky eaters, do not try new foods (Williams, Darlymple, and Neal, 2000), have strong food preferences (Kerwin, Eicher, and Geslinger, 2005), are willing to eat food that is contaminated (Kalyva, Pellizoni, Tavano, Ianello, and Siegal, 2010), while their parents often report feeding problems (Kerwin, 1999; Whiteley, Rodgers, and Shattock, 2000) that could potentially affect the course of their development. It is indicative that some children with autism spectrum disorders with severe feeding problems during their first years of life may present growth failure (Keen, 2008). Moreover, studies have found that some individuals with autism spectrum disorders tend to have very low body weight (Hebebrand et al., 1997; Sobanski, Marcus, Henninghausen, Hebebrand, and Schmidt, 1999) or comorbid eating disorders (Fisman, Steele, Short, Byrne, and Lavalee, 1996; Gillberg, Gillberg, Rastam, and Johnasson, 1996; Nilsson, Gillber, Gillberg, and Rastam, 1999). For example, Gillberg, Rastam, and Gillberg (1995) reported a comorbidity of anorexia nervosa and Asperger syndrome (AS) in 12% of their patients and Kalyva (2009) found that adolescent girls with high functioning autism reported more eating disordered attitudes than typically developing peers matched for age, IQ, and BMI.

EATING DISORDERS AND INTELLECTUAL DISABILITIES (ID)

Gravestock (2003) stated that many individuals with intellectual disabilities are overweight or obese or have other feeding and eating problems, which are often associated with considerable physical and mental health and social functioning comorbidity. It is documented that individuals with intellectual disability, such as Down syndrome, are vulnerable to anorexia nervosa (Cottrell and Crisp, 1984; Myers and Pueschel, 1991).

Gittins and Rose (2007) conducted a study with 61 adults with profound and multiple learning disabilities and discovered that 18 (29%) had eating and feeding problems. Watson, Chadwick, Stobart, and Kelly (2006) reported that the rates of eating disorders in the studies that they reviewed varied from 5% to 8% of adults with learning disabilities from community populations up to 36% for hospital populations.

Eating problems are common across the whole spectrum of intellectual disabilities, regardless of whether the individual resides in a large developmental centre or in a community group home (Matson, Cooper, Mayville, and Gonzalez, 2006). Just like individuals with other developmental disabilities, individuals with intellectual disabilities are selective with food, cannot feed themselves, they refuse to eat food and they display other feeding problems as well (O'Brien, Repp, Williams, and Christophersen, 1991). More specifically, Girolami and Scotti (2001) and Matson, Mayville, Juhn, Sturmey,

Land, and Cooper (2005) reported that most individuals with intellectual disabilities resort to food refusal, with escape being its primary function.

Interventions to Address Eating and Feeding Problems

Given the documented eating and feeding problems that are encountered by children who face developmental disabilities, it is important to design appropriate interventions to address them. When referring to treatment of eating disorders, it is imperative to assess whether the individual is at the basic stage, which are the circumstances that trigger eating disorders and how eating disorders are maintained through time. Therapists working with individuals with eating disorders should confront the developmental distortion in a way that fosters personal growth in identity, personality, emotionality, and relationship formation (Buhl, 2002).

Pharmacotherapy is often used to treat eating disorders, especially when coupled with a comorbid psychiatric disorder. For example, Dukarm (2005) suggested that psychostimulants could be used to manage bulimia due to the high rate of abstinence from bulimic symptoms and the low rate of adverse side effects. Schweikert, Stober, and Moskowitz (1997) argued for the positive effect of methylphenidate (which is prescribed to treat comorbid attention-deficit/hyperactivity disorder) on the binge eating component of bulimia nervosa. Moreover, case studies have reported that stimulant medication for treating ADHD had improved also the comorbid bulimia nervosa (Sokol, Gray, Goldstein, and Kaye, 1999).

Many parents of children with severe food refusal report that they feel incompetent and that they experience high levels of emotional stress when attempting to feed their children (de Moor et al., 2007). Children who suffer from chronic and severe food refusal are usually being fed via gastrostomy or nasal tube (Kedesdy and Budd, 1998). However, since these children usually associate oral food intake with intense gastrointestinal distress and pain, they tend to develop food refusal behaviors (such as temper tantrums, crying, vomiting or refusing to eat) (Cooper et al., 1995). If the parents withdraw food in response to their children's disruptive behaviors, then they will end up reinforcing them and rendering them part of their children's behavioral repertoire (Luiselli, 1994). In these cases food refusal can be most effectively addressed using behavioral treatments that aim to substitute unwanted disruptive behaviors with desirable ones (de Moor et al., 2005; Kerwin, 1999). Ahearn (2003), Kern and Marder (1996) and Piazza, Patel, Santana, Goh, Delia, and Lancaster (2002) suggested that simultaneous presentation of one preferred and one non-preferred food in combination with escape prevention may help address the feeding problems of children with autism spectrum disorders. Actually, parents of children with intellectual disabilities and feeding problems, such as dysphagia, are often asked to actively address their children's problems by following the advice and the recommendations of professionals. Chadwick, Jolliffe, Goldbart, and Burton (2006) conducted a relevant study and found that parents face many problems, such as

> "particular difficulties in modifying food and drinks to safe consistencies, achieving the agreed positioning during mealtimes, and in using support and prompting strategies. Problematic support and prompting strategies included difficulties with pacing correctly; facilitating people to adequately relax and concentrate; observing and prompting people to pace suitably and take safe amounts of food and drink in each mouthful. Additional barriers identified included time pressures, staff turnover and insufficient reviewing of Speech and Language Therapy management strategies by caregivers." (p. 153).

Therefore, it is important to ensure that parents are supported in their effort to implement behavior management strategies through constant training and monitoring, while individuals with intellectual disabilities should also be informed about the reasoning behind management strategies (Chadwick et al., 2006). Sleigh (2005), who conducted one of the few qualitative studies looking at mothers' experiences of feeding children with severe feeding problems, such as cerebral palsy, stressed the importance of a supportive relationship with professionals. Parents need training to learn how to practice oral or G-tube feeding with their children and emotional and practical support in dealing with the stress of raising a child with special needs at home. She also emphasized that since oral feeding is part of the bonding process between mother and child, professionals should avoid recommending very early G-tube placement for children with cerebral palsy – especially when parents want to try oral feeding. Gisel (2008) suggested on the basis of her review that sensorimotor therapies using either oral stimulation exercises or an intra-oral appliance can be quite effective in dealing with feeding problems, although there are some limitations that need to be taken into consideration.

Despite the popularity of Cognitive Behavior Therapies in treating eating disorders, there are some concerns that these therapies focus only on specific psychopathology that is associated with eating instead of dealing with other comorbid factors that coexist with disordered eating (e g. Hollon and Beck, 1994; Walters, 1999). This could partly explain why they have not been consistently effective in dealing successfully with eating disorders (Fairburn, Cooper, and Shafran, 2003). They have left out the treatment of factors such as stress (Rojo, Conesa, Bermudez, and Livianos, 2006); perfectionism, neuroticism, obsessive-compulsive behavior, negative emotions and other personality disorders (Cassin and von Ranson, 2005; Warren, Zaman, Dolan, Norton, and Evans, 2006); low self-esteem, interpersonal difficulties and mood intolerance (Sloan, Mizes, and Epstein, 2005; Westen and Harnden-Fischer, 2001). In an effort to acknowledge and address that, Fairburn et al. (2003) introduced the concept of a 'transdiagnostic' treatment for eating disorders, whereby treatment for the eating disorder would necessarily entail simultaneous treatment for the triggering or maintaining mechanism. In that prism, Fletcher, Kurshik, Uprichard, Shah, and Nasj (2008) argued that successful treatment of eating disorders should encompass the treatment of comorbid psychopathological mechanisms. Moroever, Kalyva (2009) supported that treatment of girls with Asperger Syndrome who experience eating problems should focus on addressing their social skills deficits and their misconception that thinness is linked to popularity and peer acceptance.

For children with autism spectrum disorders, it might take more time to overcome their eating and feeding problems because they have difficulties adapting to change. So, although treatment for typically developing children would include taste exposure to an unfamiliar food in a short period of time, this might not work well with children with autism spectrum disorders who will be exposed to new food, new taste, new texture, and new smell simultaneously. Therefore, the first step would be just to place the new food on the table, then to encourage the child to look at the food, to touch and finally to taste the food over a longer period of time. Apart from this adjustment, parents and professionals working with children with autism spectrum disorders should realize that their feeding and eating problems do not vary greatly from those of typically developing children (Martins et al., 2008). It is also important to teach children with autism spectrum disorders and Prader-Willi syndrome which foods they can eat and which type of food is contaminated, so that they can avoid developing gastrointestinal problems (Kalyva et al., 2010). For example, parents of children with Prader-Willi syndrome are often forced to restrict the excessive eating of their children by keeping food locked and supervising them while out of the house to make sure that they do not steal food and that they do not overeat (Butler and Thompson, 2000).

O'Reilly and Lancioni (2001) examined the effectiveness of a minimally intrusive behavioral intervention aimed at dealing with non-organic food refusal in children with intellectual disabilities. It was implemented by the mother, who played the role of the therapist, at home during daily meal schedules. The mother did not allow the child to get up and leave the meal situation for a predetermined period of time and then she praised him for every bite of food that he consumed. The child started consuming more food and decreasing the inappropriate mealtime behaviors. The mother was encouraged to keep implementing the treatment and the positive changes were maintained over time. However, when asking parents to take on the role of the therapist, it is imperative to make sure that they are properly trained and willing to do so (Kalyva, 2011).

A most recent approach to treating food refusal is multicomponent behavioural treatment packages that include positive reinforcement (Kahng, Tarbox, and Wilke, 2001). However, a potentially influential factor that has not been substantially researched is the introduction of social skills training in the treatment program. Since individuals with intellectual disabilities face problems with their social skills (Elliott, Pring, and Bunning, 2002), it is likely that they exhibit challenging or maladaptive behaviours in an attempt to be reinforced or to escape their environment (Cipani and Spooner, 1997). Therefore, Matson et al. (2006) concluded that social skills training should be incorporated in behavioural interventions to address food refusal in individuals with intellectual disabilities.

References

Ahearn, W. H. (2003). Using simultaneous presentation to increase vegetable consumption in a mildly selective child with autism. *Journal of Applied Behavior Analysis, 36*, 361-365.

Ahearn, W. H., Castine, T., Nault, K., and Green, G. (2001). An assessment of food acceptance in children with autism or pervasive developmental disorder-not otherwise specified. *Journal of Autism and Developmental Disorders, 31*, 505–511.

American Psychiatric Association. (2000). *Diagnostic and statistical manual of mental disorders* (4th ed. rev). Washington, DC: American Psychiatric Association.

Asperger, H. (1944). Die ''Autistichen Psychopathen'' in Kindersalter. *Archiv fur Psychiatrie und Nervenkrankheiten, 117*, 76–136.

Bearman, S. K., Presnell, K., Martinez, E., and Stice, E. (2006). The skinny on body dissatisfaction: A longitudinal study of adolescent girls and boys. *Journal of Youth and Adolescence, 35,* 229–241.

Berkman, N. D., Lohr, K. N., and Bulik, C. M. (2007). Outcomes of eating disorders: A systematic review of the literature. *International Journal of Eating Disorders, 40*, 239-309.

Biederman, J., Ball, S. W., Monuteaux, M. C., Surman, C. B., Johnson, J. L., and Zeitlin, S. (2007). Are girls with ADHD at risk for eating disorders? Results from a controlled five-year prospective study. *Journal of Developmental Behavioral Pediatrics, 28*, 302–307.

Biederman, J., Monuteaux, M., Mick, E., et al. (2006). Psychopathology in females with attention deficit/hyperactivity disorder: A controlled, five-year prospective study. *Biological Psychiatry, 60*, 1098–1105.

Blinder, B. J., Cumella, E. J., and Sanathara, V. A. (2006). Psychiatric comorbidities of female inpatients with eating disorders. *Psychosomatic Medicine, 68*, 454–462.

Buhl, C. (2002). Eating disorders as manifestations of developmental disorders: Language and the capacity for abstract thinking in psychotherapy of eating disorders. *European Eating Disorders Review, 10*, 138-145.

Butler, M. G., and Thompson, T. (2000). Prader–Willi syndrome: Clinical and genetic findings. *Endocrinologist, 35*, 3S–16S.

Cashdan, E. (1998). Adaptiveness of food learning and food aversions in children. *Social Science Information, 37*, 613–632.

Cassin, S. E., and von Ranson, K. M. (2005). Personality and eating disorders: A decade in review. *Clinical Psychology Review, 25*, 895–916.

Chadwick, D. D., Jolliffe, J., Goldbart, J., and Burton, M. H. (2006). Barriers to caregiver compliance with eating and drinking recommendations for adults with intellectual disabilities and dysphagia. *Journal of Applied Research in Intellectual Disabilities, 19*, 153–162.

Cipani, E., and Spooner, F. (1997). Treating problem behaviors maintained by negative reinforcement. *Research in Developmental Disabilities, 18*, 329–342.

Clark, J. H., Rhoden, D. K., and Turner, D. (1993). Symptomatic vitamin A and D deficiencies in an eight-year-old with autism. *Journal of Parenteral and Enteral Nutrition, 17*, 284–286.

Cooper, L. J.,Wacker, D. P., McComas, J. J., et al. (1995). Use of component analyses to identify active variables in treatment packages for children with feeding disorders. *Journal of Applied Behavior Analysis, 28*,139-153.

Cortese, S., Dalla Bernardina, B., and Mouren, M-C. (2007). Attention-deficit/hyperactivity disorder and binge eating. *Nutrition Review, 65*, 404–414.

Cottrell, D. J., and Crisp, A. H. (1984). Anorexia nervosa in a Down's syndrome patient: A case report. *British Journal of Psychiatry, 145*, 195-196.

de Moor, J., Didden, R., and Korzilius, H. (2007). Behavioural treatment of severe food refusal in five toddlers with developmental disabilities. *Child: Care, Health and Development, 33*, 670–676.

de Moor, J., Didden, R., and Tolboom, J. (2005) Severe feeding problems secondary to anatomical disorders: Effectiveness of behavioral treatment in three school-aged children. *Educational Psychology*, 25, 325–340.

Dimitropoulos, A., and Schultz, R. T. (2008). Food-related neural circuitry in Prader-Willi Syndrome: Response to high- versus low-calorie foods. *Journal of Autism and Developmental Disorders, 38*, 1642-1653.

Dimitropoulos, A., Feurer, I. D., Roof, E., et al. (2000). Appetite behavior, compulsivity, and neurochemistry in Prader-Willi Syndrome. *Mental Retardation and Developmental Disabilities Research Reviews, 6*, 125-130.

Dimitropoulos, A., Feurer, I., Butler, M., and Thompson, T. (2001). Emergence of compulsive behavior and tantrums in children with Prader-Willi syndrome. *American Journal on Mental Retardation, 106*, 39–51.

Dukarm, C. P. (2005). Bulimia Nervosa and Attention Deficit Hyperactivity Disorder: A possible role for stimulant medication. *Journal of Women's Health, 14*, 345-350.

Dykens, E. M. (2000). Contaminated and unusual food combinations: What do people with Prader–Willi syndrome choose? *Mental Retardation, 38*, 163-171.

Einfeld, S. L.,Tonge, B. J., and Florio, T. (1997). Behavioral and emotional disturbance in individuals with Williams syndrome. *American Journal on Mental Retardation, 102*, 45-53.

Elliott, C., Pring, T., and Bunning, K. (2002). Social skills training for adolescents with intellectual disabilities: A cautionary note. *Journal of Applied Research in Intellectual Disabilities, 15*, 91–96.

Fahy, T., and Eisler, I. (1993). Impulsivity and eating disorders. *British Journal of Psychiatry, 162,* 193–197.

Fairburn, C. G., Cooper, Z., and Shafran, R. (2003). Cognitive behaviour therapy for eating disorders: A 'transdiagnostic' theory and treatment. *Behaviour Research and Therapy, 41*, 509–528.

Fayyad, J., DeGraaf, R., Kessler, R., et al. (2007). Cross-national revalence and correlates of adult attention-deficit hyperactivity disorder. *British Journal of Psychiatry, 190*, 402–409.

Fisman, S., Steele, M., Short, J., Byrne, T., and Lavalee, C. (1996). Case study: Anorexia nervosa and autistic disorder in an adolescent girl. *Journal of the American Academy of Child and Adolescent Psychiatry, 35*, 937–940.

Flectcher, B., Kupshik, G. A., Uprichard, S., Shah, S., and Nasj, A. S. (2008). Eating disorders and concurrent psychopathology: A reconceptualisation of clinical need through Rasch analysis. *European Eating Disorders Review, 16*, 191–198.

Gillberg, I. C., Gillberg, C., Rastam, M., and Johnasson, M. (1996). The cognitive profile of anorexia nervosa: A comparative study including a community-based sample. *Comprehensive Psychiatry, 37*, 23–30.

Gillberg, I. C., Rastam, M., and Gillberg, C. (1995). Anorexia nervosa 6 years after onset: Part I personality disorders. *Comprehensive Psychiatry, 36*, 61–69.

Girolami, P. A., and Scotti, J. (2001). Use of analog functional analysis in assessing the function of mealtime behavior problems. *Education and Training in Mental Retardation and Developmental Disabilities, 36*, 207–223.

Gisel. E. (2008). Interventions and outcomes of children with dysphagia. *Developmental Disabilities Research Reviews, 14*, 165-173.

Gittins, D., and Rose, N. (2006). An audit of adults with profound and multiple learning disabilities within a West Midlands Community Health Trust – implications for service development. *British Journal of Learning Disabilities, 36*, 38–47.

Glover, D., Maltzman, I., and Williams, C. (1996). Food preferences among individuals with and without Prader-Willi syndrome. *American Journal on Mental Retardation, 101*, 195–205.

Gosch, A., and Pankau, R. (1997). Personality characteristics and behavior problems in individuals of different ages with Williams syndrome. *Developmental Medicine and Child Neurology, 39*, 527-533.

Gravestock, S. (2003). Diagnosis and classification of eating disorders in adults with intellectual disability: The diagnostic criteria for psychiatric disorders for use with adults with learning disabilities/mental retardation (DC-LD) approach. *Journal of Intellectual Disability Research, 47*, 72-83.

Hebebrand, J., Henninghausen, K., Nau, S., et al. (1997). Low body weight in male children and adolescents with schizoid personality disorder or Asperger's disorder. *Acta Psychiatrica Scandinavica, 96*, 64–67.

Hinshaw, S. P., and Blachman, D. R. (2005). Attention-deficit/hyperactivity disorder in girls. In D. Bell, S. Foster, and E. J. Mash (Eds.), *Handbook of behavioral and emotional problems in girls* (pp. 117–148). New York: Kluwer Academic/Plenum.

Hinshaw, S. P., Owens, E. B., Sami, N., and Fargeon, S. (2006). Prospective follow-up of girls with attention-deficit/hyperactivity disorder into adolescence: Evidence for continuing cross-domain impairment. *Journal of Consulting and Clinical Psychology, 74,* 489–499.

Hinton E. C., Holland A. J., Gellatly M. S., et al. (2006). Neural representations of hunger and satiety in Prader-Willi syndrome. *International Journal of Obesity, 30*, 313–321.

Ho, H. H., Eaves, L. C., and Peabody, D. (1997). Nutrient intake and obesity in children with autism. *Focus on Autism and Other Developmental Disabilities, 12*, 187–192.

Holland, A., Whittington, J., and Hinton, E. (2003). The paradox of Prader-Willi syndrome: a genetic model of starvation. *The Lancet, 362*, 989–991.

Hollon, S. D., and Beck, A. T. (1994). Cognitive and cognitive-behavioral therapies. In A. E. Bergin, and S. L. Garfield (Eds.), *Handbook of psychotherapy and behavior change* (4th ed., pp. 428–466). Oxford, England: John Wiley and Sons.

Holm, V. A., and Pipes, P. L. (1976). Food and children with Prader-Willi syndrome. *American Journal of Disabled Child, 130*, 1063–1067.

Howlin, P., Davies, M., and Udwin, O. (1998). Syndrome specific characteristics in Williams syndrome:To what extent do early behavioural patterns persist into adult life? *Journal of Applied Research in Intellectual Disabilities, 11*, 207-216.

Hudson J. I., Mangweth, B., Pope. H. G., et al. (2003). Family study of affective spectrum disorder. *Archives of General Psychiatry, 60*, 170-173.

Jacobi, C., Agras, W. S., Bryson, S., and Hamer, L. D. (2003). Behavioural validation, precursors and concomitants of picky eating in childhood. *Journal of the American Academy of Child and Adolescent Psychiatry, 42*, 76–84.

Jacobi, C., Hayward, C., de Zwaan, M., Kraemer, H. C., and Agras, W. S. (2004). Coming to terms with risk factors for eating disorders: Application of risk terminology and suggestions for a general taxonomy. *Psychological Bulletin, 130,* 19–65.

Johnson, J. G., Cohen, P., Kasen, S., and Brook, J. S. (2002). Childhood adversities associated with risk for eating disorders or weight problems during adolescence or early adulthood. *American Journal of Psychiatry, 159,* 394–400.

Johnston, C., and Mash, E. J. (2001). Families of children with attention deficit/hyperactivity disorder: Review and recommendations for future research. *Clinical Child and Family Psychology Review, 4,* 183–207.

Joseph, B., Egli, M., Koppekin, A., and Thompson, T. (2002). Food choice in people with Prader-Willi syndrome: Quantity and relative preference. *American Journal on Mental Retardation, 107,* 128–135.

Kahng, S., Tarbox, J., and Wilke, A. E. (2001). Use of a multicomponent treatment for food refusal. *Journal of Applied Behavior Analysis, 34*, 93–96.

Kalyva, E. (2009). Comparison of eating attitudes between adolescent girls with and without Asperger syndrome: Daughters' and mothers' reports. *Journal of Autism and Developmental Disorders, 39* 480-486.

Kalyva, E. (2011). *Autism: Educational and therapeutic approaches.* London: Sage.

Kalyva, E., Pellizzoni, S., Tavano, A., Iannello, P., and Siegal, M. (2010). Contamination sensitivity in autism, Down syndrome, and typical development. *Research in Autism Spectrum Disorders, 4*, 43-50.

Kedesdy, J., and Budd, K. (1998). Children who eat too little. In: J. Kedesdy and K. Budd (Eds.), *Childhood feeding disorders: Biobehavioral assessment and intervention* (pp. 159–195). Baltimore: Paul H. Brookes.

Keen, D. (2008). Childhood autism, feeding problems and failure to thrive in early infancy: Seven case studies. *European Child and Adolescent Psychiatry, 17*, 209–216.

Kern, L., and Marder, T. J. (1996). A comparison of simultaneous and delayed reinforcement as treatments for food selectivity. *Journal of Applied Behavior Analysis, 29,* 243–246.

Kerwin, M. L. (1999). Empirically validated treatments for feeding problems and failure to thrive. *Journal of Pediatric Psychology, 24,* 193–214.

Kerwin, M. L., Eicher, P. S., and Gelsinger, J. (2005). Parental report of eating problems and gastrointestinal symptoms in children with pervasive developmental disorders. *Children's Health Care, 34*, 221–234.

Lalkhem, Y. (2002). A phenomenological understanding of self-esteem in physically disabled adolescents in a non-disabled environment.

Dissertations Abstracts International Section B: Science and Engineering, 62, 4839.

Lally, G. (1999). *A survey of feeding difficulties of individuals with Williams syndrome*. Department of Psychology, University College, Dublin.

Luiselli, J. (1994). Oral feeding treatment of children with chronic food refusal and multiple developmental disabilities. *American Journal on Mental Retardation, 98*, 646–655.

Mannuzza, S., and Klein, R. G. (2000). Long term prognosis in attention deficit/hyperactivity disorder. *Child and Adolescent Psychiatric Clinics of North America, 9,* 711–726.

Marchi, M., and Cohen, P. (1990). Early childhood eating behaviors and adolescent eating disorders. *Journal of the American Academy of Child and Adolescent Psychiatry, 29,* 112–117.

Martins, Y., Young, R. L., and Robson, D. C. (2008). Feeding and eating behaviors in children with autism and typically developing children. *Journal of Autism and Developmental Disorders, 38*, 1878-1887.

Matson, J. L., Cooper, C. L., Mayville, S. B., and Gonzalez, M. L. (2006). The relationship between food refusal and social skills in persons with intellectual disabilities. *Journal of Intellectual and Developmental Disability, 31*, 47–52.

Matson, J. L., Mayville, S. B., Kuhn, D. E., Sturmey, P., Laud, R. B., and Cooper, C. (2005). The behavioral function of feeding problems as assessed by the Questions About Behavior Function (QABF). *Research in Developmental Disabilities, 26*, 399–408.

Mattos, P., Saboya, E., Ayrao, V., Segrenreich, D., Duchesne, M., and Coutinho, G. (2004). Comorbid eating disorders in a Brazilian attention deficit/hyperactivity disorder adult clinical sample. *Revista Brasileira de Psiquiatria, 26,* 248–250.

Mikami, A. Y., Hinshaw, S. P., Patterson, K. A., and Lee, J. C. (2008). Eating pathology among adolescent girls with Attention-Deficit/Hyperactivity Disorder. *Journal of Abnormal Psychology, 117*, 225-235.

Motion, S., Northstone, K., Emond, A., Stucke, S., and Golding, J. (2002). Early feeding problems in children with cerebral palsy: Weight and neurodevelopmental outcomes. *Developmental Medicine and Child Neurology, 44*, 40–43.

Myers, B. A., and Pueschel, S. M. (1991). Psychiatric disorders in persons with Down's syndrome. *Journal of Mental and Nervous Disease, 179*, 609-613.

Nicholls, R. D., Knoll, J. H. M., Butler, M. G., Karam, S., and Lalande, M. (1989). Genetic imprinting suggested by maternal heterodisomy in non-deletion Prader-Willi syndrome. *Nature, 342*, 281–285.

Nilsson, E. W., Gillberg, C., Gillberg, I. C., and Rastam, M. (1999). Ten year follow-up of adolescent-onset anorexia nervosa: Personality disorders. *Journal of the American Academy of Child and Adolescent Psychiatry, 38*, 1389–1395.

O'Brien, S., Repp, A. C., Williams, G. E., and Christophersen, E. R. (1991). Pediatric feeding disorders. *Behavior Modification, 15*, 394–418.

O'Reilly, M. F., and Lancioni, G. E. (2001). Treating food refusal in a child with Williams syndrome using the parent as therapist in the home setting. *Journal of Intellectual Disability Research, 45*, 41-45.

Pajer, K. A. (1998). What happens to "bad" girls? A review of the adult outcomes of antisocial adolescent girls. *American Journal of Psychiatry, 155,* 862–870.

Peris, T. S., and Hinshaw, S. P. (2003). Family dynamics and preadolescent girls with ADHD: The relationship between expressed emotion, ADHD symptomatology, and comorbid disruptive behavior. *Journal of Child Psychology and Psychiatry, 44,* 1177–1190.

Piazza, C. C., Patel, M. R., Santana, C. M., Goh, H., Delia, M. D., and Lancaster, B. M. (2002). An evaluation of simultaneous and sequential presentation of preferred and nonpreferred food to treat food selectivity. *Journal of Applied Behavior Analysis, 35,* 259–269.

Pipes, P. L., and Holm V. A. (1973). Weight control of children with Prader–Willi syndrome. *Journal of the American Dietetic Association, 62*, 520-524.

Rastam, M. (1992). Anorexia nervosa in 51 Swedish adolescents: Premorbid problems and comorbidity. *Journal of the American Academy of Child and Adolescent Psychiatry, 31*, 819–829.

Rojo, L., Conesa, L., Bermudez, O., and Livianos, L (2006). Influence of stress in the onset of eating disorders: Data from a two-stage epidemiologic controlled study. *Psychosomatic Medicine, 68*, 628–635.

Sarimski, K. (1996). Specific eating and sleeping problems in Prader-Willi and Williams-Beuren syndrome. *Child Care Health and Development, 22*, 143–150.

Schreck, K. A., Williams, K., and Smith, A. F. (2004). A comparison of eating behaviors between children with and without autism. *Journal of Autism and Developmental Disorders, 34*, 433–438.

Schweikert, L. A., Strober, M., and Moskowitz, A. (1997). Efficacy of methylphenidate in bulimia nervosa comorbid with attention-deficit hyperactivity disorder: A case report. *International Journal of Eating Disorders, 21*, 299-301.

Shapira, N. A., Lessig, M. C., He, A. G., James, G. A., Driscoll, D. J., and Liu, Y. (2005). Satiety dysfunction in Prader-Willi syndrome demonstrated by fMRI. *Journal of Neurology, Neurosurgery, and Psychiatry, 76*, 260–262.

Sleigh, G. (2005). Mothers' voice: A qualitative study on feeding children with cerebral palsy. *Child: Care, Health and Development, 31*, 373–383.

Sleigh, G., and Brocklehurst, P. (2004). Gastrostomy feeding in cerebral palsy: A systematic review. *Archives of Disease in Childhood, 89*, 534–539.

Sloan, D. M., Mizes, J. S., and Epstein, E. M., (2005). Empirical classification of eating disorders. *Eating Behaviors, 6*, 53–62.

Sobanski, E., Marcus, A., Henninghausen, K., Hebebrand, J., and Schmidt, M. H. (1999). Further evidence for a low body weight in male children and adolescents with Asperger's disorder. *European Child and Adolescent Psychiatry, 8*, 312–314.

Sokol, M. S., Gray, N. S., Goldstein, A., and Kaye, W. H. (1999). Methylphenidate treatment for bulimia nervosa associated with a cluster B personality disorder. *International Journal of Eating Disorders, 25*, 233–237.

Spalding, K., and McKeever, P. (1998). Mothers' experiences caring for children with disabilities who require a gastrostomy tube. *Journal of Pediatric Nursing, 13*, 234–243.

Spencer, T. J., Biederman, J., and Mick, E. (2007). Attention-deficit/hyperactivity disorder: Diagnosis, lifespan, comorbidities and neurobiology. *Journal of Pediatric Psychology, 32*, 631–642.

Stice, E., Presnell, K., and Bearman, S. K. (2001). Relation of early menarche to depression, eating disorders, substance abuse, and comorbid psychopathology among adolescent girls. *Developmental Psychology, 37*, 608–619.

Sullivan, P., Lambert, B., Rose, M., Ford-Adams, M., Johnson, A., and Griffiths, P. (2000). Prevalence and severity of feeding and nutritional problems in children with neurological impairment: Oxford Feeding Study. *Developmental Medicine and Child Neurology, 42*, 674–680.

Surman, C., Randell, E., and Biederman, J. (2006). Association between attention deficit/hyperactivity disorder in bulimia nervosa: Analysis of 4 case-control studies. *Journal of Clinical Psychiatry, 67*, 351–354.

Sweeting, H., and West, P. (2002). Gender differences in weight related concerns in early to late adolescence. *Journal of Epidemiology and Community Health, 56,* 701–702.

Townsley, R., and Robinson, C. (2000). *Food for thought? Effective support for families caring for a child who is tube fed.* Brisrtol: The Norah Fry Research Centre.

Walters, G. D. (1999). *The addiction concept: Working hypothesis or self-fulfilling prophesy?* Needham Heights, MA, US: Allyn and Bacon.

Warren, F., Zaman, S., Dolan, B., Norton, K., and Evans, C. (2006). Eating disturbance and severe personality disorder: Outcome of specialist treatment for severe personality disorder. *European Eating Disorders Review, 14,* 69–78.

Watson, F., Chadwick, D., Stobart, V., and Kelly, A. (2006). Dysphagia in adults with learning disabilities: Findings from the work conducted by the NPSA Working Party. Available online at: http://www.rcslt.org/government/NPSA_report_final_version_16th_may_2006.doc.

Webb, K., Morgan, J., and Lacey, J. H. (2009). Cerebral palsy and anorexia nervosa. *International Journal of Eating Disorders, 42,* 87–89.

Wentz, E., Lacey, J. H., Waller, G., Rastam, M., Turk, J., and Gillberg, C. (2005). Childhood onset neuropsychiatric disorders in adult eating disorder patients. A pilot study. *European Child and Adolescent Psychiatry, 14,* 431–437.

Westen, D., and Harnden-Fischer, J. (2001). Personality profiles in eating disorders: Rethinking the distinction between Axis I and Axis II. *American Journal of Psychiatry, 158,* 547–562.

Whiteley, P., Rodgers, J., and Shattock, P. (2000). MMR and autism. Autism, 4, 207–211.

Williams, P. G., Darlymple, N., and Neal, J. (2000). Eating habits of children with autism. *Pediatric Nursing, 26,* 259–264.

Wonderlich, S. A., Connolly, K. M., and Stice, E. (2004). Impulsivity as a risk factor for eating disorder behavior: Assessment implications with adolescents. *International Journal of Eating Disorders, 36,* 172–182.

Yates, W. R., Lund, B. C., Johnson, C., Mitchell, J., and McKee, P. (2009). Attention-Deficit Hyperactivity symptoms and disorder in eating disorder inpatients. *International Journal of Eating Disorders, 42,* 375–378.

Young, J., Zarcone, J., Holsen, L., et al. (2006). A measure of food seeking in individuals with Prader-Willi syndrome. *Journal of Intellectual Disability Research, 50,* 18-24.

In: Eating Disorders
Editor: C. M. Shapiro, pp. 105-125
ISBN 978-1-61209-746-6

Chapter 5

PSYCHOLOGICAL WELL-BEING AND HEALTH BEHAVIORS IN COLLEGE FEMALES WITH EATING DISORDERS: COMPARISONS WITH A NON-EATING DISORDER COHORT

Diane E. Mack[1*], Philip M. Wilson[1], Benjamin D. Sylvester[2] and Jenna D. Gilchrist[2]

ABSTRACT

Background: The peak onset of eating disorders (ED) arises predominantly between 15 to 21 years old (American Psychiatric Association, 2010). Given the alarming rates of mortality and functional impairment associated with ED (Berkman et al., 2006), it is not surprising that health professionals are targeting university/college students as an important cohort for addressing health issues stemming from ED (American College Health Association, 2000).

Objectives: The purpose of this investigation was to examine differences across indices of psychological health, weight loss strategies,

* Correspondence concerning this article should be addressed to Diane E. Mack, PhD Behavioural Health Sciences Research Lab. Department of Physical Education and Kinesiology, Faculty of Applied Health Sciences, Brock University, 500 Glenridge Ave, St. Catharines, Ontario Canada, L2S 3A1. E-mail: dmack@brocku.ca

[1] Department of Physical Education and Kinesiology, Brock University

[2] Faculty of Applied Health Sciences, Brock University

and health promoting behaviors between college females self-reporting a diagnosis of anorexia nervosa (AN) or bulimia (BN) with an age-matched comparison cohort not reporting a diagnosis of an ED.

Methods: Data were derived from the 2000 – 2004 survey period from the American College Health Association–National College Health Assessment (ACHA-NCHA). Female undergraduate students who self-reported a diagnosis of AN (n = 880) or BN (n = 1410) were compared with those not reporting a diagnosis of AN/BN (n = 56965). Participants completed a self-report instrument on a single occasion.

Results: Analyses of the data demonstrated lower perceived health, more frequent negative thoughts, and greater frequency of health promoting behaviors for individuals diagnosed with AN/BN when compared to those not reporting a diagnosis ($p < .005$). Specifically, individuals with AN or BN reported lower perceptions of overall (Cohen *d's* = 0.07 - 0.16) and psychological health (*γ's* ranged from 0.05 – 0.09) and greater use of weight loss strategies (*phi*'s = 0.07 to 35.67) than individuals not reporting AN/BN. Finally, individuals living with AN/BN reported engaging in more frequent health promoting behaviors (*d's* = 0.33 – 0.40) than individuals in the comparison group.

Conclusion: In summary, college females with AN/BN reported greater psychological health concerns and use of potentially harmful weight loss strategies. Greater reported use of health promoting behaviors reported by those with AN/BN is encouraging. As colleges and universities have been recognized as effective settings for health promotion interventions (Center for Disease Control and Prevention, 1997) because of their ability to reach a large proportion of young adults, consideration of psychological health and health promoting behaviors is essential for all members of the college community.

Enrollment in college has been associated with increased physical and psychological health concerns (American College Health Association [ACHA], 2008; Blanco et al., 2008), with the transition into college associated with the lowest levels of psychological health (Adlaf, Gilksman, Demers, and Newton-Taylor, 2001; Gall, Evans, and Bellerose, 2000). The prevalence of psychological health concerns for college students are alarming as upwards of 15% met *Diagnostic and Statistical Manual, fourth edition* (DSM-IV; American Psychiatric Association [APA], 2000), for depression and approximately 12% for an anxiety disorder (Blanco et al., 2008; Hunt and Eisenberg, 2010).

As the college years represent a developmentally challenging transition to adulthood, psychological health concerns may have significant role impairment including academic success (Kessler, Foster, Saunders, and Stang, 1995) and social relationships (Kessler, Waltern, and Forhofer, 1998).

EATING DISORDERS

Eating disorders (EDs) reflect a significant public health concern with population health data estimating lifetime prevalence rates between 0.48 - 1.50% (Hudson, Hiripi, Pope, and Kessler, 2007; Preti et al., 2009). DSM-IV criterion identifies two main classifications of EDs: Anorexia nervosa (AN) and Bulimia nervosa (BN; American Psychiatric Association (APA), 2000). AN is marked by an inability to maintain a healthy body weight (i.e., < 85 percent of ideal), whereas BN is characterized by recurrent episodes of binge eating in combination with some form of inappropriate compensatory behavior (e.g., self-induced vomiting; excessive exercise).

Classification into ED categories is based on diverse diagnostic criteria including body image disturbance, and extreme behaviors to control weight or physical shape (e.g., excessive exercise) which often result in impaired physical health and psychosocial functioning (APA, 2000). Although diagnostically independent, crossover between AN and BN has been demonstrated typically within the first 5 years of illness onset (Bulik, Sullivan, Fear, and Pickering, 1997; Tozzi et al., 2005).

With numerous biological, psychological, and social factors implicated in the etiology of AN/BN (Williams, Zucker, Martin, and Smeets, 2001), few have been consistently replicated (Berkman et al., 2006). Previous investigations suggest that characteristics are transmitted genetically and that certain personality characteristics (e.g., anxiety, perfectionism) may predispose an individual to develop AN/BN (cf. Berkman et al., 2006).

With biological factors demonstrating some association with the onset of AN/BN, the manifestation of the condition is often triggered by environmental factors (Bulik, 2004). Psychosocial factors including (but not limited to) intense fear of weight gain, body image disturbance and social pressures to be thin have also been implicated in the development of AN/BN *(Williamson, White, York-Crowe, and Stewart, 2004).*

Mid to late adolescence is associated with the peak age of onset for AN, whereas BN most often begins in late adolescence through young adulthood (APA, 2000).

In light of these observations, the higher rates of ED behavior observed in college samples (e.g., Fairburn and Berlin, 1990; Kurtzman, Yager, Landsverk, Wiesmeier, and Bodurka, 1989) may not be surprising, although differences in diagnostic criteria adopted across studies cannot be ignored (Stein, 1991).

Further speculation has been advanced that the higher rates for EDs noted in college-aged samples may be linked to known co-morbidities (e.g., depression) that become increasingly common with the transition into young adulthood (Oldehinkel, Wittchen, and Schuster, 1999) or the unique social and academic stressors embedded within the college environment (Compas, Wagner, Slavin, and Vannatta, 1986).

EATING DISORDERS: ASSOCIATIONS WITH PSYCHOLOGICAL HEALTH AND HEALTH BEHAVIORS

AN/BN are often associated with a wide range of other DSM-IV disorders (Hudson et al., 2007). For example, 42.10% of those with AN and 69.40% of those with BN met criteria for at least one of the DSM-IV disorders assessed (Preti et al., 2009). Beyond psychological consequences, AN is associated with varied medical and social consequences that can persist beyond recovery (Berkman et al., 2006). Although not typically associated with the complications linked with AN, BN is often linked with varied physical and health symptoms (e.g., fatigue, gastrointestinal problems; Berkman et al., 2006).

The extent to which college students engage in health promoting behaviors is of importance given the known associations to chronic disease (Bouchard, Blair, and Haskell, 2007; Winkleby and Cubbin, 2004). With specific reference to weight loss, health behaviors may be classified along a continuum ranging from extreme methods to potentially safe (Lietchy, 2010). *Extreme* methods (e.g., vomiting, laxative use) are associated with medical complications including thyroid functioning, cortisol regulation (Levine, 2002) and mental health concerns (APA, 2000).

Potentially unsafe weight loss strategies such as caloric restriction or rigidity in consumption have been associated with weight gain (as opposed to loss; Field et al., 2003).

Compounding the above, previous research has suggested that moderate and severe dieting in adolescence was associated with five and 18 times respectively greater likelihood of developing an ED across a two year period than non-dieters (Patton et al., 2002). *Potentially safe* weight loss practices may include consumption of healthy foods and physical activity. The beneficial outcomes associated with fruit and vegetable consumption and physical activity are well documented (Bouchard et al., 2007; Hu, 2003; US

Department of Health and Human Services, 2008; World Health Organization, 2003). Although a frequently adopted weight loss strategy (Lowry, Galuska, Fulton, Wechsler, and Kann, 2005; Wharton, Adams, and Hampl, 2008), physical activity has not been associated with an increased risk of EDs (Patton et al., 2002) and exercise (a component of physical activity) a useful adjuvant to clinical treatment. (Pendleton, Goodrick, Poston, Reeves, and Foreyt, 2002; Sundgot-Borgen, Rosenvinge, Bahr, and Schneider, 2002).

The purpose of this investigation was to examine differences across indices of psychological health, weight loss strategies, and health promoting behaviors between college females who self-reported living with AN/BN. Consistent with existing literature, it was hypothesized that individuals with AN/BN would report greater psychological health concerns (Preti et al., 2009) and greater endorsement of weight loss strategies and health promoting behaviors (Lietchy, 2010) compared to the non AN/BN cohort.

Addressing this purpose extends existing literature examining psychological health in those with AN/BN in various ways. First, the bulk of current literature considering issues of psychological health in college students has focused on those deemed 'at risk' for an ED or with 'sub-clinical' symptoms of EDs (e.g., Masuda, Price, Anderson, and Wednell, 2010; Thome, and Espelage, 2010).

Second, role impairment appears to be a widespread occurrence in EDs with upwards of 66 percent of those with EDs reporting impairment in at least one role domain (e.g., academic). As such, successful navigation through college may be impaired for those reporting AN/BN.

Finally, research has suggested that the health and well-being of college students holds considerable potential to impact public health, yet does not appear to be adequately addressed in institutions of higher education (Dories and Doherty, 2009; Stewart-Brown, Evans, Patterson, Petersen, and Doll, 2000).

With approximately half of young adults attending post-secondary schools (US Department of Education, 2007), colleges and universities have been recognized as potent settings for maximizing health promotion efforts because of their ability to reach a large proportion of young adults.

Methods and Procedures

The American College Health Association–National College Health Assessment (ACHA-NCHA) survey was developed to collect information on a broad range of health behaviors, health indices, and perceptions of college community members (The Task Force on National Health Objectives in Higher Education, 1991). The development of the ACHA-NCHA, estimates of validity and reliability for data from this survey, and sampling strategies for studies using this instrument have been documented elsewhere (ACHA, 2004; Gordon, 1995).

Participating institutions were self-selecting and participation/processing fees charged. The option of test administration via either paper-and-pencil or web-based formats was introduced in 2003 with 68.60% (n = 40311) of responses reported in the present investigation administered via paper. All geographic regions in the United States were represented with the Midwest region accounting for the greatest response rate 31.60% percent (n = 18549).

Measures

Demographic Variables

Demographic questions from the ACHA-NCHA were included for the present investigation including: Age, cultural background, marital status, number of years in school, full versus part-time status, and self-reported Body Mass Index (BMI).

AN/BN Status

Participants were asked to indicate "Within the last school year, have you had any of the following?". Separate response options were provided for those reporting AN or BN, with individuals reporting "yes" retained for further consideration. Given the concomitant nature of AN/BN (Tozzi et al., 2007) individuals reporting "yes" to both AN and BN in the last school year were excluded. A negative response to either item was used to classify the non AN/BN cohort.

Weight-loss Strategies

Participants were asked to indicate (yes or no) whether they had "exercised", "dieted", "vomited or took laxatives", or "took diet pills" in an effort to lose weight over the previous 30 days. An option for none of the aforementioned strategies was also included.

Perceived Health

Self-report estimates of perceived health were based on responses to six single-item questions embedded within the ACHA-NCHA. Global perceptions of health (Question: "Considering your age, how would you describe your general health?)" on a Likert scale anchored by 1 (*Excellent*) and 5 (*Poor*). Five items assessed the frequency over the last school year of feeling "hopeless", "overwhelmed", "exhausted", "very sad" and "depressed such that it was difficult to function". Responses were provided across a 7-point Likert scale with anchors ranging from 1 (*Never*) to 7 (*11 or more times*).

Physical Activity Behavior

Two single item indicators assessing the frequency of moderate-to-vigorous cardiovascular activity (MVPA) and resistance training (STRENGTH) behavior were included. A stem anchored the time frame for each item (i.e., "On how many of the past 7 days did you . . ."). Specific items following the stem in the ACHA-NCHA survey were as follows: (a)". . participate in vigorous exercise for at least 20 minutes or moderate exercise for at least 30 minutes?" (MVPA); and (b) ". . . do exercise to strengthen or tone your muscles, such as push-ups, sit-ups, or weight lifting?" (STRENGTH).

Fruit and Vegetable Consumption

Participants responded to a single item indicator assessing the typical number of servings of fruits and vegetables (F/V) consumed per day. Response options ranged from 1 (*I don't eat fruit and vegetables*) to 4 (*5 or more*).

Data Analysis

Sample size varied for each analysis undertaken due to the degree of missing daa evidence in sample responses across test items embedded in the ACHA-NCHA survey. Proceeding in sequential stages, descriptive statistics were first calculated across study variables. Second, appropriate parametric (e.g., independent samples *t*-tests) and non-parametric (i.e., Chi-square and Mann-Whitney *U*) tests were calculated to examine differences between AN/BN and the non AN/BN cohort on demographic variables. the frequency of various weight loss strategies, psychological health, and health behavior variables. Given the influence of sample size on null hypothesis significance tests, estimates of effect size (e.g., *phi* coefficients) were calculated to complement inferential statistics. Comparisons between the AN and BN cohort were outside the purview of this investigation.

RESULTS

Participants

Participants were 63869 female undergraduate students at varied universities and colleges in the United States (see Table 1). Participants ranged in age from 18 to 25 years (M = 20.13; SD = 1.59). The majority of respondents were enrolled in 4-year universities (96.90%; n = 56929), 97.00% (n = 56965) of whom were full-time students. Of those who responded, 1.50% (n = 880) and 2.40% (n = 1410) indicated they had AN or BN respectively over the last year. Those with AN were younger ($t(906.15) = 7.34$, $p = .001$; d = 0.24) and reported lower BMI ($t(885.20) = 11.40$, $p = .001$; $d = 0.38$) than the non AN/BN cohort. Those with BN were younger $t(1487.34) = 3.28$, p = .001; $d = 0.08$). Cultural background differences were noted, as those with AN (*phi* = 0.04) and BN (*phi* = 0.04) were more likely to identify with being "Caucasian" ($p < .01$). Consideration of the magnitude of the observed effect suggests that noted differences were somewhat negligible. Participants AN (*phi* = 0.01 to 0.25) and BN (*phi* = 0.01 to 0.44) were less likely to identify with other cultures assessed in the ACHA-NCHA with the greatest difference demonstrated for those who identified with being "*Black*".

Psychological Health

When the global estimate of General Health was considered, those with AN ($t(890.20) = 4.78$, $p = .001$; $d = 0.16$) and BN ($t(57686) = 3.07$, $p = .002$; d = 0.07) demonstrated lower perceptions of health than did those in the non AN/BN cohort (see Table 2). A series of Mann-Whitney U tests were conducted to examine differences in the frequency of experiencing various psychological health symptoms over the last school year. Consistent differences were noted as those living with AN/BN reporting more frequent concerns than the non-AN/BN cohort ($p = .001$). When considering estimates of effect size, values ranged from (γ's = 0.05 to 0.07) for the AN cohort and (γ's = 0.07 to 0.09) for the BN cohort which fell somewhat below the threshold of .10 regarded as a small effect (Cohen, 1992).

Weight Loss Strategies

Differences emerged between cohorts on the frequency of engaging in various weight loss strategies over the previous 30 days (see Table 3) with exercise uniformly endorsed as the most frequent strategy through which participants attempted to lose weight. When considering differences in the frequency of reported use, those with AN/BN reported greater engagement in exercise, diet, vomiting/laxatives and pills (*phi* = 0.07 to 0.96 and 0.45 to 35.67 respectively) compared the non AN/BN cohort. The non AN/BN cohort were more likely to do nothing in the previous 30 days in an effort to lose weight compared to either the AN (*phi* = 0.72) and BN (*phi* = 2.52) cohort.

Health Promoting Behaviors

A series of independent samples *t*-tests comparing AN/BN and the non-AN/BN cohorts on estimates of health promoting behavior were conducted with significance noted (see Table 2; $p = .001$). More specifically, individuals with AN reported greater frequency of engaging in MVPA ($d = 0.33$) and STRENGTH ($d = 0.30$) training behaviors on average across a 7 day period compared to the non AN/BN cohort. Similarly, those with BN reported engaging in MVPA and STRENGTH more frequently ($d = 0.40$ and 0.35 respectively) than the non AN/BN cohort (see Table 2). When the average number of F/V servings per day were considered, consumption was greater for those living with AN ($d = 0.35$) and BN ($d = 0.35$) than the non AN/BN cohort.

Table 1. Demographic Characteristics.

Characteristic	AN subsample			BN Subsample			Non AN/BN Subsample		
	N	%	*M (SD)*	*N*	%	*M (SD)*	*N*	%	*M (SD)*
Age	875		19.77 (1.45)	1410		20.00 (1.51)	56460		20.13 (1.59)[ab]
Marital Status									
Single	517	58.50		855	60.90		31322	55.10	
Married/engaged	363	41.30		546	38.90		25370	44.60	
Other	2	0.20		3	0.20		148	0.20	
Cultural Background									
Caucasian	756	95.90		1190	84.40		43225	93.40[ab]	
African American	22	8.40		33	7.90		3903	23.90[ab]	
Hispanic	33	12.30		72	16.10		3761	22.80[ab]	
Asian	58	20.10		72	16.10		5506	32.80[ab]	
Indian	7	2.80		11	2.70		526	3.90	
Other	29	11.20		40	9.60		1935	13.40[b]	
Year in School									
1st	338	38.40		428	30.40		16942	29.70	
2nd	223	25.30		366	26.00		13751	24.10	
3rd	182	20.70		318	22.60		13050	22.90	
4th	113	12.80		229	16.20		10343	18.10	
5th or more	24	2.70		69	4.90		2967	5.20	
Full-time Student									

Characteristic	AN subsample			BN Subsample			Non AN/BN Subsample		
	N	%	*M (SD)*	*N*	%	*M (SD)*	*N*	%	*M (SD)*
Yes	861	98.50		1367	97.70		55277	97.50	
No	13	1.50		32	2.30		1418	2.50	
Body Mass Index	857		21.49 (4.12)	1363		23.19 (3.61)	55248		23.10 (4.37)[a]
Underweight	135	15.80		43	3.20		3643	6.60	
Healthy weight	619	72.20		1018	74.70		38721	70.10	
Overweight	77	9.00		229	16.80		9113	16.50	
Obese	26	3.10		73	5.30		3771	6.80	

Note: Multiple responses could be provided for Cultural Background.

Data are presented using the mean and standard deviation for continuous variables and frequency (percentage) for categorical variables. Numbers vary due to missing data.

Age = years;

BMI = Body Mass Index (kg/m^2);

M = mean,

SD = Standard Deviation.

[a] significant difference ($p = .001$) between those with AN and non AN/BN cohort.

[b] significant difference ($p = .001$) between those with BN and non AN/BN cohort.

Table 2. Descriptive Statistics for Psychological Health and Health Behavior Variables.

Characteristic	AN subsample				BN Subsample				Non AN/BN Subsample			
	M SD		M_d	*IQR*	*M*	SD	M_d	*IQR*	*M*	SD	M_d	*IQR*
Health												
General Health	2.50	0.96			2.41	0.88			2.35	0.86		
Hopeless			3.00	4.00			3.00	4.00			2.00	3.00
Overwhelmed			5.00	3.00			6.00	3.00			5.00	4.00
Exhausted			6.00	3.00			6.00	3.00			5.00	4.00
Very Sad			5.00	4.00			5.00	4.00			3.00	3.00
Depressed			3.00	5.00			2.00	4.00			1.00	2.00
Health Behavior												
MVPA	2.93	2.28			3.04	2.03			2.22	1.98		
Strength	2.40	2.16			2.52	2.22			1.79	1.88		
F/V	2.64	0.73			2.64	0.70			2.40	0.67		

Note. Data are presented using the mean and standard deviation for continuous variables and median and inter-quartile range for variables measured at an ordinal level.

M = Univariate Mean.

SD = Standard Deviation.

M_d = Median.

IQR = Inter Quartile Range.

MVPA = Moderate and Vigorous Physical Activity (expressed as frequency per week).

STRENGTH = resistance training (expressed as frequency per week).

F/V = typical number of servings of fruits and vegetables consumed per day. Lower scores for General Health are associated with greater endorsement of health. Higher scores for all other variables are associated with a greater frequency.

Table 3. Weight loss Strategies.

	AN subsample		BN Subsample		Non AN/BN Subsample	
Strategy	*N*	%	*n*	%	*N*	%
Exercise	638	85.90	1151	90.90	34480	79.90[ab]
Diet	629	86.20	997	84.50	21164	60.70[ab]
Vomit/Laxatives	76	17.20	851	77.00	885	3.80[ab]
Pills	155	31.10	360	42.10	3711	14.70[ab]
None	129	26.50	79	11.70	33582	59.50[ab]

Note: Responses reflect those who indicated they had engaged in the weight loss strategy in the previous 30 days. None = None of the above. [a] significant difference ($p = .001$) between those with AN and non AN/BN cohort. [b]significant difference ($p = .001$) between those with BN and non AN/BN cohort.

Discussion

The overall purpose of this investigation was to examine differences between female college students who self-reported living with AN/BN across the previous year and a non AN/BN cohort. Differences between cohorts were investigated across measures of psychological health, weight loss strategies, and health promoting behaviors given their importance to academic, social, and health outcomes (e.g., ACHA, 2008; Bouchard et al., 2007; Kessler et al., 1995; Lietchy, 2010). Results demonstrated that individuals living with AN/BN report experiencing more frequent psychological health concerns over the course of the school year and greater use of potentially harmful strategies in an effort to lose weight than those in the non AN/BN cohort. Findings also demonstrate that individuals with AN/BN report greater frequency of health promoting behaviors such as physical activity and fruit and vegetable consumption.

Regardless of the cohort under consideration, a number of noteworthy observations are evident in the present study. First, it appears reasonable to contend that the college experience is associated with psychological health concerns (e.g., perceptions of being overwhelmed, exhausted). Such a finding is not confined to the present sample, and appears to be a somewhat pervasive observation within literature examining college students enrolled in post-secondary institutions (American College Health Association [ACHA], 2008; Blanco et al., 2008). Future research may want to adopt ecological frameworks (e.g., Bronfenbrenner) in an attempt consider the multiple influences on psychological health of college students.

Consistent with study hypotheses, individuals with AN/BN reported more frequent psychological health concerns than those in the non-AN/BN cohort. However caution in over-extending these findings is leveled. Consideration of the magnitude of effect (Cohen, 1992) suggests that the differences in the frequency of reporting psychological health concerns between cohorts were (at best) minimal. Prolonged and repeated psychological health concerns have been associated with long term health implications including diminished immune system functioning and exacerbated cardiovascular concerns (Howell, Kern, and Lyubomirsky, 2007). As such, noted psychological health concerns observed in college samples holds the potential for far reaching implications for an individual's health.

Weight loss strategies which hold the potential for negative health complications were adopted regardless of cohort status in ths study. While it cannot be ignored that that individuals with AN/BN reported greater endorsement of the use of weight loss strategies, data support their adoption across the female undergraduate sample examined regardless of ED status. Similar findings have been documented elsewhere in the literature (e.g., Huang, Song, Schemmel, and Hoerr, 1994; Wharton et al., 2008). Exercise, a 'potentially' safe weight loss strategy (Leitchy, 2010), was most frequently identified which is promising given known benefits of physical activity for varied health outcomes including weight loss (Bouchard et al., 2007). Given the prevalence and diversity of weight loss strategies adopted among undergraduate females, health promotion specialists on college campuses may want to visibly promote the benefits of strategies known to confer more positive than negative outcomes. The nature of the measurement of weight loss strategies embedded within the ACHA-NCHA afforded participants the opportunity to specify information specific to strategies which have been used over the previous 30 days. Future research may wish to build on this information to investigate whether a given strategy had been used, in conjunction with the perceived effectiveness and frequency of use of each strategy for weight loss.

Consideration of the extent to which specific health promoting behaviors were endorsed should raise concerns for health promotion researchers. Population health data has demonstrated that more than 73 percent of college students failed to meet public health guidelines for fruit and vegetable consumption (Center for Disease Control and Prevention, 1997). Despite longstanding health promotion efforts targeting increases in fruit and vegetable consumption (e.g., 5-A-Day), individuals in the present investigation (on average) did not consume sufficient servings of fruit and vegetables per day for health benefits. Reasons for lower than recommended consumption of fruit and vegetables on college campuses should be investigated, with possible reasons identified including price, availability, lack of awareness, etc. Similarly, when considering the frequency of physical activity, participants typically reported levels below current public health recommendations (US Department of Health and Human Services, 2008), a finding also in line with existing research (Mack, Wilson, Lightheart, Oster, and Gunnell, 2009)[1].

Data provided by individuals in the present investigation demonstrated that those who self-reported AN/BN over the previous year reported greater use of health promoting behaviors than the non AN/BN cohort. Extrapolating from the above, an optimist might suggest those who battle with extra-ordinary

[1] Data derived for MVPA cannot be compared with public health guidelines as the single item indicator does not offer the potential to tease out estimates of frequency/intensity/duration.

body concerns (i.e., the AN/BN cohorts) actively seek opportunities sufficient levels for health cannot be determined. While excessive exercise has been linked with ED (Schroff et al., 2006), physical activity patterns reported by the AN/BN cohorts were on average extreme. Future research may want to extrapolate on this observation through a detailed investigation of the utility of health promoting behaviors on psychological health in the college population regardless of ED status.

With the observations noted from the present investigation demonstrating empirical and practical utility, a number of important limitations may be raised. First, reported estimates of AN/BN should be considered lower-bound estimates of ED prevalence in the general population. Given the peak age of onset for AN (i.e., 15 – 19 years; APA, 2000) and the intermittent yet chronic nature of BN (Berkman et al., 2006), caution extrapolating to lifetime prevalence rates is warranted. Second, concerns over extrapolating to prevalence demonstrated in other literature (e.g., Preti et al., 2009) is cautioned given the non-diagnostic nature of the self-report screening questions for AN/BN embedded within the ACHA-NCHA instrument. The aforementioned limitations are identified despite the finding that the percentage of the sample who reported living with AN/BN over the previous year is generally consistent with existing literature employing more clinically accepted measures (Hudson et al., 2007; Preti et al., 2009). Third, concerns may be raised over the self-reported nature of the assessing psychological health embedded in the ACHA-NCHA instrument and the potential for construct under-representation when using a single item. With this limitation noted, the focus on measurement issues for psychological health and health behaviors has been prominent in the literature and single item approaches have been endorsed for their efficiency in large sample studies (CDC, 1997; Jackson, Morrow, Bowles, FitGerald, and Blair, 2007; Krause and Jay, 1994).

In summary, the present investigation indicated that college-age students who self-report AN/BN experience greater psychological health concerns and use of weight loss behaviors than those who did not identify a diagnosis of AN/BN. It should be highlighted however that psychological health concerns and use of potentially harmful weight loss strategies were not restricted to college-age females with AN/BN. Of particular note, is the greater use of health promoting behaviors by individuals with AN/BN compared to the non AN/BN cohort. As colleges and universities have been recognized as potentially effective settings for health promotion because of their ability to reach a large proportion of young adults (ACHA, 2008; CDC, 1997) greater attention to the academic environment and the potential stressors embedded within this environment is warranted. Moreover, doing so may have broad benefits given the significant impact that these disorders have on educational, economic, and social outcomes (Kessler et al., 1995; Kessler et al., 1998; Stewart et al., 2000).

ACKNOWLEDGMENTS

Funding support for this project was secured through the Social Sciences and Humanities Research Council of Canada. The third author was supported by a Masters scholarship awarded through the Social Sciences and Humanities Research Council of Canada during manuscript preparation.

REFERENCES

Adlaf, E. M., Gliksman, L., Demers, A., and Newton-Taylor, B. (2001). The prevalence of elevated psychological distress among Canadian undergraduates: Findings from the 1998 Canadian Campus Survey. *Journal of American College Health, 50*, 67-72.

American College Health Association (2008). *American College Health Association–National College Health Assessment: Reference Group Data Report*. Baltimore, MD: American College Health Association. American College Health Association (2004). *Healthy Campus 2010 Manual*. Baltimore, MD.

American Psychiatric Association, (2000). *Diagnostic and statistical manual of mental disorders* (4th edition, text revision). American Psychiatric Association, Washington, DC.

Berkman N. D., Bulik, C. M., Brownley, K. A., Lohr, K. N., Sedway, J. A., Rooks, A., Gartlehner, G. (2006). *Management of eating disorders. Evidence report/technology assessment* No. 135. AHRQ Publication No. 06-E010. Rockville, MD: Agency for Healthcare Research and Quality.

Blanco, C., Okuda, M., Wright, C., Hasin, D. S., Grant, B. F., Liu, S. M., and Olfson, M. (2008). Mental health of college students and their non-college-attending peers: Results from the National Epidemiologic Study on Alcohol and Related Conditions. *Archives of General Psychiatry, 65*, 1429–1437.

Bouchard, C., Blair, S. N., and Haskell, W. L. (2007). *Physical activity and health*. Human Kinetics, Champaign, IL.

Bulik, C. (2004). Genetic and biological risk factors. In Thompson K (ed.) *Handbook of eating disorders and obesity,* (p. 3 – 16). New Jersey: Wiley.

Bulik, C. M., Sullivan, P. F., Fear, J., and Pickering, A. (1997). Predictors of the development of bulimia nervosa in women with anorexia nervosa. *Journal of Nervous and Mental Disease, 185*, 704–707.

Carr, D. (1997). The fulfillment of career dreams at midlife: Does it matter for women's health? *Journal of Health and Social Behavior, 38*, 331-344.

Center for Disease Control and Prevention (1997). Youth Risk Behavior Surveillance: National College Health Risk Behavior Survey-United States, 1995. *Morbidity and Mortality Weekly Reports, 46*, 1-54.

Cohen, J. (1992). A power primer. *Psychological Bulletin, 112*, 155-159.

Compas, B. E.,Wagner, B. M., Slavin, L. A., and Vannatta, K. (1986). A prospective study of life events, social support, and psychological symptomatology during the transition from high school to college. *American Journal of Community Psychology, 14*, 241-257.

Doories, M., and Doherty, D. (2010). Healthy universities—time for action: A qualitative research study exploring the potential for a national programme. *Health Promotion International, 25*, 94-106.

Fairburn, C. G., and Beglin, S. J., (1990). Studies of the epidemiology of bulimia nervosa. *American Journal of Psychiatry, 147,* 401-408.

Field, A. E., Austin, S, B., Taylor, C. B., Malspeis, S., Rosner, B., Rockett, H. R., Gillman, M. W., and Colditz, G. A. (2003). Relation between dieting and weight change among preadolescents and adolescents. *Pediatrics, 112*, 900-906.

Gall, T. L., Evans, D. R., and Bellerose, S. (2000). Transition to first-year university: Patterns of change in adjustment across life domains and time. *Journal of Social and Clinical Psychology, 19*, 544-567.

Gordon, K. A. (1995). College health in the national blueprint for a health campus. *Journal of American College Health. 43*, 273–275.

Howell, R. T., Kern, M. L., and Lyubomirsky, S. (2007). Health benefits: Meta-analytically determining the impact of well-being on objective health outcomes. *Health Psychology Review, 1*, 83-136.

Hu, F. B. (2003). Plant based foods and prevention of cardiovascular disease: An overview. *American Journal of Clinical Nutrition, 78*, 544S-551S.

Huang, Y. L., Song, W. O., Schemmel, R. A., and Hoerr, S. M. (1994). What do college students eat? Food selection and meal pattern. *Nutrition Research, 14*, 1143-1153.

Huber, H. B., Eaker, E. D., Garrison, R. T., and Castelli, W.O. (1987). Lifestyle correlates of risk factor change in young adults: An eight-year study of coronary heart disease risk factors in the Framingham offspring. *American Journal of Epidemiology, 125*, 812-831.

Hudson J. I., Hiripi E., Pope H. G., and Kessler R. C. (2007). The prevalence and correlates of eating disorders in the national co morbidity survey replication. *Biological Psychiatry, 61,* 348-358.

Hunt, J, and Eisenberg, D. (2010). Mental health problems and help-seeking behavior among college students. *Journal of Adolescent Health, 46*, 3-10.

Jackson, A. W., Morrow, J, R., Bowles, H. R., FitGerald, S. J, and Blair, S. N. (2007). Construct validity evidence for single-response items to estimate physical activity levels in large samples studies. *Research Quartely for Exercise and Sport, 18*, 24–31.

Kessler, R. C., Foster, C. L., Saunders, W. B., Stang, P. E. (1995). Social consequences of psychiatric disorders, I: Educational attainment. *American Journal of Psychiatry 152*, 1026–1032.

Kessler, R. C., Walters, E. E., and Forthofer, M. S. (1998). The social consequences of psychiatric disorders, III: Probability of marital stability. *American Journal of Psychiatry, 155*, 1092–1096.

Krause, N. M., and Jay, G.M (1994). What do global self-rated health items measure? *Medical Care*, ***32***, 930-942.

Kurtzman, F. D., Yager, J., Landsverk, J., Wiesmeier, E., and Bodurka, D. C. (1989). Eating disorders among selected female populations at UCLA. *Journal of the American Dietetic Association, 89*, 45-52.

Liechty, J. M. (2010). Body image distortion and three types of weight loss behaviors among nonoverweight girls in the United States. *Journal of Adolescent Health, 47*, 176-182.

Levine, R. L. (2002). Endocrine aspects of eating disorders in adolescents. *Adolescent Medicine,* ***13,*** 129-143.

Lowery, R., Galuska. D. A., Fulton, J. E., Wechsler, H., and Kann, L. (2005). Weight management goals and use of exercise for weight control among U.S. high school students 1991-2001. *Journal of Adolescent Health,* ***36***, 320-326.

Mack, D. E., Wilson, P. M., Lightheart, V., Oster, K., and Gunnell, K. E. (2009). Healthy Campus 2010: Physical activity trends and the role of information provision. *Journal of Physical Activity and Health, 6*, 435-443.

Masuda, A., Price, M., Anderson, P. L., and Wendell, J. W. (2010). Disordered eating among cognition and psychological flexibility as predictors of psychological health among college students. *Behavior Modification, 34*, 3-15.

Oldehinkel, A. J., Wittchen, H. U., and Schuster, P. (1999). Prevalence, 20-month incidence and outcome of unipolar depressive disorders in a community sample of adolescents. *Psychological Medicine, 29*, 655-668.

Patton, G. C., Selzer, R., Coffey, C., Carlin, J. B., and Wolfe, R. (1999). Onset of adolescent eating disorders: Population based cohort study over 3 years. *British Medical Journal,* 318, 765-768.

Preti, A., Girolamo, G., Vilagut, G., Alonso, J., Graaf, R., Bruffaerts, R., Demyttenaere, K., Pinto-Meza, A., Haro, J. M., Morosini, P., ESEMeD-WMH Investigators (2009). The epidemiology of eating disorders in six European countries: Results of the ESEMeD-WMH project. *Journal of Psychiatric Research, 43*, 1125-1132.

Pendleton, V. R., Goodrick, G. K., Poston, W. S. C., Reeves, R. S., and Foreyt, J. P. (2002). Exercise augments the effects of cognitive-behavioral therapy in the treatment of binge eating. *International Journal of Eating Disorders, 31*, 172-184.

Shroff, H., L. Thornton, R. L., Tozzi, F., Klump, K. L., Berrettini, W. H., Brandt, H., Crawford, S., Crow, S., Fichter, M. M., Goldman, D., Halmi, K. A., Johnson, C., Kaplan, A. S., Keel, P., LaVia, M., Mitchell, J., Rotonda, A., Strober, M., Treasure, J., Woodside, D. B., Kaye, W. H., and Bulik, C. M. (2006). Features associated with excessive exercise in women with eating disorders. *International Journal of Eating Disorders, 39*, 454-461.

Stein, D. M. The prevalence of bulimia: a review of the empirical research. *Journal of Nutrition Education, 23*, 205-213.

Stewart-Brown, S., Evans, J., Patterson, J., Petersen, S., Doll, H., Balding, J., and Regis, D. (2000). The health of *students in institutes of higher education: An important and neglected public health problem? Journal of Public Health Medicine, 22, 492-499.*

Sundgot-Borgen, J., Rosenvinge, J. H., Bahr, R., and Schneider, L. S. (2002). The effect of exercise, cognitive therapy and nutritional counseling in treating bulimia nervosa. *Medicine and Science in Sports and Exercise, 34*, 190-195.

The Task Force on National Health Objectives in Higher Education (1991). *Healthy Campus 2000-making it happen.* Linthicum, MD: American College Health Association, 1991. Users manual. available at: http://www.acha-ncha. org/docs/ACHA-NCHA_USERS_MANUAL_ver2-004.pdf. Accessed March 15, 2007.

Thome, J., and Espelage, D. L. (2004). Relations among exercise, coping, disordered eating, and psychological health among college students. *Eating Behaviors, 5*, 337-351.

Tozzi, F., Thornton, L., Klump, K., Bulik, C., Fichter, M., Halmi, K., et al. (2005). Symptom fluctuation in eating disorders: correlates of diagnostic crossover. *American Journal of Psychiatry, 162*, 732-740.

US Department of Education, (2007). The condition of education 2007. *NCES 2007-064*. National Center for Education Statistics, Washington, DC.

US Department of Health and Human Services (2008). *Physical activity guidelines for Americans*. US Department of Health and Human Services, Washington DC.

Wharton, C. M., Adams, T., and Hampl, J. S. (2008). Weight loss practices and body weight perceptions among US college students. *Journal of American College Health, 56*, 579- 584.

Williamson, D. A., White, M. A., York-Crowe, E., and Stewart, T. M. (2004). Cognitive- behavioral theories of eating disorders. Behavior Modification, *28*, 711-738.

Williamson, D., Zucker, N., Martin, C., and Smeets, M. (2001). Etiology and management of eating disorders, (p. 641 - 670). In P. B. Sutker and H. E. Adams (Eds.), *Comprehensive Handbook of Psychopathology*. New York: Kluwer.

World Health Organization (WHO). Global Strategy on Diet, Physical Activity, and Health: Fruit, vegetables, and NCD disease prevention. World Health Organization, Geneva, 2003. Retrieved from the WWW on November 1, 2010: http://www.who.int/hpr/NPH/ fruit_and_vegetables/fruit_vegetables_fs.pdf

Winkleby, M. A., and Cubbin, C. (2004). Changing patterns in health behaviors and risk factor related to chronic diseases, 1990- 2000. *American Journal of Health Promotion, 19*, 19- 27.

In: Eating Disorders
Editor: C. M. Shapiro, pp. 127-139
ISBN 978-1-61209-746-6

Chapter 6

MULTIPLE FAMILY GROUP THERAPY FOR YOUNG ADOLESCENTS WITH ANOREXIA NERVOSA: A DESCRIPTIVE STUDY

Catherine Doyen*[*], *Solange Cook-Darzens and Marie-Christine Mouren

Child and Adolescent Psychiatric Department, Eating Disorders Unit, Robert Debré Hospital, Paris VII University, France

ABSTRACT

Objective: Multiple Family Group Therapy (MFGT) was recently developed for eating disordered patients and notably for adolescents with anorexia nervosa (AN). The aim of this study was to compare anorectic adolescents treated with MFGT with those treated without MFGT.

Method: BMI z-scores were obtained for two groups of anorectic adolescents at discharge.

Results: BMI z-scores showed greater improvement in the MFGT group than in the control group at 12 months.

Conclusion: MFGT seems particularly useful for severe forms of AN or for fragile or dysfunctional families.

[*] Author for correspondence: Catherine Doyen, MD, Child and Adolescent Eating Disorders Unit, Department of Child and Adolescent Psychiatry, Robert Debré Hospital, 48 boulevard Sérurier, 75 019 Paris, France. e-mail: catherine.doyen@rdb.aphp.fr

Keywords: Anorexia, Adolescents, Multiple, Family, Group.

Anorexia nervosa is a well known somatic condition with possibly life threatening prognosis but the origins of its psychological features are still debated. Studies on the efficacy of therapeutic approaches emphasize the variability of techniques available but fail to determine which type of treatment is most efficient on a short and long term basis. Furthermore, studies include mainly adults although adolescents are also sometimes included. Children and young adolescents are most often not represented and when they are child and adolescent psychiatrists have to apply therapeutic models that have not been tested on this age group. Consequently, adult therapeutic models are adapted to the developmental stage of this age group with specific involvement of parents and siblings [1]. For younger patients, outpatient treatment is strongly recommended but when inpatient treatment is needed, family therapy is the first psychotherapeutic approach to be advocated in different forms: conjoint family therapy; separated family therapy; parental counselling and multiple family group therapy [2-8]. Multiple family therapy seems to provide a hopeful approach in the treatment of younger patients with anorexia nervosa and studies are under way to clarify its modalities and efficacy. This paper describes a preliminary study on the use of multiple family group therapy (MFGT) in a French child and adolescent eating disorders unit.

CURRENT DATA ABOUT MULTIPLE FAMILY GROUP THERAPY

There are few randomized controlled trials on family therapy in anorexia nervosa but existing studies suggest efficacy in young subjects with a recent onset of the disorder [9, 10]. Efficacy of "separated" versus "conjoint" family therapy seems roughly equivalent, nevertheless the separated family model may be recommended when parental emotions towards the patient are extreme. Multiple family group therapy is a well-adapted technique devoted to family treatment and to the development of supportive links between group members. Around 1963, Carl Wells published the first paper on this technique, followed by Peter Laqueur [11,12] whose recommendations for multiple family group therapy initially addressed schizophrenic, alcoholic or maltreated patients and their families [13-16]. MFGT brings together 5 or 6 families and patients with several co-therapists. Video equipment can be used and specific strategies are described in the literature: workshops; moving workshops; family sculptures; meals and invitations; "fish in the bowl" technique, cross-parenting, and so on. Sessions are carried out in a four to five day block of therapy, followed by a shorter monthly session. Three psychological stages may be observed: "magic relief", resistance to treatment and analogical learning. According to the authors, MFGT reduces feelings of loneliness, opens a wide range of perspectives; favours mutual learning, solidarity and mutual support, as well as active parental involvement, works on chronicity and allows maintenance of confidence. Four recent studies emphasize the therapeutic value of this conjoint therapeutic model especially in adults and adolescents with eating disorders [17-21]. Although they are open studies they suggest that MFGT is accepted by patients and their families, and results in symptomatic improvement and shorter length of treatment. Within the psychodynamic field, some parent group approaches have already been described in French publications but with different objectives from those of the multiple family group therapy model developed in English speaking countries [22-23]. An initial publication by one of the authors describes in detail our team protocol for MFGT [24].

Multiple Family Group Therapy on a French Eating Disorders Unit for Children and Adolescents

Robert Debré Hospital accommodates one of four major Child and Adolescent Psychiatric Departments that exist in Paris; and it is the only one that has developed a specialised service for eating disordered youngsters aged 15 or below. In 2009, 31 patients with eating disorders (anorexia nervosa N=14; bulimia nervosa=1; eating disorders not specified N=16), mean age 13,1 ± 2,4, were followed in inpatient treatment.

For young adolescents with anorexia nervosa, we have adapted adult programs and guidelines to their developmental stage and because we care for the youngest patients with anorexia nervosa in the district we decided to promote parental counselling and family therapy. We chose to experiment multiple family group therapy for several reasons. First, family therapy is central in the treatment of our young anorexic population and we provide conjoint (and sometimes separated) family therapy. But as indicated in the literature, this form of therapy sometimes fails with families who perceive it as intrusive or with some young patients who do not fare well with strong expression of parental emotion, and end up feeling very guilty. Secondly, as suggested by international teams, MFGT is indicated for severely ill patients and we needed an alternative therapeutic approach for these patients. Thirdly, as the number of young anorexic patients increased, we hoped that multiple family group therapy would facilitate the follow-up of a higher number of subjects. And finally, families of inpatient subjects repeatedly expressed their need to join a parents group which had not been developed until then. We have presented the modalities of our MFGT program in another publication (for more details see Cook-Darzens et al., 2005). Briefly, between 2002 and 2004 we treated a total of 15 families, in successive groups of 5 to 7 families. We adapted the British model and planned sessions as follows: every other week, parents and young patients attended group sessions. Two sessions were devoted to separate parent and patient groups and the third session followed a multifamily group format. The parent group was facilitated by the second author, a family therapist assisted by two co-therapists (social worker and dietician); the patient group was led by the first author, a child and adolescent psychiatrist, along with two co-therapists (social worker and dietician, different from those in the parents group). After two separate sessions, families, patients, and therapists from both groups were brought together to the multifamily session. During each 2-hour multifamily meeting, multiple themes were dealt with, using different techniques: understanding and management of anorexia nervosa ; family relationships and family identity ; fighting loneliness, etc... The objective of this study was to compare the symptomatic outcome of anorexic inpatients after discharge depending on whether they received MFGT or a routine therapeutic program.

METHOD

Participants

From 2002 to 2004, we recruited 15 anorexic patients and their families into the MFGT modality. Patients' mean age was 15.6 (13.83 to 17.08 years), all were female and had just been discharged from inpatient treatment. At the beginning of inpatient treatment, they all fulfilled DSM-IV [25] diagnostic criteria for anorexia nervosa, or eating disorder not otherwise specified for prepubertal patients but with clinical signs of anorexia nervosa. During the same period (2002-2004), we collected descriptive data from a control group (CT) of 28 anorexic patients matched for age (mean age 15.1; 13.1 to 16.4 years) who did not benefit from MFGT but received our routine therapeutic program. These 28 anorexic patients had also received inpatient treatment and were discharged during 2002-2004. They also met DSM-IV diagnostic criteria for anorexia nervosa or eating disorder not otherwise specified at the beginning of inpatient treatment. In our psychiatric department, "routine treatment" consists of psychiatric consultations combined with dietary guidance, for some families a family approach (family counselling or family therapy), and individual psychotherapy for the anorexic patients. Descriptive data on this cohort are given in Table 1. As can be seen, patients from the multiple family group therapy and from the control group tend to have similar BMI z-scores at the beginning and at the end of inpatient treatment. MFGT patients have longer inpatient treatment, higher rates of comorbidity and higher frequencies of previous hospitalizations.

Table 1. Descriptive Medical Data from Multiple Family Therapy Group (MFTG, N=15) and Control Group (CTG, N=28).

	Mean age	Mean BMI at beginning of IT	Mean BMI at discharge of IT	Length of IT (months; days)	Number of hospitalizations (%) (1, 2 or >2 hospitalizations)	Comorbidity*
MFTG N=15	15.6	14.31 z-score -1.65	17.68 z-score -0.79	6;15	1= 46.2% 2= 23.1% >2= 30.7%	69%
CTG N= 28	15.1	13.94 z-score -1.69	17.43 z-score -0.79	3;7	1= 85.7% 2= 10.7% >2= 3.6%	35.7%

* At least one associated mental disorder on axis I or II of DSM-IV.
MFGT: Multifamily group therapy.
CTG: Control Group with Inpatient Treatment.
IT: Inpatient Treatment.

As mentioned above, we chose this population for our MFGT because we felt these patients were particularly fragile with risk factors such as one or more previous hospitalizations, high comorbidity and complex family functioning. All patients and families gave their consent to participate in the study. Two families expressed their wish to drop out of the MFGT program after one or two multifamily meetings.

Procedure

Three quantitative variables were selected for describing MFGT and CT group outcomes: weight, height and BMI expressed in percentiles and z-scores. For MFGT, Morgan and Russell scores were also calculated [26]. Patients were weighed and measured at each session and BMI scores were plotted on the Rolland-Cachera French curves, revised in 1991 with T.J. Cole's collaboration. This method was validated by WHO in 1995 then by the Centre for Disease Control (CDC) in 1995 [27, 28]. Somatic data were also computerized with a palm program which calculates growth percentiles and z-scores based on the June 2000 revision of the Centre for Disease Control (CDC) Growth Charts (smoothing method, LMS). There is no computerized program specifically validated on European populations but we hypothesized that CDC Growth Charts based on US populations were suited for Caucasian populations as well. With regard to somatic data, Morgan and Russell scores ("General outcome") were evaluated at 6 and 12 months (after discharge?) according to the following criteria: poor outcome (score 1): weight under 15% of mean weight and persistent amenorrhoea; intermediate outcome (score 2): weight around 15% of mean weight but not steady or abnormal menses; good outcome (score 3): steady weight at 15% of mean weight and regular menses [26]. Due to the small size of the samples, no formal statistical analyses were carried out.

RESULTS

After 12 months, the mean BMI z-score of MFGT patients was –1.07 (versus –1.10 for the CT group) with equivalent percentiles of 5% in both groups (Table 2). Morgan and Russell scores were estimated at 2 at the end of the one year MFGT session.

A comparison of MFGT and CT group outcomes shows that at 6 months, the CT group seems to have a higher mean BMI z-score than the MFGT group. At 12 months, the mean BMI is higher for the MFGT than for the CT group but with age correction, z-scores become similar for both therapeutic modalities. In fact, z-scores suggest that BMI stabilized in the MFGT group but decreased in the CT group (Table 3). No patient from the MFGT group needed to be hospitalized during the first year after discharge and only one needed inpatient treatment during the second year.

Table 2. Outcome of anorexia nervosa in Multiple Family Therapy Group (MFTG) and in ConTrol Group (CTG) evaluated on somatic data: Weight, Height, BMI.

	T6		T12	
	MFTG Mean age : 16.39 N= 9	CTG Mean age : 15.84 N= 10	MFTG Mean age : 16.65 N= 8	CTG Mean age : 16.09 N= 8
Weight (kg)	44.22	46.08	45.45	45.06
Percentiles	6	15	9	10
Z scores	- 1.53	- 1.02	- 1.36	- 1.27
Height (cm)	1.62	1.63	1.63	1.64
Percentiles	46	53	51	59
Z scores	- 0.11	0.07	0.02	0.21
BMI	16.84	17.34	17.10	16.75
Percentiles	4	10	5	5
Z scores	-1.11	-0.91	-1.07	- 1.10

Table 3. BMI z-scores at T0, T6 and T12 for Multiple Family Therapy Group (MFTG) and ConTrol Group (CTG).

	T0		T6		T12	
	MFTG Mean age : 15.6 N= 15	CTG Mean age : 15.1 N= 28	MFTG Mean age : 16.39 N= 9	CTG Mean age : 15.84 N= 10	MFTG Mean age : 16.65 N= 8	CTG Mean age : 16.09 N= 8
BMI	17.68	17.43	16.84	17.34	17.10	16.75
Z scores	-0.79	-0.79	-1.11	-0.91	-1.07	-1.10

DISCUSSION

Specific treatment of anorexia nervosa for young children and adolescents is seldom described in the eating disorders literature. Few studies have yielded precise inpatient or outpatient treatment protocols and for young subjects, most treatment programs are derived from adult therapeutic programs. Nevertheless, some authors suggest that treatment for younger patients with anorexia nervosa has to be applied by specialized teams who are knowledgeable in child development and respect fundamental needs: ongoing family support and proximity, schooling, somatic development [1]. Family approaches are strongly recommended and within this field multiple family group therapy is a new psychotherapeutic approach that is intensively developed by specialized teams through day-care programs for severely ill anorexic patients. Our therapeutic experience is the first one to be described in a French psychiatric department.

As in Scholz and Asen's (2001) and Colahan and Robinson's studies (2002), we observed symptom improvement, and no relapse occurred during the first year for MFGT patients. The main result was a tendency for BMI stabilization after 12 months of MFGT which was less marked in the CT group with routine treatment. Nevertheless this mean BMI remains low and testifies that weight gain is difficult to achieve after discharge. Probably, although we target a healthy weight range, it is not always reached even after a long period of inpatient treatment. Target weight is also difficult to define for young anorexic patients. It changes with age, height and chronic course of illness and has to be readjusted on a regular basis. Consensus is lacking on the method to define the BMI target for this population probably because we ignore long-term outcome for younger patients after in or outpatient treatment. Our data also suggest that duration of treatment after discharge has to be of at least one year, following an intensive mode, especially in severe forms of anorexia nervosa. Overall, the MFGT approach was more intensive and more efficient than individual family therapy for most of these families. And considering that MFGT patients suffered from more severe anorexia with a potentially more chronic course than the CT group (as suggested by a higher number of previous hospitalizations, a longer duration of the index hospitalization, and higher rates of comorbidity), the MFGT modality seems particularly efficient indeed.

There are many biases in our study and results should be interpreted with caution. The size of our samples is small and some data were lacking for the control group after 6 and 12 months. Nevertheless we may hypothesize that those 20/28 who dropped out of follow-up belong to a group with an intermediate or good outcome (similar to frequencies of 2/3 mentioned in outcome studies) and that the 8/28 CT patients who were evaluated at 12 months represented the 1/3 with worse outcome described in literature and in need of close specialized supervision even after discharge. Another bias was that we did not control for therapeutic variables and that subjects from the control group had different types of psychotherapy. Prepubertal and pubertal subjects were also combined in the MFGT group, even though very young patients (younger than 13 years old) were not included.

Independently from somatic outcome measures, we found that the MFGT had positive effects on mothers and fathers who regained a feeling of competence. For instance relationships at home were less explosive during meals. Young subjects were surprised to discover they could be appraised in other ways than the "anorexic daughter" during their exchanges with other parents. For a while, they became adolescents and it was an intense experience to observe these "normally" functioning girl in a triad of adolescents and parents. Difficulties expressed by young subjects were heard in a different manner by parents who consequently created different and new ways of responding. The family therapist addressed themes that are essential in anorexia nervosa: impact of the illness on family relationships, autonomy, perfectionism, friendships and these topics were subsequently developed during separate group sessions. Families and patients listened and learned from others as to how to cope when they lived uncomfortable or distressful situations. Some of them became leaders in the group, providing a model of adequate parental relations with an anorexic adolescent. Others were sometimes encouraged and "comforted". As indicated earlier, the families we selected for MFGT had an adolescent with quite a severe form of disease: most of them were hospitalized for the second time, or more, and they had high comorbidity rates. Clinically, we found that therapy was well-accepted by families and adolescents, particularly by those who previously experienced individual family therapy as intrusive. For one family with a very severely ill adolescent who had successive relapses, severe hyperactivity and self-injuries, we observed a surprisingly positive outcome. After repeated hospitalizations, the patient achieved for the first time weight stabilization after discharge. Her family was less defensive and parents regained a sense of competence and confidence in her ability to manage the eating disorder. The somatic measures of outcome confirmed this clinical perception.

We have already described our therapeutic program in previous publications [5, 24, 29] and emphasized the fact that we treat anorexic children and adolescents without practicing separation from the parents although in France Charcot's model of treatment for anorexia nervosa remains widely used regardless of developmental needs. With this study, we hope to encourage the use of a novel approach to psychological treatment.

We expect that multifamily group therapy will soon be broadened in its application and that a group for very young prepubertal anorexic subjects may also be developed. As a family-oriented approach is recommended in the literature for younger anorexic subjects we may hypothesize that MFGT for younger patients will prove to be efficient as well.

CONCLUSION

This preliminary study on Multifamily Group Therapy in young anorexic subjects points to the therapeutic value of this family approach, at least with regard to somatic stabilization of severely ill patients. Other therapeutic assets are family change in perception of illness, families learning from one another, and mutual support. This therapeutic experimentation should be evaluated more precisely over the next few years: outcome, quality of life, family functioning, and self-esteem in adolescents and relatives may be interesting variables to assess in future studies on multiple family group therapy.

REFERENCES

[1] Gowers S. and Bryant-Waugh R. (2004): Management of child and adolescent eating disorders: the current evidence base and future directions. *J. Child Adolesc. Psychol. Psychiat.*, 45, 1: 63-83.

[2] Minuchin S., Rosman B.L., Baker L. (1978): Psychosomatic families: Anorexia nervosa in context. Harvard University Press, Cambridge.

[3] Russel G.M.F, Dare C., Eisler I. and Legrange D.: Controlled trials of family treatments in anorexia nervosa. In: Psychobiology and treatment of anorexia nervosa and bulimia. Nervosa, K. Halmi (Eds), American Psychiatric Press, Inc. Washington D.C., 1992, pp 237-262.

[4] Eisler I., Dare C., Hodes M., Russell G.F., Dodge E., Le Grange D.(2000): Family therapy for adolescent anorexia nervosa: The results of a controlled comparison of two family interventions. *Journal of Child Psychology and Psychiatry*, 41 (6),727-736.

[5] Cook-Darzens S., Doyen C., Mouren-Siméoni M.C.(2001): A « joint family consultation approach » to the initial treatment of early onset

anorexia nervosa in a French paediatric hospital. *Journal of Family Psychotherapy*, 12(3), 55-77.

[6] Cook-Darzens S., Doyen C., Brunaux F., Rupert F., Bouquet M.J., Bergametti F. et Mouren M.C.(2005): Thérapie multifamiliale de l'adolescent anorexique. *Thérapie familiale*, 26, 3 : 223-245.

[7] Eisler I., Simic M., Russell G., Dare C.: A randomised controlled treatment trial of two forms of family therapy in adolescent anorexia nervosa: a five-years follow-up. *J. Child Psychol. Psychiatry*, 2007, 48: 552-560

[8] Cook-Darzens S., Doyen C., Mouren M.C.: Family therapy in the treatment of adolescent anorexia nervosa: current research evidence and its therapeutic implications. *Eat. Weight Dis.*, 2008, 13, 4: 157-170.

[9] Russel G.M.F, Dare C., Eisler I. and Legrange D.: Controlled trials of family treatments in anorexia nervosa. In: Psychobiology and treatment of anorexia nervosa and bulimia. Nervosa, K. Halmi (Eds), American Psychiatric Press, Inc. Washington D.C., 1992, pp 237-262.

[10] Lock J., Couturier J., Agras W.S.: Comparison of a long-term outcomes in adolescents with anorexia nervosa treated with family therapy. *J. Am. Child Adolesc. Psychiatry*, 2006, 45: 666-672

[11] Laqueur H.P., La Burt H.A., Morong E.(1964): Multiple family therapy : Further developments. *International Journal Society Psychiatry*, 10, 69-80.

[12] Laqueur H.P.: Mechanisms of change in multiple family therapy. In C.J. Sajer and H.S. Kaplan (Eds.) Progress in group and family therapy. Bruner/Mazel, New York, 1972.

[13] Asen E.(2002): Multiple family therapy : An overview. *Journal of Family Therapy*, 24, 3-16.

[14] Berkowitz C.B., Gunderson J.G. (2002): Multifamily psycho educational treatment of borderline personality disorder (pp.268-290). In W.R. McFarlane (Ed.), Multifamily groups in the treatment of severe psychiatric disorders. Guilford Press, New York.

[15] Keitner G.I., Drury L.M., Ryan C.E., Miller I.W., Norman W.H. and Solomon D.A. (2002): Multifamily group treatment for major depressive disorder (pp.244-267). In W.R. McFarlane (Ed.), Multifamily groups in the treatment of severe psychiatric.

[16] McFarlane W.R. (2002): Multifamily groups in the treatment of severe psychiatric disorders. Guilford Press, New York.

[17] Slagerman M., Yager J.(1989): Multiple family group treatment for eating disorders: A short term discussion groups for patients with chronic medical illness. *Families, Systems and Health*, 16, 55-70.

[18] Dare C., Eisler I.: A multi-family group day treatment programme for adolescent eating disorder (2000). European Eating Disorders Review, 8, 4-18. Voir traduction française, *Générations*, 24, 9-16.

[19] Scholz M., Asen E.(2001): Multiple family therapy with eating disordered adolescents: Concepts and preliminary results. *European Eating Disorders Review*, 9, 33-42.

[20] Colahan M., Robinson P.(2002): Multi-family groups in the treatment of young adults with eating disorders. *Journal of Family Therapy*, 24, 17-30.

[21] Le Grange D. and Eisler I. (2009): Family interventionsin adolescent anorexia nervosa. *Child Adolesc. Psychiatr. Clin. N. Am., Jan* ; 18 (1) : 159-73.

[22] Jeammet Ph.(1984): Le groupe de parents: Sa place dans le traitement de l'anorexie mentale. *Neuropsychiatrie de l'Enfance*, 32(5-6), 299-303.

[23] Poinso F., Lalande M., Battista M., Rufo M. (1998): Un groupe de parents d'adolescentes anorexiques : Du soutien des familles d'adolescentes anorexiques à la psychothérapie de groupe. *Psychiatrie de l'Enfant*, 41 (2), 511-544.

[24] Cook-Darzens S. (2002) : Thérapie familiale de l'adolescent anorexique : Approche systémique intégrée. Dunod, Paris.

[25] American Psychiatric Association : Diagnostic and Statistical Manual of Mental Disorders, 4th edition, Washington DC, 1995, Traduction française J.D. Guelfi et al: Manuel diagnostique et statistique des troubles mentaux, Masson, Paris 1996, 1056 pages.

[26] Morgan H.G. and Russel G.F.M.(1975): Value of family background and clinical features as predictors of long-term outcome in anorexia nervosa: four year follow-up study of 41 patients. *Psychol. Med.*, 5: 355-371.

[27] Rolland-Cachera M.F., Cole T.J., Sempe M., Tichet J., Rossignol C., Charrauda A. (1991) : Body Mass Index variations : centiles from birth to 87 years. *Eur. J. Clin. Nut.*, 45: 13-21.

[28] WHO expert Committee (1995). Physical status: the use and interpretation of anthropometry. WHO technical reports, series n° 854, Geneva: WHO, 452p.

[29] Yon L., Doyen C., Asch M., Cook-Darzens S., Mouren M.C., Traitement de l'anorexie mentale du sujet jeune en unité d'hospitalisation spécialisée : recommandations et modalités pratiques. *Arch. Pédiatr.*, 2009, 16, 11: 1491- 8.

In: Eating Disorders
Editor: C. M. Shapiro, pp. 141-153
ISBN 978-1-61209-746-6

Chapter 7

RISK FACTORS OF EATING DISORDERS IN FEMALES

Tamara Yousef Mousa*
Researcher Assistant, Department of Nutrition and Food Science,
University of Jordan, Amman 11196 – Jordan

ABSTRACT

Eating disorders are described as a persistent disturbance in eating behavior intended to control body weight and accompanied by body image dissatisfaction. These disturbances impair both physical health and psychosocial functioning. Hence, the recognition of risk factors of eating disturbances and vulnerable groups is considered an effective intervention before developing eating disorders. This is important to prevent the health hazards related to eating disorders such as amenorrhea and osteopenia.

The current paper, therefore, will discuss the predisposing factors of eating disorders in females including biological variables, particularly genetic predisposition, individual, familial and social variables, as well as westernization. Individual variables such as low self-esteem, pubertal timing in adolescent girls and negative body image, as well as parental pressures towards thinness and negative family relations have influenced eating disorders occurrence. Similarly, socio-cultural variables including

* Correspondence to: Tamara Yousef Mousa, MSc. Researcher Assistant, Department of Nutrition and Food Science, University of Jordan, P.O. Box: 960364. Amman 11196 – Jordan. Telephone / Fax number: 00962-6-5604301.E-mail: mousa_tamara@yahoo.com

socioeconomic status, exposure to thin media messages, and pressure from peers have increased the risk of exhibiting eating disorders.

INTRODUCTION

Eating disorders (ED) are described as a persistent disturbance in eating behavior intended to control body weight and accompanied by body image dissatisfaction. These disturbances impair both physical health and psychosocial functioning (Afifi-Soweid, Kteily, and Shediac-Rizkallah, 2002; Klein and Walsh, 2004). Disordered eating behaviors usually begin with dieting accompanied by unhealthy eating behaviors and attitudes such as skipping meals, binging, purging, self-induced vomiting, excessive exercise, as well as administrating laxatives, diuretics and diet pills (Jones, Bennett, Olmsted, Lawson, and Rodin, 2001; Abraham, 2003). Eating disorders are associated with several health hazards such as gastrointestinal problems, dermatologic abnormalities, emaciation, anemia, amenorrhea and osteopenia (Klein and Walsh, 2004; Fairburn and Harrison, 2003). The current paper, therefore, will discuss the predisposing factors of ED in females. The literature has signified that the occurrence of ED in females in general and in adolescent girls in particular, is highly correlated with many factors including individual, familial and social variables (Littleton and Ollendick, 2003), as well as westernization (Lake, Staiger, and Glowinski, 2000).

1. INDIVIDUAL VARIABLES

Individual variables include genetics, physiological and psychological aspects of females. Beginning with genetic predisposition, both anorexia nervosa (AN) and bulimia nervosa (BN) appeared to be common among female relatives of anorectic as well as bulimic probands, and thus seemed to be familial syndromes (Steiger, Stotlan, Ghadirian, and Whitehead., 1995). A recent report has verified that the lifetime prevalence of AN or BN among female relatives of an individual with ED is seven to twenty times higher than that of the general population (Klein and Walsh, 2004). The concordance rate of AN in twin studies was approximately 55% in monozygotic twins and 5% in dizygotic twins; corresponding figures for BN were 35% and 30%, respectively. This has suggested a significant heritability for AN but not for BN (Fairburn and Harrison, 2003). Environmental influences have been found to have greater contribution on BN than genetic factors regarding the development of the overvalued ideas that triggered BN (Wade, Martin, and Tiggemann., 1998). Finally, genotypes and environmental factors are assumed to affect ED transmission in one of three ways: passive transmission where a specific genetic vulnerability in the high-risk child upon which parent traits and attitudes have provoking effects, reactive transmission through the interaction of familial processes with a third factor such as peers or other social influences, and active transmission in which the severity of the psychopathology in affected children is linked to the severity of familial disturbances (Strober, Lampert, Morrell, Burroughs, and Jacobs, 1990; Steiger et al., 1995; Steiger, Stotlan, Trottier, and Ghadirian, 1996).

The second individual variable, which has been observed in adolescent girls, is physiological changes associated with puberty including menstruation, accumulation of body fat and increased body weight (Archibald, Graber, and Brooks-Gunn, 1999; Spear, 2002). Littleton and Ollendick (2003) has indicated that early adolescence is one of the modal ages for the development of body image dissatisfaction and ED. Pubertal changes have been shown to cause the bodies of adolescent girls to deviate from the pre-pubertal thin body considered ideal (Abraham and O'Dea, 2001; Sweeting and West, 2002). In a study conducted in Zarka, Jordan, data showed that post-menarcheal girls (10-15 years) had higher body weight and percentage fat than pre-menarcheal girls (As'ad, 1999). In addition, a few researchers who compared between pre- and post-menarcheal girls have found that the latter group has exercised more, considered themselves too fat and has been more dissatisfied with their body shape than pre-menarcheal girls had (O'Dea and Abraham, 1999). Our research (Mousa, Al-Domi, Mashal, and Jibril, 2010) that investigated ED occurrence among adolescent girls (10-16 years) in Amman, Jordan has provided similar findings. Data has shown that the risk of developing ED among participants who were overweight or at risk for overweight has increased by almost 2 folds ($p<0.01$). Hence, physiological changes of puberty have led to body weight and shape concerns predisposing adolescent girls to develop ED (Levine, Smolak, Moodey, Shuman, and Hessen, 1994; Presnell, Bearman, and Stice, 2004).

Finally, several psychological problems such as depression and low self-esteem have been argued to account for body image dissatisfaction and ED in females (Fairburn and Harrison, 2003; Steinhausen, Gavez, and Metzke, 2005). Stressful life events and unpleasant childhood events such as bullying and teasing regarding body weight and/or shape have been observed to promote weight and shape concerns in schoolgirls (Levine et al., 1994;

Gowers and Shore, 2001). Further, personality characteristics such as negative affectivity, dysphoria, stress, and temperament have contributed to negative body image perception, which provided a fertile environment for females' acknowledgement of ED (Leon, Fulkerson, Perry, Keel, and Klump, 1999; Littleton and Ollendick, 2003). Studies have also verified that the increase in body image dissatisfaction was positively correlated with ED among Western females (Hill and Bhatti, 1995; Littleton and Ollendick, 2003; Eapen, Mabrouk, and Bin-Othman, 2006). In accordance with the previous finding, a recent study has designated that being dissatisfied with body image has increased the risk of acknowledging ED among adolescent girls by almost 5 folds ($p<0.001$) (Mousa et al., 2010). Moreover, perfectionism is a personality style that has been assessed in female university students, verifying that self-imposed expectations of perfection were related to anorectic attitudes. The perception that others are imposing expectations of perfection on oneself, and the need to appear perfect, to avoid appearing imperfect, and to avoid disclosure of imperfection, as well as low appearance self-esteem and body image avoidance were related to ED symptoms (Hewitt, Flett, and Ediger, 1995). Situational stress has been argued to exacerbate the inability to maintain perfectionistic ideals and attributed to binge eating. Researchers concluded that distress induced overeating has functioned as a source of distraction from the actual source of dysphoria and alleviated the symptoms of distress (Polivy and Herman, 1999). Low self-esteem has also been signified to be negatively correlated with body dissatisfaction and initiating negative emotions regarding physical appearance in females, contributing to aberrant eating behaviors (Wertheim, Paxton, Maude, Szmuckler, Gibbons, and Hiller, 1992; Littleton and Ollendick, 2003).

2. Familial Variables

Parents and siblings negative comments regarding body weight and encouragement to lose weight were implicated to initiate females to view their body negatively and to engage in aberrant eating behaviors (Gowers and Shore, 2001). Parents stressing on the importance of thinness, and receiving more feedback regarding physical appearance from parents were associated with developing weight concerns in adolescent girls (Schwartz, Phares, Tantieff-Dunn, and Thompson, 1999). For instance, mothers who dieted or encouraged their daughters to lose weight has affected negative body image and eating problems development in adolescent schoolgirls (Levine et al.,

1994). Another study has indicated that the risk of developing ED has increased by 1.5 folds ($p<0.001$) among adolescent schoolgirls who received negative comments regarding body weight from their parents (Mousa et al., 2010). Finally, poor family relations, weak communication, more confliction and arguments, as well as negative family emotional climate such as low-caring and less cohesive families, weak family connectedness, and stressed family environment have been suggested to increase the risk of eating disturbances in females (Archibald et al., 1999; French, Story, Downes, Resnick, and Blum, 1995; Steinhausen, et al., 2005).

3. Social Variables

Social variables include socioeconomic status, exposure to thin media messages, and receiving negative comments regarding body weight from peers. High social class (Gowers and Shore, 2001) and socioeconomic status including income, parental education and occupation have been signified to be associated with the importance of physical appearance and thinness, contributing to ED among females (Al-Subaie, 2000; Khawaja and Afifi-Soweid, 2004; Ho, Tai, Lee, Cheng, and Liow, 2006). Additionally, socioeconomic status has been documented to be associated with greater desire for thinness, dieting, binging, and vigorous exercise to control body weight in female college students (Drewnowski, Kurth, and Krahn, 1994).

The second social variable is peers reinforcement regarding socially esteemed body which has contributed to poor body image and ED in females. Peers have played an important role in modeling a variety of disordered eating behaviors such as dietary restraint, binge eating, self-induced vomiting, and preoccupation with body weight and shape (French et al., 1995; Littleton and Ollendick, 2003). However, peers relationships and the importance of thinness to peers have been indicated to be neither associated with weight concerns nor with ED in schoolgirls (Field, Camargo, Taylor, Berkey, Roberts, and Colditz, 2001). These findings were opposed by numerous studies which described that pressures from peers towards thinness have maintained the development of negative body image perception and ED because females seek to achieve a socially esteemed body to establish connection with, and to gain approval from peers (Levine et al., 1994; McCabe and Ricciardelli, 2001; Presnell et al., 2004). In line with this, Mousa and colleagues (2010) have reported that perceiving negative feedback regarding body weight from peers or friends have significantly increased the probability of ED by 1.4 folds ($p<0.01$).

The last social indicator that is documented to affect ED occurrence among females is Mass media. Messages from mass media have promoted a narrow standard of attractiveness and have often presented other potentially harmful messages as defining self-worth in terms of the individual appearance (Littleton and Ollendick, 2003). Several studies have stated that media messages have generated a clear image of the societal ideal for females and attributed to engaging in dieting, as well as developing weight and shape concerns (Field et al., 2001; McCabe and Ricciardelli, 2001; Eapen et al., 2006). Further, thin female models and celebrities are socially desirable; the worship and admiration of a celebrity with an unrealistic thin body shape has led to poor body image and ED in adolescent girls (Vandereycken, 2006). It has also been demonstrated that the frequency of reading fashion magazines was positively associated with dieting and exercising to lose weight or improve body shape (Field, Cheung, Wolf, Herzog, Gortmaker, and Colditz, 1999). A previous study, however verified that neither exposure to, nor perceived pressure to be thin from mass media has contributed to poor body image and exaggerated eating behaviors (Gibbs, 1986). Nevertheless, adolescent schoolgirls in Amman, Jordan who made efforts to look like females in the media as well as who exercised and/or went on a diet to lose weight because of a magazine article or picture were at higher risk to endorse ED by 1.3 and 1.5 folds, respectively ($p \leq 0.001$) (Mousa et al., 2010).

4. Cultural Differences and Eating Disorders

Eating disorders are considered as a result of "westernization" and modernization of the society (Lester, 2004). In the Western society, females in general and adolescent girls in particular have often engaged in ED (Al-Subaie, 2000; Jones et al., 2001). These abnormal behaviors resulted from the stringent Western standards of beauty, leading to preoccupation with thinness and body dissatisfaction (Abdollahi and Mann, 2001; Lester, 2004). Thus, ED are perceived as Western culture-bound syndromes (Keel and Klump, 2003) associated with sociocultural influences that exert pressures on young females to conform to, and to internalize body ideals of the Western society (Dolan, 1991; Lake et al., 2000).

On the other hand, a study that investigated the impact of Western culture on ED occurrence among Iranian women living in Iran and in the United States of America has reported that neither exposure to Western media nor acculturation to Western norms appeared to be related to symptoms of disordered eating behavior and body image concerns (Abdollahi and Mann, 2001). Conversely, Australian female college students had greater body image distortion than Chinese ones, who consist of traditional and acculturated Chinese subgroups. There was no significant difference between the Australian and Chinese females regarding their attitudes towards eating. Nevertheless, the effect of cultural conflict has significantly influenced eating attitudes and body image of the traditional Chinese subgroup, but not the Western acculturated subgroup (Lake et al., 2000). This has been ascribed to intra-familial conflict experienced by non-Western females, when their attempts to emulate the relative independence of their Western peers is contradicted by the cultural, religious as well as gender-based norms and values held by their families (Hill and Bhatti, 1995; Lake et al., 2000). Hence, a cultural clash between a traditional culture and adopted Westernized culture heightened the risk for eating and body image disturbances in females (Soh, Touyz, and Surgenor, 2006).

Eating disorders have been conceptualized as illnesses of Western industrialized countries (Le Grange, Telch, and Tibbs, 1998) in which being slim and fit is highly rated because it symbolizes certain notions such as social acceptance, competitiveness, and social class. Nonetheless, non-Western populations including Arab populations have been found to place value on plumpness; a sign of beauty, fertility, and good health (Shuriquie, 1999; Abdollahi and Mann, 2001). Many developing countries, however, have recently undergone rapid social and economic changes, leading to a wide spread adoption of Western styles, habits and attitudes. Cultural changes in non-Western developing populations have involved identification with Western norms of body shape and weight contributing to ED development (Mumford, Whitehouse, and Choudry, 1992; Latzer, Tzischinsky, and Asaiza, 2007). For instance, several studies have verified that ED are emerging in developing countries including Pakistan (Mumford et al., 1992) and Iran (Nobakht and Dezhkam, 2000). Eating problems have also been observed in Arab countries such as Jordan (33.4%) (Mousa et al., 2010), Oman (29.4%) (Eapen et al., 2006), United Arab Emirates (23.4%), and Saudi Arabia (19.6%) (Al-Subaie, Al-Shammari, Bamgbove, Al-Sabhan, Al-Shehri, and Bannah, 1996). Arab Females, therefore, might be acquiring a conflict between Western and Arabic norms of body image (i.e.; causing body image dissatisfaction) attributing to ED occurrence in the Arabic society (Shuriquie, 1999). Moreover, it has been proposed that Western standards of beauty have contributed for the negative perception of body image in non-Western and Arabic females through the accessibility of, and the readiness to assimilate

Western values through mass media (Mousa, Mashal, Al-Domi, and Jibril, 2010).

5. Athletes and Eating Disorders

A final interesting variable is the eating behavior of female athletes. An earlier study demonstrated that dancers and skaters were leaner, more perfectionist and exhibited more restraint eating, binging or purging behaviors than swimmers and non-athletes, dancers in particular exhibited greater eating pathology than skaters (Brooks-Gunn, Burrow, and Warren, 1988). This is explained by that competitive pressures for exceptional performance have enhanced preexisting socio-cultural pressures for females to be thin, predisposing athletes to eating problems (Fulkerson, Keel, Leon, and Dorr, 1999; Anderson et al., 2000). Furthermore, ED in athletes are likely to be associated with sports endeavor dimensions including: the preferred body size, personality characteristics as perfectionism, the type of sport as aesthetics, and the need for high achievement. These dimensions were suggested to increase the risk of ED occurrence in athletic females (Brooks-Gunn et al., 1988).

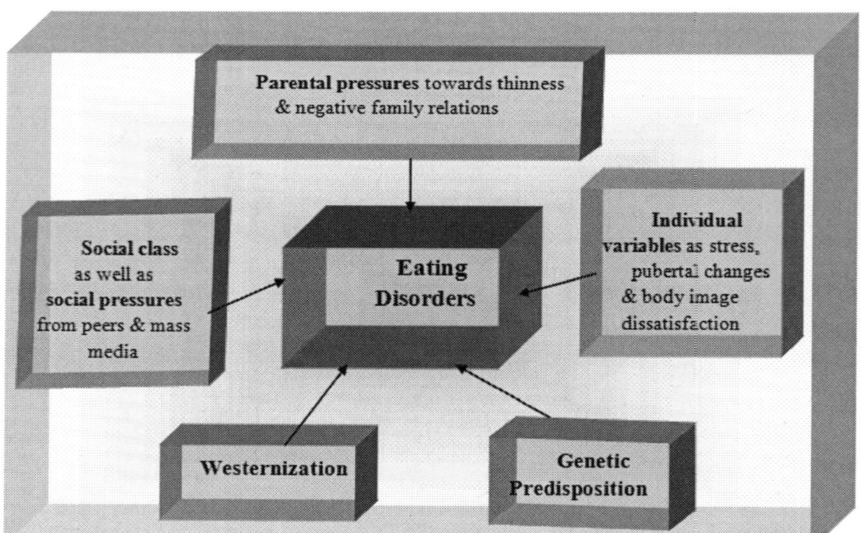

Figure 1. Risk Factors of Eating Disorders in Females.

Overall, the current paper concluded that genetic predisposition, individual variables such as stress, pubertal timing in adolescent girls and negative body image, as well as parental pressures towards thinness and negative family relations have influenced ED occurrence in females. Similarly, westernization and social variables including socioeconomic status, exposure to thin media messages, and pressure from peers have predisposed ED in females as it is summarized in Figure (1).

Therefore, identification of risk factors of eating disturbances and vulnerable groups is considered an effective intervention before developing ED. This is important to prevent or at least control the incidence of the health hazards related to ED such as anemia, amenorrhea and osteopenia (Fairburn and Harrison, 2003). Future research, hence, should focus on conducting epidemiologic studies as well as developing interventional studies to help in managing ED occurrence among females.

REFERENCES

Abdollahi, P., and Mann, T. (2001). Eating disorders symptoms and body image concerns in Iran: Comparisons between Iranian women in Iran and in America. *International Journal of Eating Disorders*, 30, 259-268.

Abraham, S. (2003). Dieting, body weight, body image, and self-esteem in young women: Doctors' dilemmas. *Medical Journal of Australia*, 178, 607-611.

Abraham, S., and O'Dea, J. (2001). Body mass index, menarche, and perception of dieting among peripubertal adolescent females. *International Journal of Eating Disorders*, 29, 23-28.

Afifi-Soweid, R.A., Kteily, M.B., and Shediac-Rizkallah, M.C. (2002). Preoccupation with weight and disordered eating behaviors of entering students at a university in Lebanon. *International Journal of Eating Disorders*, 32, 52-57.

Al-Subaie, A. (2000). Some correlates of dieting behavior in Saudi schoolgirls. *International Journal of Eating Disorders*, *28*, 242-246.

Al-Subaie, A., Al-Shammari, S., Bamgbove, E., Al-Sabhan, K., Al-Shehri, S., and Bannah, A. (1996). Validity of the Arabic version of the eating attitude test. *International Journal of Eating Disorders*, 20, 321-324.

Anderson, S., Griesemer, B., Johnson, M., Martin, T., McLain, L., Rowland, T., and Small, E. (2000). Medical Concerns in female athletes. *Pediatrics*, 106, 610-613.

Archibald, A., Graber, J., and Brooks-Gunn, J. (1999). Associations among parent-adolescent relationships, pubertal growth, dieting, and body image in young adolescent girls: A short-term longitudinal study. *Journal of Research on adolescence*, 9, 395-415.

As'ad, L. (1999). *Some anthropometric measurements as indicators for the nutritional status and menses for a group of girls aged (10-15) years.* Unpublished Master Dissertation, University of Jordan, Amman, Jordan.

Brooks-Gunn, J., Burrow, C., and Warren, M. (1988). Attitudes toward eating and body weight in different groups of female adolescent athletes. *International Journal of Eating Disorders*, 7, 749-757.

Dolan, B. (1991). Cross-cultural aspects of anorexia nervosa and bulimia: A review. *International Journal of Eating Disorders*, 10, 67-78.

Drewnowski, A., Kurth, C., and Krahn, D. (1994). Body weight and dieting in adolescence: Impact of socioeconomic status. *International Journal of Eating Disorders*, 16, 61-65.

Eapen, V., Mabrouk, A-A., and Bin-Othman, S. (2006). Disordered eating attitudes and sympto-matology among adolescent girls in the United Arab Emirates. *Eating Behaviors*, 7, 53-60.

Fairburn, C., and Harrison, P. (2003). Eating disorders. *The Lancet*, 361, 407-416.

Field, A., Camargo, C., Taylor, B., Berkey, C., Roberts, S., and Colditz, G. (2001). Peer, parent, and media influences on the development of weight concerns and frequent dieting among preadolescent and adolescent girls and boys. *Pediatrics*, 107, 54-60.

Field, A., Cheung, L., Wolf, A., Herzog, D., Gortmaker, S., and Colditz, G. (1999). Exposure to the mass media and weight concerns among girls. *Pediatrics*, 103, e36-e40.

French, S.A., Story, M., Downes, B., Resnick, M.D., and Blum, R.W. (1995). Frequent dieting among adolescents: Psychosocial and health behavior correlates. *American Journal of Public Health*, 85, 695-701.

Fulkerson, J., Keel, P., Leon, G., and Dorr, T. (1999). Eating-disordered behaviors and personality characteristics of high school athletes and nonathletes. *International Journal of Eating Disorders*, 26, 73-79.

Gibbs, R. (1986). Social factors in exaggerated eating behavior among high school students. *International Journal of Eating Disorders*, 5, 1103-1107.

Gowers, S., and Shore, A. (2001). Development of weight and shape concerns in the aetiology of eating disorders. *British Journal of Psychiatry*, 179, 236-242.

Hewitt, P., Flett, G., and Ediger, E. (1995). Perfectionism traits and perfectionistic self-presentation in eating disorder attitudes, characteristics, and symptoms. *International Journal of Eating Disorders*, 18, 317-326.

Hill, A., and Bhatti, R. (1995). Body shape perception and dieting in preadolescent British Asian girls: Links with eating disorders. *International Journal of Eating Disorders*, 17, 175-183.

Ho, T.F., Tai, B.C., Lee, E.L., Cheng, S., and Liow, P.H. (2006). Prevalence and profile of females at risk of eating disorders in Singapore. *Singapore Medical Journal*, 47, 499-503.

Jones, J.M., Bennett, S., Olmsted, M.P., Lawson, M.L., and Rodin, G. (2001). Disordered eating attitudes and behaviors in teenaged girls: A school-based study. *Canadian Medical Association Journal*, 165, 547-552.

Keel, P., and Klump, K. (2003). Are eating disorders culture-bound syndromes? Implications for conceptualizing their etiology. *Psychological Bulletin*, 129, 747-769.

Khawaja, M., and Afifi-Soweid, R.A. (2004). Images of body weight among young men and women: Evidence from Beirut, Lebanon. *J Epidemiology and Community Health*, 58, 352-353.

Klein, D., and Walsh, B. (2004). Eating disorders: clinical features and pathophysiology. *Physiology and Behavior*, 81, 359-374.

Lake, A., Staiger, P., and Glowinski, H. (2000). Effect of Western culture on woman's attitudes to eating and perceptions of body shape. *International Journal of Eating Disorders*, 27, 83-89.

Latzer, Y., Tzischinsky, O., and Asaiza, F. (2007). Disordered eating related behaviors among Arab schoolgirls in Israel: An epidemiological study. *International Journal of Eating Disorders*, 40, 263-270.

Le Grange, D., Telch, C.F., and Tibbs, J. (1998). Eating attitudes and behaviors in 1,435 South African Caucasian and non-Caucasian college students. *American Journal of Psychiatry*, 155, 250-254.

Leon, G., Fulkerson, J., Perry, C., Keel, P., and Klump, K. (1999). Three to four year prospective evaluation of personality and behavioral risk factors for later disordered eating in adolescent girls and boys. *Journal of Youth and adolescence*, 28, 181, 196.

Lester, R. (2004). Commentary: Eating disorders and the problem of "Culture" in acculturation. *Culture, Medicine and Psychiatry*, 28, 607-615.

Levine, M., Smolak, L., Moodey, A., Shuman, M., and Hessen, L. (1994). Normative developmental challenges and dieting disturbances in middle school girls. *International Journal of Eating Disorders*, 15, 11-20.

Littleton, H., and Ollendick, T. (2003). Negative body image and disordered eating behavior in children and adolescents: What places youth at risk and how can these problems be prevented? *Clinical Child and Family Psychology Review*, 6, 51-66.

McCabe, M., and Ricciardelli, L. (2001). Parent, peer, and media influences on body image and strategies to both increase and decrease body size among adolescent boys and girls. *Adolescence*, *36*, 225-240.

Mousa, T., Al-Domi, H., Mashal, R., and Jibril, M. (2010). Eating disturbances among adolescent schoolgirls in Jordan. *Appetite,* 54, 196-201.

Mousa, T., Mashal, R., Al-Domi, H., and Jibril, M. (2010). Body image dissatisfaction among adolescent schoolgirls in Jordan. *Body Image: An International Journal of Research*, 7, 46-50

Mumford, D.B., Whitehouse, A.M., and Choudry, I.Y. (1992). Survey of eating disorders in English-medium schools in Lahore, Pakistan. *International Journal of Eating Disorders*, 11, 173-184.

Nobakht, M., and Dezhkam, M. (2000). An epidemiological study of eating disorders in Iran. *International Journal of Eating Disorders*, 28, 265-271.

O'Dea, J., 7 Abraham, S. (1999). Onset of disordered eating attitudes and behaviors in early adolescence: Interplay of pubertal status, gender, weight, and age. *Adolescence*, 34, 671-679.

Polivy, J., and Herman, P. (1999). Distress and eating: Why do dieters overeat? *International Journal of Eating Disorders*, 26, 153-164.

Presnell, K., Bearman, S., and Stice, E. (2004). Risk factors for body dissatisfaction in adolescent boys and girls: A prospective study. *International Journal of Eating Disorders*, 36, 389-401.

Schwartz, D., Phares, V., Tantieff-Dunn, S., and Thompson, J. (1999). Body image, psychological functioning, and parental feedback regarding physical appearance. *International Journal of Eating Disorders*, 25, 339-343.

Shuriquie, N. (1999). Eating disorders: A transcultural perspective. *Eastern Mediterranean Health Journal*, 5, 354-360.

Soh, N., Touyz, S., and Surgenor, L. (2006). Eating and body image disturbances across cultures: A review. *European Eating Disorders Review*, 14, 54-65.

Spear, B. (2002). Adolescent growth and development. *Journal of American medical Association*, 102, S23-S29.

Steiger, H., Stotlan, S., Trottier, J., and Ghadirian, A. (1996). Familial eating concerns and psychopathological traits: Causal implications of transgenerational effects. *International Journal of Eating Disorders*, 19, 147-157.

Steiger, H., Stotlan, S., Ghadirian, A., and Whitehead, V. (1995). Controlled study of eating concerns and psychopathological traits in relatives of eating-disordered probands: Do familial trait exist? *International Journal of Eating Disorders*, 18, 107-118.

Steinhausen, H-C., Gavez, S., and Metzke, C. (2005). Psychosocial correlates, outcome, and stability of abnormal adolescent eating behavior in community samples of young people. *International Journal of Eating Disorders*, 37, 119-126.

Strober, M., Lampert, C., Morrell, W., Burroughs, J., and Jacobs, C. (1990). A controlled family study of anorexia nervosa: Evidence of familial aggregation and lack of shared transmission with affective disorders. *International Journal of Eating Disorders*, 9, 239-253.

Sweeting, H., and West, P. (2002). Gender differences in weight related concerns in early to late adolescence. *J Epidemiology and Community Health*, 56, 700-701.

Vandereycken, W. (2006). Media influences and body dissatisfaction in young women. *Eating Disorders Review*, 17, 5.

Wade, T., Martin, N., and Tiggemann, M. (1998). Genetic and environmental risk factors for the weight and shape concerns characteristic of bulimia nervosa. *Psychological Medicine*, 28, 761-771.

Wertheim, E., Paxton, S., Maude, D., Szmuckler, G., Gibbons, K., and Hiller, L. (1992). Psychosocial predictors of weight loss behaviors and binge eating in adolescent girls and boys. *International Journal of Eating Disorders*, 12, 151-160.

In: Eating Disorders
Editor: C. M. Shapiro, pp. 155-165
ISBN 978-1-61209-746-6

Chapter 8

DISSOCIATION AND THE ESCAPE FROM AWARENESS OF APPEARANCE THREATS

Matthew Fuller-Tyszkiewicz and Alexander J. Mussap
School of Psychology, Deakin University
221 Burwood Highway, Melbourne, Victoria 3125

ABSTRACT

Although extant literature demonstrates a link between dissociation and disordered eating symptomatology, the nature of this relationship remains unclear. One prominent explanation is based on an 'escape from awareness' model of dissociation, in which binge eating reflects a maladaptive cognitive response to the appearance-threatening aspects of certain foods. This is typically conceptualized as an initial hyper-vigilance aimed at detecting a potential appearance threat – for example, an item of high calorie food identified by an individual who is preoccupied with her/his weight, currently dieting, and hungry – followed by a rapid cognitive disengagement from awareness of the identified threat. In this chapter, we review evidence for this two stage model in individuals with elevated levels of disordered eating symptomatology. In addition, we report on our own findings that suggest that dissociation in the context of food and bingeing may be more closely related to the initial hyper-vigilance stage of threat processing. This chapter concludes with recommendations for future research into the role of threat processing in binge eating.

INTRODUCTION

Dissociation refers to disturbances to the usual integration of key facets of one's identity (i.e., consciousness, memory, and behavioural control; American Psychiatric Association; APA, 2000). Clinical observations and correlational studies indicate that symptoms of dissociation, such as depersonalization, derealisation, and absorption, are over-represented in individuals diagnosed with an eating disorder (Chandarana and Malla, 1989; Katz and Gleaves, 1996; McCallum, Lock, Kulla, Rorty and Wetzel, 1992; Torem, 1986; 1990; Vanderlinden, Vandereycken, van Dyck and Vertommen, 1993), particularly those with bulimic symptoms (Beato, Cano and Belmonte, 2003; Demitrack, Putnam, Brewerton, Brandt and Gold, 1990; Everill, Waller and MacDonald, 1995; Goldner, Cockhill, Bakan and Birmingham, 1991; Groth-Marnat and Michel, 2000; McManus, 1995; Waller et al., 2003). Despite this accumulated evidence suggesting a link between dissociation and disordered eating symptoms, the nature of this relationship remains unclear.

The most commonly proposed 'traumatogenic' explanation is that the relationship is non-causal and indirect, and simply reflects a common origin for dissociation and disordered eating in abuse experienced in childhood (Beato et al., 2003). However, there are at least two reasons to suspect a causal relationship between dissociation and disordered eating. First, correlations between child abuse and disordered eating symptoms are neither strong nor consistent, and are weaker than the relationship between dissociation and disordered eating symptoms (Ball, Kenardy, and Lee, 1999). Second, the need to escape from awareness of abuse would predict widespread symptoms of psychological disturbance consistent with generalised dissociation. Contrary to this, case reports and correlational studies indicate that dissociative experiences may be relevant specifically to eating psychopathology (Chandarana and Malla, 1989; McCallum et al., 1992; Torem, 1986) and particularly to the frequency of binge-eating episodes (Everill et al., 1995; Fuller-Tyszkiewicz, 2008; Fuller-Tyszkiewicz and Mussap, 2008; Waller et al., 2001; although see Covino, Jimerson, Wolfe, Franko, and Frankel, 1994). This is consistent with dissociation influencing binge eating directly (Fuller-Tyszkiewicz and Mussap, 2009).

In this chapter, we review empirical support for an alternative and indirect causal explanation for the relationship between dissociation and disordered eating. According to the 'escape from awareness' explanation, binge eating is an indirect result of the application of dissociative cognitive strategies to appearance-threatening food stimuli (Everill and Waller, 1995; Heatherton and

Baumeister, 1991). A key advantage of the escape from awareness model over the traumatogenic explanation is that the former can incorporate the background conditions of childhood abuse as well as the findings that specific aspects of eating disorders are relevant to dissociation.

COGNITIVE PROCESSING OF THREAT STIMULI

Heatherton and Baumeister's (1991) escape from awareness model challenges the traditional view of cognitive distraction-based coping which suggests that an individual will shift her/his attention away from an identified threat stimulus. Heatherton and Baumeister (1991) proposed that some individuals may instead alleviate heightened negative emotions and cognitions by focusing on a different aspect of the threat. Central to the escape from awareness model is the notion that each stimulus (e.g. object, action, event, etc.) has multiple levels of meaning. It is argued that lower levels of awareness emphasize the concrete aspects of the stimulus, such as movement and sensation, which are tied to the immediate stimulus environment. In contrast, high levels emphasize the broader meaning of the stimulus, considering its relation to standards and norms, the implications and consequences (both personal and interpersonal). Because these high levels of awareness can involve consideration of consequences of an action as well as comparison with societal norms and personal expectations, it is thought that engagement in this level of awareness is important for maintaining behavioural control, including control over eating (Everill and Waller, 1995; Heatherton and Baumeister, 1991).

Reports of the phenomenological experience of binge-eaters are consistent with key elements of the escape from awareness model. It has been demonstrated that:

i) negative affect is highest on days when eating disordered individuals binge eat (Crowther, Sanffner, Bonifazi and Shepherd, 2001)
ii) there is a steady increase in negative affect prior to a binge episode (Cooper et al., 1988; Davis, Freeman, and Garner, 1988), and
iii) negative affect decreases during and after a binge episode (Lingswiler, Crowther, and Stephens, 1989; Tachi, Murakami, Murotsu, and Washizuka, 2001). Moreover, binge eaters report feelings of loss of control over eating, experience displacement of time and insensitivity to satiety cues, and have difficulty recalling

what and how much they ate during the binge the episode (Elmore and De Castro, 1990; Heilbrun and Worobow, 1991; Johnson and Larson, 1982; Polivy, 1976).

Everill and Waller (1995) suggest that these phenomenological experiences are reminiscent of dissociative processes, and that dissociation may thus be the underlying mechanism by which individuals escape from awareness. Specifically, an individual may attempt to minimize the psychological impact of a threatening stimulus by cognitively suppressing the negative aspects of the stimulus, thereby achieving a temporary reduction in negative arousal. Waller, Quinton and Watson (1995) suggest that this is accomplished in two distinct and sequential stages: an initial hyper-vigilance designed to facilitate identification of the threats, followed by an attentional shift away from the identified threat.

Empirical Evidence for Two-Stage Threat Processing Model

Experimental investigations of threat-induced cognitive avoidance have typically involved simple word-based tasks in which individuals are required to engage with threat words (e.g., 'lonely') in order to successfully complete the task. For instance, in a modified version of the Stroop Interference task (Meyer and Waller, 2000; Waller, Watkins, Shuck, and McManus, 1996), participants are asked to identify the colour of a presented word – some of which are threat words. In this and similar tasks (e.g., anagram solving and word search exercises), slower reaction times are thought to reflect interference due to cognitive suppression of the presented word. Results from these studies have generally shown that individuals with a diagnosis of bulimia nervosa or with elevated levels of bulimic symptomatology are slower than controls in these tasks (McManus, Waller, and Chadwick, 1996; Meyer et al., 2005; Waller and Mijatovich, 1998; Waller et al., 1995; Waller et al., 1996; although see Mountford, Waller, Watson, and Scragg, 2004; Seddon and Waller, 2000; Waller and Meyer, 1997). Furthermore, experimental exposure to threatening stimuli has been shown to elicit dissociative symptoms and increased food consumption in individuals with heightened disordered eating symptoms, consistent with cognitive models linking suppression to binge eating (Hallings-Pott, Waller, Watson, and Scragg, 2005; Meyer and Waller, 1999; Waller and Barter, 2005; Waller and Mijatovich, 1998).

Unfortunately interpretation of these findings is complicated by several methodological issues. First, several researchers (e.g., Amir, Elias, Klumpp, and Przeworski, 2003; Buckner, Maner, and Schmidt, 2010; Koster, Crombez, Verschuere, and De Houwer, 2004) argue that the results of reaction-based tasks are ambiguous as it is unclear whether the reaction time data reflect increased attention to the threat stimuli (and, hence, difficulty *disengaging* from this in order to complete the task) or cognitive disengagement from the task (and hence evidence of the cognitive avoidance hypothesized). Meyer, Waller, and Watson (2000) have raised a similar concern that these tasks may be inadvertently accessing the hyper-vigilance stage of threat processing rather than the suppression phase. They varied the interval between initial display of a target stimulus (threat, positive, or neutral word) and subsequent word search task, finding that the interference effect occurred when the interval was larger than 1500 ms. Thus, prior inconsistencies may be, at least in part, attributable to comparison of results across studies which have accessed different aspects of the threat processing.

Due to ethical considerations, this previous research has also relied extensively on symbolic representations of threats rather than threats per se. These representations, usually in the form of words, have limited ecological validity and are of questionable salience to individuals (Stormark and Torkildsen, 2004). Furthermore, previous studies have employed generic threat cues rather than cues that are relevant to the food and appearance concerns that characterise individuals with an eating disorder (APA, 2000). Given that the general threat processing model is likely to generalize beyond eating disordered populations, a more robust test of threat processing relevant to disordered eating might involve use an ambiguous threat; that is, a stimulus which is threatening for the target group, but not for others. Heatherton and Baumeister (1991) suggest that individuals utilise escape from awareness strategies to suppress negative thoughts and emotions which, they argue, are often self-directed. As ED individuals are preoccupied with food and appearance, it is reasonable to assume that many of these (self-directed) thoughts they seek to escape result from consideration of food and its effects on appearance. Food is a particularly salient threat because individuals with disordered eating symptoms have conflicting feelings towards it.

OUR STUDY

In an attempt to address the limitations of prior research, Fuller-Tyszkiewicz (2008) tracked processing of food-related words immediately prior to and following actual presentation of a tray containing tempting but appearance threatening food items (pastries). Three categories of words were used, representing three characteristics of an individual's evaluation of, and reaction to food: the aesthetic properties (e.g., 'sweet'), appearance-threatening aspects of food (e.g., 'obese'), and compensatory/purgative responses to food (e.g., 'exercise'). Attentional bias towards the threatening aspects of the food cue was evaluated by measuring reaction times (RTs) for making 'good/bad' judgments of these words. To rule out the possibility that RTs for the appearance-threatening aspects of food reflect cognitive suppression, recall of the three word types were compared pre- and post-exposure to the pastries.

The findings of this study were inconsistent with the notion that the dissociative mechanism operates by suppressing awareness of the threatening aspects of food. First, dissociative symptoms were unrelated to pre- or post-exposure RTs for appearance-threatening words. Second, dissociation was unrelated to recall of appearance-threatening words at either time point. Fuller-Tyszkiewicz explored the possibility that the pattern was obscured by assuming that the relationship between dissociative symptoms and RTs would hold for all individuals regardless of their level of disordered eating symptomatology. Reasoning that the relationship between dissociation and RTs for appearance-threat words may only occur for individuals with heightened appearance concerns, the extent to which the interaction between appearance concerns and dissociative symptoms was predictive of RTs was tested. Interestingly, while this interaction term was unrelated to pre-exposure RTs, it was related to change in RTs for appearance-threatening words from pre- to post-exposure. Heightened appearance concerns coupled with the tendency to dissociate resulted in relatively faster post-exposure RTs for classifying appearance-threatening words as 'bad' versus 'good'. Importantly, the interaction term did not reliably predict change in reaction time for either the aesthetic or the compensatory aspects of food, suggesting that the moderating influence of dissociation is restricted to the personally threatening aspects of the food cue (i.e., appearance threats). Additionally, accuracy of classifying words as 'good' or 'bad' was unrelated to dissociation or appearance concerns, ruling out the possibility that individuals with heightened symptoms simply responded quickly (and without engaging the stimulus) in order to escape the threat.

CONCLUSION

Collectively, these findings suggest that the relevance of dissociation to food and eating behaviours is consistent with an escape from awareness model. However, unlike Everill and Waller's (1995) assertion that dissociation is responsible for the cognitive suppression phase of threat processing, our findings instead/also implicate dissociation in the prior, threat detection phase. Nijenhuis, Spinhoven, van Dyck, van der Hart, and Vanderlinden (1998) argue that dissociation may serve as a survival function by providing earlier detection of threat and thus affording an individual more time to effectively deal with the threat.

Due to the aforementioned limitations inherent in research of this sort, it remains unclear what happens after a threat is identified. Given that the task used by Fuller-Tyszkiewicz (2008) required participants to pay attention to the semantic meaning of the presented stimuli, is perhaps not surprising that a suppression effect for the appearance-threatening words was not found. And, as mentioned above, other studies have found a negative relationship between RTs and disordered eating symptomatology which could be interpreted as cognitive avoidance or difficulty disengaging from the threat.

Clearly, more research is needed to disambiguate this effect. For example, the eye tracking paradigm, which has recently been used to evaluate difficulty disengaging in populations of individuals with an anxiety disorder (e.g., Buckner et al., 2010), may better inform our understanding of the second phase of the threat processing (namely, the cognitive suppression stage).

ACKNOWLEDGMENTS

This review paper was supported by a grant from the Australian Research Council (DP0556370).

REFERENCES

American Psychiatric Association. (2000). *Diagnostic and statistical manual of mental disorders* (4th ed. rev.). Washington, DC.

Amir, N., Elias, J., Klumpp, H., and Przeworski, A. (2003). Attentional bias to threat in social phobia: Facilitated processing of threat or difficulty disengaging attention from threat? *Behaviour Research and Therapy, 41*, 1325-1335.

Ball, K., Kenardy, J., and Lee, C. (1999). Relationships between disordered eating and unwanted sexual experiences: A review. *Australian Psychologist, 34*, 166-176.

Beato, L., Cano, T.R., and Belmonte, A. (2003). Relationship of dissociative experiences to body shape concerns in eating disorders. *European Eating Disorders Review, 11*, 38-45.

Buckner, J.D., Maner, J.K., and Schmidt, N.B. (2010). Difficulty disengaging attention from social threat in social anxiety. *Cognitive Therapy Research, 34*, 99-105.

Chandarana, P.C., and Malla, A. (1989). Bulimia and dissociative states: A case report. *Canadian Journal of Psychiatry, 34,* 137-139.

Cooper, J.L., Morrison, T.L., Bigman, O.L., Abramowitz, S.I., Levin, S., and Krener, P. (1988). Mood changes and affective disorder in the bulimic binge-purge cycle. *International Journal of Eating Disorders, 7,* 469-474.

Covino, N.A., Jimerson, D.C., Wolfe, B.E., Franko, D.L., and Frankel, F.H. (1994). Hypnotizability, dissociation, and bulimia nervosa. *Journal of Abnormal Psychology, 103*, 455-459.

Crowther, J.H., Sanffner, J., Bonifazi, D.Z., and Shepherd, K.L. (2001). The role of daily hassles in binge eating. *International Journal of Eating Disorders, 29*, 449-454.

Davis, R., Freeman, R.J., and Garner, D.M. (1988). A naturalistic investigation of eating behaviour in bulimia nervosa. *Journal of Consulting and Clinical Psychology, 56(2),* 273-279.

Demitrack, M.A., Putnam, F.W., Brewerton, T.D., Brandt, H.A., et al. (1990). Relation of clinical variables to dissociative phenomena in eating disorders. *American Journal of Psychiatry, 147*, 1184-1188.

Elmore, D.K., and de Castro, J.M. (1990). Self-rated moods and hunger in relation to spontaneous eating behaviour in bulimics, recovered bulimics, and normals. *International Journal of Eating Disorders, 9*, 179-190.

Everill, J.T., and Waller, G. (1995). Dissociation and bulimia: Research and theory. *European Eating Disorders Review, 3*, 129-147.

Everill, J.T., Waller, G., and MacDonald, W. (1995). Dissociation in bulimic and non-eating-disordered women. *International Journal of Eating Disorders, 17*, 127-134.

Fuller-Tyszkiewicz, M. (2008). *On the relationship between dissociation and disordered eating*. Unpublished manuscript.

Fuller-Tyszkiewicz, M., and Mussap, A. (2008). The relationship between dissociation and binge eating. *Journal of Trauma and Dissociation, 9*, 445-462.

Fuller-Tyszkiewicz, M., and Mussap, A. (2009). Short communication on the relationship between dissociation and binge eating. In Chambers, Natalie (eds), *Binge eating: Psychological factors, symptoms, and treatment.* Nova Science Publishers, New York, N.Y.

Goldner, E.M., Cockhill, L.A., Bakan, R., and Birmingham, C.L. (1991). Dissociative experiences and eating disorders. *American Journal of Psychiatry, 148*, 1274-1275.

Groth-Marnat, G., and Michel, N. (2000). Dissociation, comorbidity of dissociative disorders, and childhood abuse in a community sample of women with current and past bulimia. *Social Behavior and Personality, 28*, 279-292.

Hallings-Pott, C., Waller, G., Watson, D., and Scragg, P. (2005). State dissociation in bulimic eating disorders: An experimental study. *International Journal of Eating Disorders, 38*, 37-41.

Heatherton, T.F., and Baumeister, R.F. (1991). Binge eating as an escape from self-awareness. *Psychological Bulletin, 110*, 86-108.

Heilbrun, A.B., and Worobow, A.L. (1991). Attention and disordered eating behaviour: 1. Disattention to satiety cues as a risk factor in the development of bulimia. *Journal of Clinical Psychology, 47*, 3-9.

Johnson, C.L., and Larson, R. (1982). Bulimia: An analysis of moods and behaviour. *Psychosomatic Medicine, 44*, 341-351.

Katz, B.E., and Gleaves, D.H. (1996). Dissociative symptoms among patients with eating disorders: Associated feature or artefact of a comorbid dissociative disorder? *Dissociation: Progress in the Dissociative Disorders, 9*, 28-36.

Koster, E.H.W., Crombez, G., Verschuere, B., and De Houwer, J. (2004). Selective attention to threat in the dot probe paradigm: Differentiating vigilance and difficulty to disengage. *Behaviour Research and Therapy, 42*, 1183-1192.

Lingswiler, V.M., Crowther, J.H., and Stephens, M.A. (1989). Affective and cognitive antecedents to eating episodes in bulimia and binge eating. *International Journal of Eating Disorders, 8*, 533-539.

McCallum, K.E., Lock, J., Kulla, M., Rorty, M., and Wetzel, R.D. (1992). Dissociative symptoms and disorders in patients with eating disorders. *Dissociation: Progress in the Dissociative Disorders, 5,* 227-235.

McManus, F. (1995). Dissociation and the severity of bulimic psychopathology among eating-disordered and non-eating-disordered women. *European Eating Disorders Review, 3*, 185-195.

McManus, F., Waller, G., and Chadwick, P. (1996). Biases in the processing of different forms of threat in bulimic and comparison women. *Journal of Nervous and Mental Disease, 184*, 547-554.

Meyer, C., Serpell, L., Waller, G., Murphy, F., Treasure, J., and Leung, N. (2005). Cognitive avoidance in the strategic processing of ego threats among eating-disordered patients. *International Journal of Eating Disorders, 38,* 30-36.

Meyer, C., and Waller, G. (1999). The impact of emotion upon eating behaviour: The role of subliminal visual processing of threat cues. *International Journal of Eating Disorders, 25,* 319-326.

Meyer, C., Waller, G., and Watson, D. (2000). Cognitive avoidance and bulimic psychopathology: The relevance of temporal factors in a nonclinical population. *International Journal of Eating Disorders, 27,* 405-410.

Meyer, C., and Waller, G. (2000). Subliminal activation of abandonment- and eating-related schemata: Relationship with eating disordered attitudes in a nonclinical population. *International Journal of Eating Disorders, 27,* 328-334.

Mountford, V., Waller, G., Watson, D., and Scragg, P. (2004). An experimental analysis of the role of schema compensation in anorexia nervosa. *Eating Behaviours, 5,* 223-230.

Nijenhuis, E.R.S., Spinhoven, P., van Dyck, R., van der Hart, O., and Vanderlinden, J. (1998). Degree of somatoform and psychological dissociation in dissociative disorder is correlated with reported trauma. *Journal of Traumatic Stress, 11,* 711-730.

Polivy, J. (1976). Perception of calories and regulation of intake in restrained and unrestrained subjects. *Addictive Behaviors, 1*, 237-243.

Seddon, K., and Waller, G. (2000). Emotional processing and bulimic psychopathology: Age as a factor among nonclinical women. *International Journal of Eating Disorders, 28*, 364-369.

Stormark, K.M., and Torkildsen, O. (2004). Selective processing of linguistic and pictorial food stimuli in females with anorexia and bulimia nervosa. *Eating Behaviours, 5,* 27-33.

Tachi, T., Murakami, K., Murotsu, K., and Washizuka, T. (2001). Affective states associated with bingeing and purging behaviours in Japanese patients with bulimia nervosa. *British Journal of Medical Psychology, 74,* 487-496.

Torem, M.S. (1986). Dissociative states presenting as an eating disorder. *American Journal of Clinical Hypnosis, 29,* 137-142.

Torem, M.S. (1990). Covert multiple personality underlying eating disorders. *American Journal of Psychotherapy, 44,* 357-368.

Vanderlinden, J., Vandereycken, W., van Dyck, R., and Vertommen, H. (1993). Dissociative experiences and trauma in eating disorders. *International Journal of Eating Disorders, 13*, 187-193.

Waller, G., Babbs, M., Milligan, R., Meyer, C., Ohanian, V., and Leung, N. (2003). Anger and core beliefs in the eating disorders. *International Journal of Eating Disorders, 34*, 118-124.

Waller, G., and Barter, G. (2005). The impact of subliminal abandonment and unification cues on eating behaviour. *International Journal of Eating Disorders, 37*, 156-160.

Waller, G., and Meyer, C. (1997). Cognitive avoidance of threat cues: Association with Eating Disorder Inventory scores among a non-eating-disordered population. *International Journal of Eating Disorders, 22,* 299-308.

Waller, G., and Mijatovich, S. (1998). Preconscious processing of threat cues: Impact on eating among women with unhealthy eating attitudes. *International Journal of Eating Disorders, 24,* 83-89.

Waller, G., Ohanian, V., Meyer, C., Everill, J., and Rouse, H. (2001). The utility of dimensional and categorical approaches to understanding dissociation in the eating disorders. *British Journal of Clinical Psychology, 40*, 387-397.

Waller, G., Quinton, S., and Watson, D. (1995). Processing of threat-related information by women with bulimic eating attitudes. *International Journal of Eating Disorders, 18,* 189-193.

Waller, G., Watkins, H., Shuck, V. and McManus, F. (1996). Bulimic psychopathology and attentional biases to ego threats among non-eating-disordered women. *International Journal of Eating Disorders, 20,* 169-176.

In: Eating Disorders
Editor: C. M. Shapiro, pp. 167-175
ISBN 978-1-61209-746-6

Chapter 9

Commentary: Motivation for Exercise in Eating Disorders: New Insight Gives Relevance for the Diagnostic Criteria

S. Bratland-Sanda[*1]

Abstract

Exercise is defined as one of several possible weight compensatory behaviors in the DSM-IV criteria for bulimia nervosa. However, little knowledge exists about other reasons for exercise among patients with eating disorders.

Aim: To review the literature about reasons for exercise among patients with eating disorders compared to non-clinical controls.

Methods: Literature search in PubMed and ISI Web of Science was carried out. To be included the studies had to involve patients diagnosed with DSM-IV anorexia nervosa, bulimia nervosa or eating disorders not specified.

Results: A total of six papers met the inclusion criteria. Of these, four had examined a wider range of motives for exercise than just weight and shape. One paper found weight and shape as a more important reason for exercise among patients than controls. Three papers found exercise for

[*] Correspondence: solfrid.bratland-sanda@hit.no
[1] Department of sport science and outdoor life studies, Telemark University College, Bo Norway Institute of research, Modum Bad Psychiatric Center, Vikersund Norway

regulation of affects and mood as more important among the patients than the controls. Furthermore, one study found exercise for affect regulation, but not weight regulation, as a more important motive among the excessive exercising patients compared to the non-excessive exercisers.

Conclusion: Exercise in eating disorders is not necessarily all about the body weight, especially not among patients with longstanding eating disorders. These findings suggest that the DMS-IV criteria should emphasize assessment of all types of exercise among the patients, regardless of the exercise motives.

INTRODUCTION

Excessive exercise is a phenomenon that has been shown across all three DSM-IV diagnoses for eating disorders (Solenberger, 2001). Studies have found the prevalence of excessive exercise to range from 40 – 80% for anorexia nervosa, 21 – 57% for bulimia nervosa and 21 – 50% for eating disorders not otherwise specified (Davis, et al., 1997; Shroff, et al., 2006; Solenberger, 2001). The prevalence seems to be higher in the acute phase of the disorder (Davis, et al., 1997). Individuals with eating disorders who are exercising excessively have shown more severe eating disorder psychopathology, higher frequency of acute and overuse exercise related injuries, and higher frequency of comorbidity such as depression or anxiety (D. Bamber, Cockerill, and Carroll, 2000; D. J. Bamber, Cockerill, Rodgers, and Carroll, 2003; Brewerton, Stellefson, Hibbs, Hodges, and Cochrane, 1995; Klein, et al., 2004; Symons Downs and Hauseblas, 2003). The excessive exercising individuals are furthermore characterized with longer duration of treatment, poorer outcome of treatment and higher risk of relapse (Kaye, Gwirtsman, George, Ebert, and Petersen, 1986; Strober, Freeman, and Morrell, 1997).

In the diagnostic criteria, excessive exercise is defined and recognized as one of several possible weight compensatory behaviors in the DSM-IV criteria for bulimia nervosa, and as one of the symptoms of anorexia nervosa in the ICD-10 (American Psychiatric, 1994; Who, 1993). The weight and appearance related motives for exercise are common also among individuals without eating disorders (Furnham, Badmin, and Sneade, 2002; Mond and Calogero, 2009). The exercise motives can be intrinsic (i.e. motivation that comes from inside oneself), extrinsic (i.e. external reward) or a combination of these. Examples of such motives can be health related, fitness related, socializing, well-being, and affect regulation (Cash, Novy, and Grant, 1994; Plonczynski, 2000).

Affect regulation can be defined as the process of increasing positive and/or decreasing negative affects (Larsen, Prizmic, Baumeister, and Vohs, 2004). Affects are defined as a set of bodily based reactions that evolve to respond to life events and to motivate and guide behavior (Tomkins, 1995). The basic affects are fear, disgust, anger, sadness and happiness, also referred to as sad, mad, glad and scared (McCullough, 2003). Exercise can be used to both activate positive affects and well-being, and suppress negative affects. Furthermore, studies have found moderate intensity exercise to be linked to positive affects, whereas vigorous intensity exercise or exercise in excessive amounts were associated with an increase in negative affects (Koltyn, Lynch, and Hill, 1998; Lind, Ekkekakis, and Vazou, 2008). The terms negative and positive affect regulation can be used in the meaning of regulation negative and positive affects, but it can also be an expression of maladaptive or preferable affect regulation strategies respectively (Fonagy, Gergely, Jurist, and Target, 2002). Mostly, exercise can be viewed as a positive affect regulation strategy, but in excessive amounts it becomes a maladaptive strategy.

In the normal population, the motives for exercise have been shown to be very complex, and it can vary over time. Among individuals with eating disorders, the clinical experience is that the exercise motives are solely weight and appearance related. However, it is interesting to examine the scientific knowledge about reasons for exercise among patients with eating disorders compared to non-clinical controls, and among the excessive compared to the non-excessive exercising patients.

Methods

A literature search in PubMed and ISI Web of Science was carried out. To be included, the studies had to involve patients or individuals diagnosed with DSM-IV anorexia nervosa, bulimia nervosa or eating disorders not otherwise specified. Furthermore, the study had to include data regarding exercise motivation. Search terms included *exercise, physical activity, motivation,* and *eating disorders*. The search gave a total of 89 hits; of these six matched the inclusion criteria (Boyd, Abraham, and Luscombe, 2007; Bratland-Sanda, et al., 2010a, 2010b; Mond and Calogero, 2009; Penas-Lledo, Vaz Leal, and Waller, 2002; Vansteelandt, Rijmen, Pieters, Probst, and Vanderlinden, 2007).

RESULTS

Differences between Individuals with and without Eating Disorders

Boyd et al. (2007) found no differences in perceived importance of exercise for weight loss among females with and without eating disorders. This was also found in a study by Bratland-Sanda et al.(2010a). Mond and Calogero (2009) found that exercise primarily for weight and shape related reasons were more common among females with eating disorders compared to the healthy controls. Bratland-Sanda et al. (2010a) found that exercise for health and fitness related reasons were less important, and exercise for regulation of negative affects was more important, in females with longstanding eating disorders compared to non-clinical age matched controls. This difference was not found in the studies by Boyd et al. (2007), and Mond and Calogero (2009). The inconsistency regarding exercise motivation between females with and without eating disorders can be due to differences in the different studies' clinical samples. It seems that weight and shape related reasons might be more important during the acute phase of an eating disorder, and that the importance of exercise as an affect regulation strategy is more important among individuals with a long illness duration.

Differences between Excessive and Non-Excessive Exercising Patients

Exercise dependence, which is characterized by uncontrollable excessive exercise behavior, includes symptoms such as withdrawal, continuance, reduction in other activities, and increased tolerance (Hausenblas and Symons Downs, 2002). One of the key features of this behavior is the experience of intense guilt when exercise cannot take place (Adkins and Keel, 2005; Mond, Hay, Rodgers, and Owen, 2006). When it comes to reported exercise motivation between excessive and non-excessive exercising individuals with eating disorders, three studies support the importance of affect regulation as a motive among the excessive exercisers (Bratland-Sanda, et al., 2010b; Penas-Lledo, et al., 2002; Vansteelandt, et al., 2007). None of these studies reported differences in importance of exercise for weight and appearance related reasons between the excessive and non-excessive exercisers.

Furthermore, Calogero and Pedrotty (2004) found reduction in compulsive exercise in patients following a specialized treatment program where healthy exercise was part of the treatment. Bratland-Sanda et al., (2010b) followed a group of adult female inpatients with longstanding eating disorders from admission to discharge. We found that reduced eating disorder psychopathology was correlated with reduction in exercise dependence and reduced importance of exercising as regulation strategy for negative affects. However, no correlation was observed between reduced eating disorder psychopathology and reduced importance of exercising for regulation of body weight.

Practical and Clinical Implications of the Findings

Exercise in eating disorders is not necessarily all about the body weight, especially not among patients with longstanding eating disorders. It is a problem that most of the published studies regarding motives for exercise among patients with eating disorders have only assessed weight and appearance related reasons. In that way, the studies are biased, and the studies by Peñas-Lledo et al., (2002), Boyd et al., (2007), Vansteelandt et al., (2007) and Bratland-Sanda et al., (2010a, 2010b) shows that there are other important aspects to the exercise motivation as well. Of these aspects, the affect regulation seems the most important one. Furthermore, exercise for body weight, shape and appearance related reasons are important for females regardless of the presence of an eating disorder, and regardless of the actual quantity of the exercise (i.e. the duration, intensity and frequency of the exercise). This indicates that the focus in the diagnostic criteria, especially DSM-IV, is somewhat misleading. Therefore, the excessive exercise should not be viewed solely as a weight compensatory behavior, but as a possible symptom of eating disorders regardless of the motivation behind. Furthermore, several studies have reported excessive exercise to be a common feature across the various eating disorder diagnoses (Bratland-Sanda, et al., 2010b; Davis, et al., 1997; Solenberger, 2001). Excessive exercise should therefore be included as a symptom in the DSM-IV diagnoses for anorexia nervosa, bulimia nervosa and eating disorders not otherwise specified, and in the ICD-10 diagnoses for anorexia nervosa, atypical anorexia nervosa, bulimia nervosa and atypical bulimia nervosa.

In the assessment of excessive exercise, it is important to include all features and aspects of the behavior. As of today, the instrument considered as gold standard for assessing eating disorders is the Eating Disorders Examination clinical interview. In this interview, all questions about exercise include only exercise to control weight and shape, or burn calories (Fairburn, Cooper, and Wilson, 1993). Because of the complexity of exercise motives among the individuals with eating disorders, quantity of exercise should be assessed regardless of the exercise motives. Furthermore, it is important to cover all aspects of the behavior, and therefore elements such as guilt when exercise cannot take place, withdrawal symptoms, tolerance and lack of control should also be assessed. Important questions to ask the individuals are:

- What type of exercise do you engage in?
- How hard or intense are your exercises (do you get sweaty, heavy breathing, can you have a conversation while you are exercising etc.)?
- How often do you exercise?
- For how long do your exercise sessions last?
- How long has this behavior been consistent?
- Why do you exercise?
- Are you able to skip your exercise?
- How do you feel when you cannot or do not exercise?
- What can you do instead of exercising?

CONCLUSION

Exercise, especially in excessive amounts, is a complex feature among individuals with eating disorders. Due to the seriousness of this behavior, it is important that it is given attention in assessment and treatment of the eating disorder. Because of the complexity of the exercise motives, excessive exercise should not only be viewed as a weight compensatory behavior. Furthermore, it is a feature seen across the various eating disorder diagnoses, and it should therefore be mentioned as a possible symptom within all these diagnoses. Proper screening of the quantity (e.g. duration, intensity, frequency) and quality (e.g. motives and attitudes) of the behavior is essential, and as of today the instruments for assessing exercise in eating disorders are inadequate. It is therefore recommended to assess all performed exercise regardless of the motives, and assess attitudes such as lack of control, withdrawal symptoms and feelings when exercise is not performed.

REFERENCES

Adkins, E. C., and Keel, P. K. (2005). Does "excessive" or "compulsive" best describe exercise as a symptom of bulimia nervosa? *Int.J Eat.Disord., 38*(1), 24-29.

American Psychiatric, A. (1994). *Diagnostic and Statistical Manual of Mental Disorders (DSM-IV).* Washington DC: APA.

Bamber, D., Cockerill, I. M., and Carroll, D. (2000). The pathological status of exercise dependence. *Br.J.Sports Med., 34*(2), 125-132.

Bamber, D. J., Cockerill, I. M., Rodgers, S., and Carroll, D. (2003). Diagnostic criteria for exercise dependence in women. *Br.J.Sports Med., 37*(5), 393-400.

Boyd, C., Abraham, S., and Luscombe, G. (2007). Exercise behaviours and feelings in eating disorder and non-eating disorder groups. *Eur Eat Disord Rev, 15*(2), 112-118.

Bratland-Sanda, S., Sundgot-Borgen, J., Ro, O., Rosenvinge, J. H., Hoffart, A., and Martinsen, E. W. (2010a). "I'm not physically active - I only go for walks": physical activity in patients with longstanding eating disorders. *Int J Eat Disord, 43*(1), 88-92.

Bratland-Sanda, S., Sundgot-Borgen, J., Ro, O., Rosenvinge, J. H., Hoffart, A., and Martinsen, E. W. (2010b). Physical activity and exercise dependence during inpatient treatment of longstanding eating disorders: an exploratory study of excessive and non-excessive exercisers. *Int J Eat Disord, 43*(3), 266-273.

Brewerton, T. D., Stellefson, E. J., Hibbs, N., Hodges, E. L., and Cochrane, C. E. (1995). Comparison of eating disorder patients with and without compulsive exercising. *Int.J.Eat.Disord., 17*(4), 413-416.

Calogero, R. M., and Pedrotty, K. N. (2004). The practice and process of healthy exercise: an investigation of the treatment of exercise abuse in women with eating disorders. *Eat Disord, 12*(4), 273-291.

Cash, T. F., Novy, P. L., and Grant, J. R. (1994). Why do women exercise? Factor analysis and further validation of the Reasons for Exercise Inventory. *Percept.Mot.Skills, 78*(2), 539-544.

Davis, C., Katzman, D. K., Kaptein, S., Kirsh, C., Brewer, H., Kalmbach, K., et al. (1997). The prevalence of high-level exercise in the eating disorders: etiological implications. *Compr.Psychiatry, 38*(6), 321-326.

Fairburn, C. G., Cooper, Z., and Wilson, G. T. (1993). The Eating Disorders Examination (12th ed.) *Binge eating: Nature, assessment and treatment* (pp. 317-360). London: Guilford.

Fonagy, P., Gergely, G., Jurist, E. L., and Target, M. (2002). *Affectregulation, Mentalization, and the Development of the Self.* New York: Other Press.

Furnham, A., Badmin, N., and Sneade, I. (2002). Body image dissatisfaction: gender differences in eating attitudes, self-esteem, and reasons for exercise. *J Psychol, 136*(6), 581-596.

Hausenblas, H. A., and Symons Downs, D. (2002). Exercise dependence: a systematic review. *Psychol Sports Exerc, 3*, 89-123.

Kaye, W. H., Gwirtsman, H., George, T., Ebert, M. H., and Petersen, R. (1986). Caloric consumtion and activity levels after weight recovery in anorexia nervosa: a prolonged delay in normalization. *Int.J.Eat.Disord., 5*(3), 489-502.

Klein, D. A., Bennett, A. S., Schebendach, J., Foltin, R. W., Devlin, M. J., and Walsh, B. T. (2004). Exercise "addiction" in anorexia nervosa: model development and pilot data. *CNS.Spectr., 9*(7), 531-537.

Koltyn, K. F., Lynch, N. A., and Hill, D. W. (1998). Psychological responses to brief exhaustive cycling exercise in the morning and the evening. *Int J Sport Psychol, 29*(2), 145-156.

Larsen, R. J., Prizmic, Z., Baumeister, R. F., and Vohs, K. D. (2004). Affect regulation *Handbook of self-regulation: research, theory, and application* (pp. 40-61). New York: The Guilford Press.

Lind, E., Ekkekakis, P., and Vazou, S. (2008). The affective impact of exercise intensity that slightly exceeds the preferred level: 'pain' for no additional 'gain'. *J Health Psychol, 13*(4), 464-468.

McCullough, L. (2003). *Treating Affect Phobia: A Manual for Short-Term Dynamic Psychotherapy*. New York: The Guilford Press.

Mond, J. M., and Calogero, R. M. (2009). Excessive exercise in eating disorder patients and in healthy women. *Aust.N.Z.J Psychiatry, 43*(3), 227-234.

Mond, J. M., Hay, P. J., Rodgers, B., and Owen, C. (2006). An update on the definition of "excessive exercise" in eating disorders research. *Int.J Eat.Disord., 39*(2), 147-153.

Penas-Lledo, E., Vaz Leal, F. J., and Waller, G. (2002). Excessive exercise in anorexia nervosa and bulimia nervosa: relation to eating characteristics and general psychopathology. *Int.J Eat.Disord., 31*(4), 370-375.

Plonczynski, D. (2000). Measurement of motivation for exercise. *Health.Ed.Res., 15*(6), 695-705.

Shroff, H., Reba, L., Thornton, L. M., Tozzi, F., Klump, K. L., Berrettini, W. H., et al. (2006). Features associated with excessive exercise in women with eating disorders. *Int.J Eat Disord, 39*(6), 454-461.

Solenberger, S. E. (2001). Exercise and eating disorders: a 3-year inpatient hospital record analysis. *Eat.Behav., 2*(2), 151-168.

Strober, M., Freeman, R., and Morrell, W. (1997). The long-term course of severe anorexia nervosa in adolescents: survival analysis of recovery, relapse, and outcome predictors over 10-15 years in a prospective study. *Int.J Eat Disord, 22*(4), 339-360.

Symons Downs, D., and Hauseblas, H. A. (2003). I cant stop: The relationship among exercise dependence symptoms, injury and illness behaviors, and motives for exercise continuance. *J Human Movement Stud, 45*, 359-375.

Tomkins, S. S. (1995). *Exploring affects.* Cambridge, UK: Cambridge University Press.

Vansteelandt, K., Rijmen, F., Pieters, G., Probst, M., and Vanderlinden, J. (2007). Drive for thinness, affect regulation and physical activity in eating disorders: a daily life study. *Behav Res Ther., 45*(8), 1717-1734.

Who (1993). *The ICD-10 classification of mental and behavioural disorders: diagnostic criteria for research.* Geneva: World Health Organization.

INDEX

A

Abraham, 45, 53, 78, 142, 143, 149, 152, 169, 173
abuse, 11, 65, 156, 157, 163, 173
academic success, 106
access, 45
accessibility, 147
accounting, 71, 110
acculturation, 146, 151
activity level, 174
adjustment, 26, 35, 93, 122
adolescent boys, 33, 152
adolescent female, 77, 79, 81, 149
adulthood, 6, 99, 107, 108
adults, 23, 24, 29, 90, 95, 97, 103, 109, 128, 129
advancement, 52
adverse effects, 9
aesthetic, 10, 73, 160
aesthetics, 148
aetiology, 67, 150
affective disorder, 153, 162
African Americans, 9
age, ix, 2, 6, 7, 11, 15, 23, 25, 49, 62, 63, 65, 66, 67, 68, 71, 73, 77, 81, 90, 106, 107, 111, 112, 120, 128, 129, 130, 131, 132, 133, 134, 152, 170
aggregation, 153
agonist, 48
agoraphobia, 60
alcohol abuse, 13
alcohol dependence, 23
alters, 57
amenorrhea, viii, x, 2, 6, 11, 23, 61, 63, 64, 65, 66, 68, 70, 72, 73, 74, 76, 77, 78, 80, 81, 141, 142, 149
American Psychiatric Association (APA), ix, 2, 5, 6, 1516, 22, 23, 27, 53, 57, 89, 94, 105, 106, 107, 121, 138, 156, 161, 162
amygdala, 42, 53
anemia, 12, 142, 149
anger, 169
antidepressant, 17, 22, 54
antidepressant medication, 17
anxiety, 12, 13, 15, 19, 21, 22, 23, 42, 44, 46, 47, 48, 49, 53, 57, 58, 106, 107, 161, 168
anxiety disorder, 13, 15, 23, 53, 57, 106, 161
appetite, 23, 59, 60, 64, 65
Arab countries, 147
arousal, 158
assessment, xi, 42, 51, 58, 59, 77, 94, 99, 121, 168, 172, 174
assets, 136
athletes, 10, 37, 73, 76, 80, 81, 148, 149, 150
Attention Deficit Hyperactivity Disorder (ADHD), 85, 86, 91, 95, 96, 101
attentional bias, 42, 54, 165
audit, 97

autism, ix, 83, 85, 89, 92, 93, 94, 95, 98, 99, 100, 101, 103
autonomy, 135
autosomal dominant, 87
aversion, 43, 48
avoidance, 25, 42, 45, 46, 48, 52, 65, 144, 158, 159, 161, 164, 165
awareness, x, 20, 24, 119, 155, 156, 157, 158, 159, 160, 161

B

barriers, 92
base, 136
behavior therapy, 38
behavioral aspects, 52
behavioral problems, 86
beneficial effect, 74
benefits, 18, 25, 73, 119, 121, 122
bias, 134, 160, 162
bingeing, x, 155, 165
blame, 24
bleeding, 75
blood, 11
blood pressure, 11
blueprint, 122
body composition, 77
body dissatisfaction, 8, 9, 10, 30, 31, 36, 95, 144, 146, 152, 153
body fat, 64, 66, 67, 143
body image, x, 14, 33, 35, 41, 42, 50, 51, 53, 58, 63, 84, 86, 87, 107, 141, 142, 143, 144, 145, 146, 147, 149, 150, 152
body mass index (BMI), x, 22, 63, 64, 65, 67, 68, 76, 90, 110, 112, 115, 127, 131, 132, 133, 134
body shape, vii, 3, 39, 40, 41, 51, 73, 143, 146, 147, 151, 162
body size, 41, 55, 58, 59, 148, 152
bonding, 92
bone, viii, 61, 62, 66, 67, 68, 69, 70, 71, 72, 73, 74, 76, 77, 78, 79, 80, 81, 82
bone form, 66, 67, 71
bone growth, 68
bone mass, viii, 61, 66, 67, 70, 72, 73, 74, 76, 77, 79, 81
bone resorption, 66, 72
bone volume, 68
bones, 72
borderline personality disorder, 137
brain, 7, 42, 47, 53, 54, 59
brain damage, 59
breathing, 172
bullying, 143
burn, 172

C

calcium, 62, 66, 67, 70, 74
calcium carbonate, 74
caloric intake, 51, 62, 64, 66, 67
caloric restriction, 65, 108
calorie, x, 72, 88, 96, 155
carbohydrate, 12, 38, 88
carbohydrate metabolism, 12
carbohydrates, 7
carboxyl, 67
cardiomyopathy, 29
cardiovascular disease, 122
caregivers, 92
case studies, 91, 99
case study, 27
Caucasian population, 132
Caucasians, 5
causal relationship, 12, 156
CDC, 120, 132
cerebral palsy, 85, 86, 87, 92, 100, 102
challenges, 28, 46, 151, 157
chemical, 7, 46
chemicals, 7
child abuse, 156
child development, 134
childhood, 33, 78, 84, 85, 98, 100, 143, 156, 157, 163
children, 11, 24, 28, 35, 53, 71, 73, 78, 80, 84, 86, 88, 89, 91, 92, 93, 94, 95, 96, 97, 98, 99, 100, 101, 102, 103, 133, 135, 143, 152
chromosome, 88
chronic diseases, 125

City, 39, 83
classification, 64, 78, 97, 102, 175
clients, 18
climate, 145
clinical application, 49
clinical psychology, 55
clinical trials, 71
CNS, 174
cognition, 89, 123
cognitive dimension, 49
cognitive level, 46
cognitive models, 158
cognitive process, 59
cognitive processing, 59
cognitive profile, 97
cognitive science, 55
cognitive therapy, 21, 27, 32, 33, 124
cognitive-behavioral therapy, 124
collaboration, 132
collagen, 67
college campuses, 119
college students, ix, 26, 105, 106, 108, 109, 118, 119, 121, 122, 123, 124, 125, 145, 147, 151
colleges, ix, 106, 109, 112, 120
communication, 89, 145, 163
community, ix, 29, 34, 90, 97, 106, 110, 124, 153, 163
comorbidity, 28, 30, 32, 45, 84, 90, 101, 131, 134, 135, 163, 168
compensation, 56, 164
competitiveness, 147
compilation, vii
complement, 112
complete blood count, 28
complexity, 40, 172
compliance, 95
complications, 11, 12, 62, 108, 118
composition, 67
compulsive behavior, 93, 96
computer, 55
concordance, 142
conditioned response, 43
conditioned stimulus, 47
conflict, 147
consciousness, 156
consensus, 71
consent, 131
construct validity, 37
consumption, 4, 45, 88, 94, 108, 113, 118, 119, 158
contraceptives, 69, 71, 74
control group, x, 127, 131, 134
controlled trials, 128
controversial, viii, 9, 23, 61, 63, 69, 73, 74
coordination, 37
coronary heart disease, 123
correlation, 8, 66, 68, 71, 171
correlations, 44, 156
cortex, 53
cortical bone, 81
cortisol, 66, 67, 78, 108
cost, 14, 36, 37
counseling, 37, 124
counseling psychology, 37
critical value, 67
Croatia, 35
cross sectional study, 79
CTA, 48
cues, 40, 41, 42, 43, 46, 50, 55, 157, 159, 163, 164, 165
cultural clash, 147
culture, 9, 146, 151
cure, 22
cycles, 2
cycling, 174
cytokines, 67

D

dancers, 73, 74, 76, 80, 81, 148
database, 37
deficiencies, 71, 95
deficit, ix, 83, 85, 91, 95, 96, 97, 98, 99, 100, 102
deformation 51
dehydration, 84
denial, 2
Department of Education, 109, 125

Department of Health and Human Services, 125
depersonalization, 156
depression, 12, 15, 21, 22, 23, 30, 32, 33, 35, 66, 102, 106, 108, 143, 168
depressive symptoms, 12, 29, 33
dermatology, 29
desensitization, 51
detection, 13, 26, 46, 161
developing countries, 147
developmental disorder, 89, 94, 95, 99
Diagnostic and Statistical Manual of Mental Disorders, 2, 63, 138, 173
diagnostic criteria, vii, 1, 2, 6, 63, 68, 77, 89, 97, 107, 130, 168, 171, 175
diet, 9, 110, 113, 142, 146
diet pill, 110, 142
dieting, x, 6, 9, 14, 23, 24, 31, 49, 68, 72, 79, 108, 122, 142, 145, 146, 149, 150, 151, 155
disability, 90, 97
disclosure, 144
discrimination, 29, 88
discussion groups, 138
diseases, 84
disgust, 169
displacement, 157
dissatisfaction, x, 8, 9, 14, 86, 141, 142, 143, 147, 152, 174
dissociation, x, 155, 156, 158, 160, 161, 162, 163, 164, 165
dissociative disorders, 163
distortions, vii, 39, 40, 41, 42
distress, 5, 86, 91, 144
diversity, 119
dizygotic, 142
dizygotic twins, 142
dizziness, 23
doctors, 25
dopamine, 7, 45
dopaminergic, 28
dosage, 22, 69
double-blind trial, 27, 31
Down syndrome, 90, 99
drug abuse, 54
drugs, 13, 28, 71
dysphagia, 92, 95, 97
dysphoria, 87, 144

E

eating disturbances, x, 78, 141, 145, 149
economic change, 147
education, 125, 145
electrolyte, 11, 12
elementary school, 36
e-mail, 127
emotion, 8, 10, 14, 36, 101, 130, 164
emotion regulation, 14, 36
emotional problems, 98
emotional processes, viii, 40, 43, 44, 45, 46, 48
emotional reactions, 84
emotional responses, 50, 54, 55
emotional state, vii, 39, 40, 41, 42, 44, 46, 47, 48, 52
emotionality, 91
empirical studies, 25
encouragement, 144
endocrine, 11, 62
enemas, 3
energy, 65, 66, 72
energy expenditure, 72
England, 98
environment, 49, 51, 57, 58, 94, 99, 108, 120, 144, 157
environmental factors, 24, 107, 143
epidemiologic studies, 149
epidemiology, vii, 1, 29, 122, 124
equipment, 129
estrogen, 2, 74, 79
etiology, vii, 1, 7, 49, 58, 62, 107, 151
evidence, viii, x, 7, 19, 23, 25, 28, 36, 37, 41, 43, 44, 45, 49, 54, 61, 64, 85, 87, 88, 89, 102, 111, 123, 136, 137, 155, 156, 159
exposure, x, 9, 10, 42, 47, 48, 50, 51, 53, 55, 56, 57, 93, 142, 145, 146, 149, 158, 160
extinction, 53

F

failure to thrive, 99
families, x, 24, 103, 127, 128, 130, 131, 134, 135, 136, 145, 147
family conflict, 20
family environment, 145
family functioning, 131, 136
family members, 7, 19, 25
family relationships, 130, 135
family support, 134
family therapy, 16, 19, 35, 128, 129, 131, 134, 135, 137, 138
fasting, 3, 5, 6
fat, 2, 8, 43, 64, 66, 67, 88, 143
fear, 2, 19, 25, 41, 53, 107, 169
feelings, 16, 45, 129, 157, 159, 173
female rat, 5, 6
femur, 76
fertility, 78, 147
fetal development, 71
fights, 47
Fiji, 9
fish, 129
fitness, 168, 170
flexibility, 49, 123
fluid, 11, 12
fluoxetine, 22, 32
follicle, 70
follicles, 70
food intake, viii, 9, 24, 45, 46, 47, 49, 56, 58, 59, 83, 91
Ford, 86, 102
formation, 66, 91
fractures, 68, 73, 77, 81
France, 127, 135
fruits, 111, 116
functional analysis, 97
fundamental needs, 134

G

gender differences, 7, 174
generalized anxiety disorder, 13
genetic factors, 24, 143
genetic predisposition, x, 141, 142, 149
genetics, 53, 142
Greece, 83
group therapy, 16, 128, 129, 131, 134, 136
growth, 2, 11, 37, 66, 68, 84, 90, 91, 132, 150, 152
growth factor, 66
guidance, 51, 34, 131
guidelines, 2, 23, 119, 125, 129
guilt, 170, 172
guilty, 5, 130
gymnastics, 10

H

happiness, 169
hazards, x, 141, 142, 149
headache, 23
health care, vii, 1, 6, 14
health effects, 84
health insurance, 37
health problems, 123
health promotion, ix, 106, 109, 119, 120
hearing impairment, 24
height, 2, 6, 15, 63, 77, 132, 134
heritability, 7, 142
high school, 122, 123, 150
higher education, 109, 124
history, viii, 33, 37, 61, 64, 76, 82
Hong Kong, 51
hormone, 2, 56, 81
hormones, 66, 67, 69
hospitalization, 5, 15, 16, 17, 64, 134
housing, 57
human, 46, 50, 51, 58, 59, 78
Hunter, 60
hyperactivity, ix, 83, 85, 91, 95, 96, 97, 98, 99, 100, 102, 135
hyperglycemia, 11
hypersensitivity, 54
hypertension, 11, 29
hypoglycemia, 11
hypogonadism, 74, 81
hypophosphatemia, 38
hypotension, 11

hypothalamus, 7, 48, 66
hypothesis, 42, 103

I

ideal, 8, 9, 17, 31, 36, 64, 70, 76, 107, 143, 146
idealization, 9
ideals, 9, 144, 146
identification, 46, 147, 149, 158
identity, 9, 19, 26, 84, 91, 130, 156
image, x, 33, 36, 41, 51, 54, 58, 59, 67, 84, 87, 123, 144, 145, 146, 147, 152, 174
images, 9, 36, 37, 41, 42, 59
immigrants, 9
immune system, 12, 118
impairments, 44, 89
imprinting, 101
improvements, 18, 21, 70, 76
impulsivity, 58, 86
incidence, viii, 61, 62, 69, 73, 124, 149
income, 145
independence, 147
individual differences, 49
industrialized countries, 147
infancy, 99
infertility, 11
ingestion, 46
inhibition, 42
inhibitor, 22
initiation, 66, 73
injuries, 135, 168
insomnia, 23
institutions, 109, 110
insulin, 12, 66, 67
integration, vii, 18, 39, 40, 42, 48, 49, 52, 156
intellectual disabilities, ix, 83, 85, 90, 92, 94, 95, 96, 100
interface, 50
interference, 158, 159
internalization, 8, 31
internalizing, 86
interpersonal factors, 18
interpersonal relations, 16
interpersonal relationships, 16
intervention, x, 16, 32, 77, 87, 94, 99, 141, 149
Ipecac, 29
Iran, 146, 147, 149, 152
irritability, 45
isolation, 16, 57
Israel, 151
issues, ix, 14, 16, 17, 19, 24, 79, 105, 109, 120, 159

J

Jordan, 141, 143, 146, 147, 150, 152

K

kidney, 11
kidney failure, 11

L

labeling, 8
lack of control, 3, 4, 172, 173
later life, viii, 49, 61, 62
laxatives, 3, 11, 110, 113, 142
lead, 9, 11, 23, 47, 66, 77, 84, 86, 87
lean body mass, 68
learning, 46, 53, 90, 95, 97, 98, 103, 129, 136
learning disabilities, 90, 97, 98, 103
Lebanon, 149, 151
leptin, 66, 67, 70, 71
lifetime, 5, 13, 14, 32, 64, 65, 107, 120, 142
light, 23, 48, 107
loneliness, 16, 129, 130
longitudinal study, 11, 12, 37, 76, 80, 81, 82, 95, 150
loss of appetite, 24
lumbar spine, 71, 74, 76, 82
luteinizing hormone, 70

M

machinery, 53
magazines, 9, 146

magnitude, 71, 112, 118
major depressive disorder, 137
majority, 5, 13, 23, 24, 62, 87, 112
malaise, 47, 48
malnutrition, 5, 65, 84
mammals, 46, 47
management, viii, 27, 34, 61, 62, 69, 79, 92, 123, 125, 130
marital status, 110
mass, 63, 66, 67, 69, 72, 76, 80, 81, 146, 148, 149, 150
mass media, 146, 148, 150
matter, iv, 57, 122
measurement, 59, 119, 120
measurements, 68, 150
media, x, 9, 24, 35, 36, 142, 145, 146, 149, 150, 152
media messages, x, 142, 145, 146, 149
median, 116
medical, vii, viii, 1, 11, 14, 15, 16, 17, 25, 34, 61, 62, 63, 64, 75, 77, 84, 86, 87, 108, 138, 152
medical care, 63
medication, 15, 20, 23, 91, 96
medicine, 80
Mediterranean, 152
memory, 156
menarche, 11, 37, 63, 58, 73, 81, 102, 149
menopause, 23, 28, 62
menstruation, 11, 54, 66, 70, 143
mental disorder, 13, 27, 77, 94, 121, 131, 162
mental health, 14, 55, 77, 90, 108
mental illness, 37
mental retardation, 87, 98
messages, 146
meta-analysis, 54
metabolism, 12, 66, 67, 79
methylphenidate, 91, 102
mice, 54, 56
misuse, 3
models, viii, 9, 40, 41, 46, 48, 51, 52, 54, 59, 128, 146
modernization, 146
modifications, 46
molecules, 46
monozygotic twins, 142
mood disorder, 65
morbidity, 55, 123
morphology, 70
mortality, viii, ix, 5, 13, 83, 105
mortality rate, viii, 5, 13, 83
motivation, 15, 42, 53, 168, 169, 170, 171, 175
MRI, 59
multidimensional, vii, 1, 58
multiple factors, 62
multiple personality, 165
muscle strength, 72, 80
muscles, 111
myopathy, 29

N

National Center for Education Statistics, 125
necrosis, 67
negative affectivity, 144
negative effects, 9, 74
negative emotions, 8, 21, 45, 93, 144, 157
negative outcomes, 119
negative reinforcement, 88, 95
negative relation, 86, 161
neurobiology, 102
neuroimaging, 43
neurons, 56, 66
neurotransmission, 57
neurotransmitter, 47
neutral, 42, 159
New England, 27
New Zealand, 35
North America, 9, 27, 35, 100
novelty seeking, 65
nucleus, 48, 56
null, 111
null hypothesis, 111
nursing, 77
nutrition, 69, 72
nutritional status, 65, 66, 67, 150

O

obesity, 27, 58, 63, 88, 98, 122
obsessive-compulsive disorder, 35
OCD, 13, 22
old age, 24
oligomenorrhea, viii, 61, 64, 65, 66, 72, 77
opportunities, 120
organ, 11, 12
organic food, 94
osteoporosis, viii, 11, 61, 62, 67, 68, 69, 71, 72, 77, 80, 81, 82
outpatients, 8
ovaries, 70
overweight, 7, 19, 33, 34, 38, 51, 90, 143
ovulation, 70, 72

P

pacing, 92
pain, 48, 91, 174
pairing, 48
Pakistan, 147, 152
palpitations, 12
panic disorder, 60
parent-adolescent relationships, 150
parental involvement, 37, 129
parental pressure, x, 141, 149
parental relationships, 19
parenting, 129
parents, 10, 19, 37, 86, 89, 91, 92, 93, 94, 128, 130, 135, 138, 144
participants, 21, 65, 113, 119, 143, 158, 161
pathogenesis, 30
pathology, 12, 21, 32, 36, 37, 47, 86, 100, 148
pathophysiological, 74
pathophysiology, 57, 67, 78, 151
pathways, 43, 56, 59
peptide, 67
perfectionism, 8, 10, 93, 107, 135, 144, 148
personality, 8, 91, 93, 97, 102, 103, 107, 144, 148, 150, 151
personality characteristics, 107, 144, 148, 150
personality disorder, 93, 97, 102, 103
personality factors, 8
pharmacological treatment, 22, 25, 52
phenotype, 89
phobia, 13
photographs, 50, 51, 55
physical activity, 45, 73, 80, 108, 118, 119, 120, 123, 169, 173, 175
physical exercise, 66, 67, 72
physical health, x, 64, 107, 141, 142
physiological mechanisms, 66
physiology, 64
pilot study, 18, 81, 85, 103
placebo, 22, 23, 27, 28, 31, 32, 38, 69, 74, 80
pleasure, 46
polymorphism, 34
polymorphisms, 58
population, viii, 6, 10, 13, 14, 23, 24, 28, 30, 32, 33, 77, 83, 85, 107, 120, 129, 131, 134, 142, 164, 165, 169
positive attitudes, 17
positive correlation, 8
positive reinforcement, 94
post-secondary institutions, 118
Prader-Willi syndrome, ix, 83, 85, 88, 89, 93, 96, 97, 98, 99, 101, 102, 103
preadolescents, 122
predators, 47
prefrontal cortex, 42, 53, 60
pregnancy, 10, 63
preparation, iv, 42, 121
prevention, viii, 13, 24, 26, 33, 35, 36, 37, 62, 79, 80, 92, 122, 125
primary function, 91
primate, 59
probability, 89, 145
probands, 142, 153
probe, 163
problem behavior, 95

problem behaviors, 95
professionals, ix, 87, 92, 93, 105
progesterone, 70
prognosis, vii, 1, 5, 13, 100, 128
project, 121, 124
psychiatric disorders, 23, 98, 123, 137
psychiatric illness, 15
psychiatrist, 130
psychiatry, 27, 30, 36
psychoactive drug, 22
psychological distress, 121
psychological health, vii, viii, ix, 1, 83, 105, 106, 109, 111, 112, 118, 120, 124, 125
psychological problems, 143
psychological stress, 62
psychological variables, 58
psychology, 27, 28, 36, 58
psychopathology, 7, 27, 33, 50, 54, 58, 59, 65, 93, 97, 102, 143, 156, 164, 165, 168, 171, 175
psychosis, 15
psychosocial functioning, x, 107, 141, 142
psychosocial stress, 49
psychostimulants, 91
psychotherapy, 20, 27, 32, 33, 35, 38, 95, 98, 131, 135
psychotropic medications, 22
puberty, 11, 63, 73, 143
public health, 107, 109, 119, 124

Q

qualitative research, 122
quality of life, 136
quartile, 116

R

radius, 77
Rasch analysis, 97
reaction time, 158, 159, 160
reactions, 42, 169
reactivity, 20, 42, 50, 54, 56, 58
reading, 146
real time, 51
realism, 50, 55
reality, 21, 40, 49, 51, 52, 53, 55, 58, 59, 60
reasoning, 92
recall, 160
recalling, 157
receptors, 48, 54, 56
recognition, x, 26, 34, 141
recommendations, iv, xi, 27, 92, 95, 99, 119, 128, 155
recovery, viii, 5, 14, 15, 19, 24, 25, 61, 69, 70, 76, 80, 82, 108, 174, 175
recovery process, 14, 16
recreation, 51
recreational, 49
regression, 78
rehabilitation, 24, 50, 59
reinforcement, 45, 55, 99, 145
rejection, 45
relapses, 135
relatives, 136, 142, 153
relaxation, 44
relevance, 161, 164
reliability, 110
relief, 129
replication, 123
reproduction, 70
reproductive age, 62
requirements, 17, 37
researchers, 24, 119, 143, 159
resistance, 111, 116, 129
resources, 42, 43, 45
response, x, 22, 42, 43, 54, 56, 57, 60, 91, 110, 123, 155
responsiveness, 59
restoration, 15, 19, 70, 72, 75, 76
retardation, 11, 84
rewards, 17, 53, 57
risk factors, vii, x, 7, 8, 10, 25, 31, 40, 98, 122, 123, 131, 141, 149, 151, 153
risks, 68, 69, 71, 73, 77
rodents, 48
routines, 16

S

sadness, 169
safety, 47
Saudi Arabia, 147
schema, 164
schemata, 164
schizoid personality disorder, 98
schizophrenia, 14, 55
scholarship, 121
school, 28, 96, 110, 111, 112, 118, 151, 152
schooling, 134
science, 28, 37, 167
scientific knowledge, 169
scoliosis, 73
secondary schools, 109
secretion, 12, 66, 67, 74
selective attention, 42
selectivity, 99, 101
self esteem, 8
self-awareness, 56, 163
self-concept, 87
self-esteem, x, 8, 14, 29, 36, 84, 85, 87, 93, 99, 136, 141, 143, 149, 174
self-fulfilling prophesy, 103
self-image, 59, 84
self-presentation, 151
self-regulation, 174
self-worth, 146
sensation, 157
sensations, 14, 21
sensitivity, 57, 99
sensitization, 45, 54
sensory modalities, vii, 39, 47
serotonin, 7, 22, 34, 47, 53, 56, 57
serum, 66, 68
sexual abuse, 9, 84
sexual experiences, 162
shape, xi, 2, 9, 10, 17, 40, 41, 51, 63, 77, 84, 107, 143, 145, 146, 150, 151, 153, 167, 170, 171, 172
shortness of breath, 12
showing, 72, 76
siblings, 128, 144
side effects, 22, 23, 71, 91
signals, 41, 43, 44, 48, 49, 54
signs, 130
Singapore, 151
skeleton, 71
skills training, 94, 96
skin, 55
sleeping problems, 101
smoking, 13, 30
smoothing, 132
snacking, 38
soccer, 72
social acceptance, 147
social anxiety, 162
social behavior, 45, 47, 48, 51
social behaviour, 48
social class, 145, 147
social consequences, 108, 123
social hierarchy, 47
social impairment, 56
social indicator, 146
social influence, 143
social influences, 143
social interactions, 40, 47, 52
social phobia, 13, 45, 58, 162
social relations, 106
social relationships, 106
social situations, 51
social skills, 93, 94, 100
social skills training, 94
social status, 47
social stress, 53
social support, 9, 87, 122
social withdrawal, 45, 47, 48
society, 23, 146, 147
socioeconomic status, x, 142, 145, 149, 150
solidarity, 129
South Africa, 151
specialists, 119
speculation, 108
speech, 86
spine, 69, 71, 74, 76, 77
spine fractures, 76
stability, 15, 16, 17, 123, 153

stabilization, 134, 135, 136
standard deviation, 115, 116
starvation, 5, 45, 98
state, 7, 45, 48, 56, 65, 66
states, vii, 39, 41, 45, 46, 65, 73, 162, 165
statistics, 111
stigma, 25
stimulant, 91, 96
stimulus, 20, 47, 50, 72, 157, 158, 159, 161
stomach, 21, 51
stress, 20, 49, 54, 66, 67, 72, 81, 91, 92, 93, 101, 144, 149
stress fracture, 72, 81
stressors, 108, 120
striatum, 53, 57
structure, 51
style, 8, 144
subgroups, 147
substance abuse, 15, 33, 37, 102
substance use, 12, 14, 29
substrates, 53
success rate, 15
suicide, 5, 15
supervision, 19, 134
supplementation, 70
suppression, 11, 66, 67, 158, 159, 160, 161
survival, 161, 175
susceptibility, 49, 58
symptomology, 8, 9, 12, 21
syndrome, 12, 64, 72, 85, 87, 88, 90, 93, 95, 96, 97, 98, 99, 100, 101

T

target, 15, 134, 159
taste aversion, 48, 56
taxonomy, 31, 99
teams, 130, 134
techniques, 18, 20, 51, 128, 130
technologies, 50, 53
technology, 121
temperament, 144
test items, 111
testosterone, 71
texture, 93
therapeutic approaches, 99, 128
therapeutics, 52
therapist, 51, 94, 101, 130, 135
therapy, 15, 16, 17, 18, 19, 20, 21, 27, 29, 31, 32, 33, 34, 35, 38, 52, 58, 60, 70, 74, 75, 79, 81, 97, 128, 129, 135, 136, 137
thoughts, ix, 17, 20, 21, 106, 159
threats, 158, 159, 160, 164, 165
threshold level, 66
thyroid, 72, 108
time frame, 111
time pressure, 92
tinnitus, 58
tobacco, 13, 32, 55
toddlers, 96
toxicity, 47
training, 20, 21, 73, 76, 92, 111, 113, 116
traits, 143, 151, 152, 153
transition to adulthood, 106
translation, 48
transmission, 47, 143, 153
trauma, 164, 165
trial, 28, 31, 35, 69, 74, 79, 80, 137
triggers, 48, 56
turnover, 78, 92

U

United Kingdom (UK), 25, 175
ultrasound, 70
unconditioned, 47
underlying mechanisms, 54
unification, 165
United, 14, 57, 61, 71, 110, 112, 122, 123, 146, 147, 150
United States, 14, 57, 71, 110, 112, 122, 123, 146
universities, ix, 106, 109, 112, 120, 122
urban, 30

V

validation, 98, 173
variables, x, 7, 96, 111, 115, 116, 132, 135, 136, 141, 142, 145, 149, 162
variations, 138
vegetables, 111, 116, 119, 125
victims, 84
visual processing, 164
vitamin A, 95
vitamin D, 70
vitamin D deficiency, 71
volleyball, 10
vomiting, 3, 4, 11, 64, 65, 84, 91, 107, 108, 113, 142, 145
vulnerability, 53, 84, 143

W

Wales, 61
Washington, 27, 77, 94, 121, 125, 136, 137, 138, 162, 173
weakness, 12
web, 110
weight changes, 10
weight control, 123
weight gain, viii, 2, 3, 17, 61, 69, 70, 71, 72, 74, 107, 108, 134
weight loss, ix, 2, 4, 11, 15, 17, 18, 23, 24, 34, 37, 45, 48, 62, 63, 65, 105, 106, 108, 109, 111, 113, 117, 118, 119, 120, 123, 153, 170
weight management, 18
weight reduction, 18
well-being, 109, 122, 169
western culture, 9
withdrawal, 46, 47, 48, 75, 170, 172, 173
World Health Organization (WHO), 109, 125, 132, 138 175
worldwide, viii, 83
wrestling, 10
WWW, 125

Y

young adults, ix, 23, 106, 109, 120, 123, 138
young people, 153
young women, 62, 63, 67, 68, 69, 71, 72, 73, 74, 78, 79, 81, 82, 85, 149, 153